Instructor's Manual

Mosaic 2

Grammar

4th Edition

Prepared by

Diana Renn

Michael Ryall

McGraw-Hill

McGraw-Hill 
A Division of The ***McGraw-Hill*** *Companies*

Mosaic 2 Grammar Instructor's Manual, 4th Edition

Published by McGraw-Hill a business unit of The McGraw-Hill Companies, Inc., 1221 Avenue of the Americas, New York, NY 10020.

This book is printed on recycled, acid-free paper containing 10% postconsumer waste.

2 3 4 5 6 7 8 9 0 QSR QSR 0 9 8 7 6 5

ISBN 0-07-232997-1

Editorial director: *Tina B. Carver*
Series editor: *Annie Sullivan*
Development editor: *Jennifer Monaghan, Annie Sullivan*
Director of marketing: *Thomas P. Dare*
Production and composition: *A Good Thing, Inc.*
Printer: *Quebecor World Dubuque*

www.mhcontemporary.com/interactionsmosaic

TABLE OF CONTENTS

General Teaching Suggestions

Using the Introductory Material (Setting the Context)

This section can be a dialog, a reading passage, a class discussion or a paired interview. The purpose of the introductory section is to contextualize the material for the students as an aid to understanding. Although the passage highlights the first grammar point/s, its main purpose here is to introduce the theme.

Using Introductory Conversations

These dialogs can be used in a variety of ways.

- Call on students to read the parts aloud.
- After students have read and completed the comprehension activity, divide them into pairs or small groups to personalize by substituting their own information for the information in the conversation.
- Have the students relate sections of the conversation to the illustrations.
- Use it as the basis for a grammar discovery technique.

Using Introductory Picture Activities

- Have the students do the activity in pairs or groups and then share their answers with the class.
- Later on, have students find or draw another picture which illustrates the same grammar point and then present it to the class.

Using Introductory Readings

- You may wish to first use it as a reading skills activity by asking students to skim or scan for particular information.
- Tell the students to look up as soon as they are done. Time the students as they are reading. Then check their comprehension

Presenting Grammar

Many teachers prefer to present grammar rules and then practice them. Mosaic 2 Grammar is organized in this way. However, some teachers prefer to teach grammar deductively, using example sentences or exercises prior to studying the grammar charts. In this way, students deduce the rules and simply use the charts to check their hypotheses.

These techniques can be especially useful in classes with false beginners who have incomplete understanding of a number of basic grammar points and may be turned off by yet another explanation of the use of the present simple, for example. Discovery techniques will allow students to use what they know and fill in the gaps.

When possible, avoid having the students look at the Grammar Chart immediately. The techniques presented in the teacher's manual give you ideas for using context sentences and situations that will help the students understand the meaning of the new structure and allow them to guess the rules for forming it.

This technique can be very powerful. It allows students to think about the grammar and come up with their own rules and interpretations before you actually give them the correct information. Even though, student-generated rules will not always be exactly correct, the students will gain a lot by having had an opportunity to think about the structure first.

The teacher's manual often gives example context sentences and situations. However, you should feel free to modify these as you see fit. One of the best methods of explaining a grammar point is to give students examples from their own lives. This particularly important when you are asking them to guess the meaning of a particular structure.

Draw from current news stories, places of local interest, TV programs and movies. Above all, include information on your students' own interests, hobbies or careers. This type of personalization often clarifies a point when impersonal example sentences fail.

Using the Video

The video gives the students the opportunity to hear authentic, unscripted American English. This is particularly important for students of English as a foreign language. Therefore, neither you nor your students should expect to understand every word. The purpose is to allow them to practice listening for specific facts and/or general information. For this reason, the activities do not cover all the points discussed in every video clip.

Although the video transcripts are included in the teacher's manual, try not to use them except for general comprehension. It is much better to have your students watch the video several times and struggle with comprehension, than it is to have you read the transcript aloud. You should preview the video for your class. If there is a word, such as a name that you feel certain will cause comprehension problems, feel free to write it on the board for them. However, do not be tempted to preteach long vocabulary lists.

The *Before You Watch* activity asks students to call on their own prior knowledge to answer some questions related to the video. When appropriate, bring in visual material such as maps and photographs that may help students build background that will help them understand what they are about to see.

Before playing the tape, discuss the *Watch* section with students. Make sure they understand the meanings of all the words and that they also know what information the questions are asking them to watch for.

The *Watch Again* section asks students to look for more specific information than they did in the *Watch* section. Again, go over the questions carefully before replaying the tape and answer any questions students may have. Invite individuals to put their responses on the board and have the class check their own answers.

You can have the *After You Watch* discussion in the whole-class setting, or divide students into small groups. If you choose to have small groups, move among them to be sure they are focusing on the questions in the book and to provide language support. Afterwards, ask the groups to report back to the whole class.

them do so after the class has finished the activities.

Dealing With Unknown Vocabulary

As always, look the exercise over beforehand to try to catch problem words. Many times you will find them listed in the teacher's manual. If students encounter an unknown word, supply the definition (or translation) as quickly as possible and move on. Don't get sidetracked into a vocabulary lesson. Your class will forget what you are trying to teach.

Feedback and Error Correction

Be happy about errors. They show you the problem areas. Correct answers simply tell you what students already know. Keep reminding students that errors are necessary for progress because they learn how a language works by experimenting and receiving feedback. Students should be working slightly above their ability, so if they aren't making errors, they are not getting the right amount of challenge.

When/What to Correct

As a general rule, errors that interfere with communication are more important than those that don't. Distinguish between error correction in accuracy activities and error correction in fluency activities. Accuracy activities such as the grammar exercises demand that the teacher point out errors. When the objective is fluency, as in the *Using What You've Learned* activities, tolerate some errors and note others to be worked on later.

Don't rush correction. First of all, make sure that you are reasonably certain what the student is trying to say. Then indicate that they have made an error and give them a chance to correct it if it is reasonable to assume that they will be able to do that. The decision should be made based on the level of the error. If a low-level student makes a present tense error, he or she can reasonably be expected to be able to correct it. However, if the same student makes a passive voice error, you can simply supply the correct form and move on.

Class Correction

Class correction is a good way of focusing students' attention on errors made in fluency activities.

- Collect errors from students' written work or notes you have made during fluency activities.
- Write them on a transparency (if you have an overhead projector), type them out and

distribute them to the class or write them on the board. Reword them if necessary to make them anonymous.

- Ask students to correct them as a class or in pairs.

Homework

The amount of homework you assign will depend on the amount of time you can realistically expect your students to spend doing it. Assign as homework work that students do at different speeds and generally do alone. Feel free to assign an exercise that students did as group or pair work in class, particularly if it is on a difficult grammar point.

If a particular assignment is crucial to the next day's activities, warn the students in advance. If you do not, you may find yourself with a large group of unprepared students and lesson you can't teach. Assign homework before the students are packing up to leave, Make sure that there is enough time for them to ask questions.

Working with Multi-level Classes

Very few language classes contain students of equal abilities and experience. One of the best ways to cope with a multi-level class is through the use of pair work and group work. These techniques give the teacher time to work with small groups of students while the others work on their own.

When appropriate, you can work on the same activity that has been assigned to the rest of the class. At other times, you may find some other activity would be more helpful. For instance, while the rest of the class is working on a pair activity, you can be working as a partner of one of the students. Or if one group is doing a fluency activity in *Using What You've Learned*, you may choose to reinforce a difficult grammar point with a select group.

You can also use these special instruction sessions to ask students what they need help with. Sometimes covering everything on the page with every student may not be the best use of your time. Asking students what kind of help they need, and providing the support they ask for is one important way to advance the language-learning process.

Same or Mixed-Ability Grouping?

In general, mixed ability groups work best and allow you to take advantage of different ability levels of your students. More advanced students will gain confidence when they realize that they know the material well enough to help others. Middle-range students often feel more comfortable in small group settings and lower ability students may understand student explanations better than explanations which come from teachers. In addition, over-reliance on same ability groups tends to increase the difference in ability among the more and less capable students. Same ability grouping works well when you want to give one group of students more guidance, or a task more suited to their level.

If possible, divide the activity into different tasks and make sure that each student has a task to perform. Some possible tasks are moderator (the person who keeps everything going) time-keeper, (the person who makes sure that the work is being completed in a specified time and who also makes sure that everyone participates) the reporter (the person who reports back to the class. Students are usually more engaged in group work so even unmotivated students tend to work harder.

Teacher as Groupwork Facilitator

Teachers have an important role to play in pair and group work. This is not the time to correct papers! Circulate as unobtrusively as possible. Try not to interrupt the flow of conversation unless the students are confused, not on task or not doing the activity correctly. If students need vocabulary help, give it to them. Do not let the activity founder for lack of one or two crucial words. Carry a small notebook in which to note errors. However, do not hover writing furiously. Make notes as unobtrusively as possible, then use this information to plan future lessons.

Individualized Instruction

A third way to deal with mixed ability levels in your classroom is to work with individuals or small groups of less advanced learners while others are working on their own. At many points in this Instructor's Manual you will find instructions such as, *Move around the room offering language support as needed.* At these times you may wish to focus a single student or a small group of students who can benefit from special instruction.

When appropriate, you can work on the same activity that has been assigned to the rest of the class. At other times, you may find some other aspect of the listening/speaking skills requires additional attention. For instance, while the rest of the class may be working on writing vocabulary items in an activity, you might be working with an individual or a small group on the pronunciation of these same words. For these students, it is most important that they learn to say and understand the words at this point.

You can also use these special instruction sessions to ask students what they need help with. Sometimes covering everything on the page with every student may not be the best use of your time. Asking students what kind of help they need, and providing the support they ask for is one important way to advance the language-learning process.

Administering the Grammar Placement Test

The Grammar Placement test helps teachers and administrators place students into the Grammar strand of the **Interactions Mosaic** series. All of the placement tests have been carefully designed to assess a student's language proficiency as it correlates to the different levels of the **Interactions Mosaic** series.

The Grammar Placement Test assesses whether or not students can use grammar in context. The structures or notions come from both academic and conversational language. There are two sections to the grammar test. In the first part of the test, students are asked to find the best word to complete each sentence. In the second part of the test, students are asked to find the error in each sentence. The test follows a multiple choice format for easy administration and scoring. The test has been designed to be given during a one-hour class period.

Placement Chart for the Grammar Test

Number of Items Correct	Place in
0–6	Needs a more basic text.
6–17	Interactions Access
18–30	Interactions 1
31–43	Interactions 2
44–56	Mosaic 1
57–70	Mosaic 2

Using Chapter Quizzes

Each chapter in **Mosaic 2 Grammar** is accompanied by a quiz. All quizzes are worth 50 points. If you are using a system based on 100, simply multiply the results by two. In general, the chapter quizzes measure achievement. However, using quizzes can be an important diagnostic tool as well if you use the information to guide your teaching in the lessons that follow. If the majority of the class does particularly badly on any portion of the test, a review of that point may be required. If only a few students appear to have a problem, you may want to assign them extra practice. Otherwise, you can simply make note of students who appear to have a problem and pay close attention to them when that point comes up again.

Here are some suggestions for making use of these quizzes.

- Explain that the purpose of the quizzes is to give students an idea of how they are doing and what areas they may need to work on.
- Emphasize that the quizzes are a learning device.
- Go over the instructions for all the exercises. Make sure students understand what they are supposed to do before they begin writing their answers.
- Allow students time to complete the quiz. They are meant to be brief and should take about fifteen minutes to complete.
- Always correct quizzes as soon as possible so that students find out about their errors while the questions and answers are still fresh in their minds.

- One way to give immediate feedback is to have students correct each other's papers in class. This provides the additional advantage of allowing for a classroom discussion of the questions most people missed.

Using Your Own Quizzes

You may want to prepare and administer quizzes on specific items that students must memorize such as irregular past tense and past participles.

- Announce the quiz in advance to give students a chance to prepare.
- Don't spend longer than ten minutes administering the quiz.
- Let the students exchange papers to correct.
- Set a minimum score, for example 80% and keep testing students until they achieve it.

Language and Learning

Goals

- The sentence and its parts
- The simple tenses
- The continuous tenses
- The perfect and perfect continuous tenses and verb tense review
- Modal auxiliaries

Introduction

This chapter is intended to present a quick review of verb tenses and choosing when to use them. Have students read the brief introduction paragraph. Before having students read the passage about language, have a brief pre-reading discussion as a class or in small groups. Ask them to read the first sentence only and predict what the writer might say on this topic. Then have students read the passage individually.

Discussing Ideas

Have students discuss the questions in small groups and report their ideas to the class.

Part 1 The Sentence and Its Parts

Setting the Context

Have students discuss the prereading questions in pairs or groups. If students in the class can easily be grouped according to language or similar languages, it might be interesting to have them discuss similarities of their languages with English in groups that are linguistically similar; afterwards, they could share their knowledge with the class. Then have students read the passage individually.

Discussing Ideas

Have students discuss the questions in small groups or pairs. The issue of language versus dialect may generate a lot of conversation; if time permits, you could have students from different language groups explain some examples of dialect to the rest of the class.

A. Parts of Speech

Read the explanation of parts of speech above the example in the box. Have students read the examples and the labels. Point out that for verbs which use an auxiliary to form a particular tense, both parts of the verb (auxiliary and main verb) should be labeled "verb." (For example: *may have*). Write one sentence from the reading passage on the board and have students work together as a class to label the parts of speech.

1 Page 3.

Read the instructions and the example. Have students complete the exercise in pairs, groups, or as a class.

Answers: 1. *The* = article; *world* = noun; *Mandarin* = adjective; *but* = conjunction; *it* = pronoun; *inside* = preposition 2. *are* = verb; *speakers* = noun 3. *Almost* = adverb; *population* = noun; *Indo-European* = adjective 4. *English* = noun; *popular* = adjective; *in* = preposition; *and* = conjunction; *its* = pronoun; *popularity* = noun 5. *If* = conjunction; *included* = adjective (or: *are included* = verbs, in passive voice)

B. Sentences

Read the explanation above the chart or elicit a definition of what constitutes a sentence (versus a phrase or a clause; phrases and clauses will also be covered in Part C). Have students take turns reading the four examples and notes. Elicit additional examples of each kind of sentence.

C. Subjects

Read the explanation above the chart or elicit a definition of a subject. Have students take turns reading the four examples and notes in the chart. Elicit additional examples of sentences with different types of subjects.

D. Verbs, Objects, and Complements

Read the explanation above the chart. Have students take turns reading the examples and notes in the chart. Elicit additional examples.

Optional Activity: Have pairs or groups write sentences with various types of verbs and then exchange sentences with other/groups pairs to label as transitive, linking, etc. To add a game element and make the activity more challenging, set a time limit and have groups compete to correctly label the most sentences within the time limit.

2 Page 5.

Read the instructions and the example. Have students complete the exercise individually or in pairs. Check answers as a class; have students identify what type of verb, subject, and object is used in each sentence when they give their answers.

Answers: 1. linguists (noun subject), have identified (transitive verb) over four thousand languages (direct object) 2. Some languages (subject phrase), are (linking verb) relatively new (complement) 3. Others (Pronoun subject), were used (intransitive verb) 4. Over four thousand languages and dialects (subject phrase), are (linking verb), currently being used (complement) 5. Many (pronoun subject), have (transitive verb), no written form (direct object) 6. Linguists (noun subject), have given (transitive verb), writing systems (direct object), to some of these language (indirect object)

3 Page 5.

Read the instructions and the example. You may need to review the terms *dependent clause and independent clause*. A clause always has a subject and a verb. If it can stand on its own as a sentence, it is an independent clause. If it cannot stand on its own because it begins with a word like because, while, or if, it is a dependent clause and must be attached to an independent clause with a comma and a conjunction, or with a semicolon and a conjunctive adverb (however, nevertheless, etc.). Have students complete the exercise individually or in pairs.

Answers: 1. The Aranda people lead simple lives (main clause); who live in the Australian desert (dependent clause; also called a relative/adjective clause); who = connecting word (relative pronoun) 2. their language is incredibly complex (independent clause) 3. While the English verb system is considered complex (dependent clause); while = connecting word; it is much simpler than the Arandan system (independent clause) 4. Every Arandan verb can take about a thousand different endings (independent clause); and = connecting word (conjunction); each ending changes the meaning of the verb (independent clause) 5. It is as if English verbs like *run* had one thousand different forms (independent clause) 6. Nobody knows (independent clause); why = connecting word; why the Arandan verb system is so complex (dependent clause)

E. Preview of the Tense System

Have students read the information about the tense system. You could also begin by eliciting what they do know about the tense system, though Exercise 4 is designed as a diagnostic activity. Emphasize the fact that *functions* can change.

4 Page 6.

Have students work individually or in pairs to complete this diagnostic exercise. Give minimal or no guidance; this exercise can be a useful tool to help you determine what to emphasize in the coming sections. Go over the answers as a class. A common mistake to watch out for is the confusion of gerunds and infinitives with verbs. You might remind students that these words look like verbs but act like nouns. They can always check to see if a word is a verb, gerund, or infinitive by labeling all the parts of a sentence and examining the function of each word.

Answers: 1. have been using = present perfect continuous (or present perfect progressive; students may have learned either term) 2. don't know = simple present; began = simple past 3. are studying = present continuous 4. were writing = past continuous 5. had learned = past perfect 6. had been speaking = past perfect continuous 7. are = simple present; are = simple present 8. have learned = present perfect 9. learns = simple present; will change = future 10. will be talking = future continuous 11. will have begun = future perfect 12. will have been speaking = future perfect continuous; learns = simple present

Using What You've Learned

5 Page 7.

Read the instructions. This is a nice icebreaker activity to help to warm up a new class. Encourage them to think of at least two additional questions to ask a classmate. Remind them that in most cases there is more than one way to ask these questions. After they have written out their questions, allow ample time for them to conduct interviews. You can also use this exercise as a diagnostic activity by going around the room and taking notes on common mistakes/problems that you hear. This information can help you choose what to emphasize in the coming sections of this chapter, as well as what you might want to go over as a class when the interviews are over.

Sample Answers: 1. What is your name? 2. How old are you? 3. What is your native country? / What country are you from? / Where are you from? / What is your native language? / What language do you speak? 4. How long have you been here? / How much time have you spent here? 5. Why are you studying English? / What is your reason for studying English? 6. How long have you been studying English? / How many years have you studied English? 7. What is your major/job? / What are you majoring in? / Where are you working? 8. Are you single or married? / Do you have children? 9. What are your hobbies and interests? / What hobbies and interests do you have? / Where have you traveled? / Where do you like to travel? / Where would you like to travel?

6 Page 7.

Read the instructions. Note that this activity follows from the discussion of the first passage at the beginning of this section; they may wish to form groups or pairs with people from that discussion, or new ones. As with Activity 5, you can use this exercise as a diagnostic activity by going around the room and taking notes on common mistakes/problems that you hear. This information can help you choose what to emphasize in the coming sections of this chapter, as well as what you might want to go over as a class when the interviews are over.

Optional Activity: Have students arrange their comparison of English versus another language in a chart or graph. Then have them present it to the class.

7 Page 7.

Read the instructions. You may need to reassure students that they need not become expert linguists; there are some simple Web and library searches that they could do to obtain some basic information, using the name of the language as a search term. Even an encyclopedia will give enough information for the presentation. If students are describing a language from a region that many people may not be familiar with, encourage them to bring in pictures and give a little information about the region and its people.

8 Page 8.

Read the instructions. This is a fun trivia activity that can be conducted individually, in pairs, or in groups.

Optional Activity: To add a game element to Activity 8, have students work in pairs or groups and compete to answer the questions the fastest. You could also expand this activity by having students interview native English speakers to test their knowledge of their own language. Students could then compare the results in groups or present their findings in a brief presentation to the class.

Part 2 The Simple Tenses

Setting the Context

Have students discuss the prereading questions in groups or as a class. Then have students read the passage individually.

Discussing Ideas

Have students discuss the passage in pairs or small groups and debate the question. Encourage them to list other possible differences between humans and animals and share them with the class.

A. The Simple Tenses: An Overview

Begin reviewing the simple tenses by eliciting from students what rules they have learned about the simple tenses and when they might choose to use this these tenses. Read the explanation above the chart. Have students read the chart individually. Quickly review question and negative form by having students form questions and negative statements from the examples in the chart.

B. The Simple Present Tense

Read the explanation above the charts. Have students read the charts individually. Be sure to review third person singular; even fairly advanced students may sometimes forget to use or pronounce the *-s* ending. Refer students to Appendix 2 for spelling rules and Appendix 3 for pronunciation rules.

Optional Activity: Elicit additional sentences in the simple present by having students go around and state one sentence about themselves using one of the time expressions in the chart. Alternatively, have students ask and answer questions in the simple present tense by going around the room in a chain. If you feel your students need review or practice in pronouncing *-s* in third person singular, have them make statements about each other.

C. Special Uses of the Simple Present Tense

Read the explanation above the chart. Emphasize the fact that the simple present tense used in reference to the past gives a sense of immediacy or urgency to the story. You might also point out that the simple present tense used in reference to the future is used when future plans are definite. It would be inappropriate, for example, to use this tense to discuss possible or tentative future plans or schedules. Elicit additional examples of each of these uses of the simple present tense.

1 Page 10.

Read the instructions and the example. Have students write out their schedules individually. Then have them work with a partner to explain their schedules. Encourage students to ask questions to get the information (For example: What is something you always do on weekend mornings?) and to ask follow-up questions to make the activity more conversational. Answers will vary.

2 Page 10.

Read the instructions and the example. You might want to have students first write out a calendar of plans for the month (you could hand out blank copies of a calendar for the month to fill in) or have them do this activity while looking at their schedules/planners, if they have them. Then have them ask and answer questions about future plans using the simple present tense. If students need practice using or pronouncing *-s* in third person singular, have them report some of their partner's plans to the class. Answers will vary

3 Page 10.

Read the instructions and the beginning of the story. Have students work in pairs to complete the story. This activity can be done orally or in writing.

Optional Activity: Do Activity 3 as a chain storytelling activity by going around the room and having students add to the story one sentence at a time. This can be done orally, with all students listening for correct use of the verb tense and noting any other errors they might hear; it can also be done in writing by passing around a piece of paper to add on to and then read aloud and checked for errors after everyone has written a sentence.

D. The Simple Future Tense and *Be Going To*

Ask students if they can explain the reasons for choosing *will* versus *be going to* make statements about the future. Then have them read the information above the chart. Have them take turns reading the examples in the chart out loud. Emphasize the difference in certainty: *be going to* indicates definite plans. Elicit additional examples.

4 Page 11.

Read the instructions and the example. Have students complete the exercise individually and then compare answers with a partner. Encourage students to refer back to the chart when they go over their answers and state the reason for choosing *will* versus *be going to* for each sentence.

Answers: 1. I'm going to have 2. Will 3. come 4. is going to come 5. am going to invite 6. I'll bring 7. I'll come 8. won't need (or: am not going to need)

Optional Activity: Have students look back at Activity 4 and determine which sentences could also use the simple present tense.

Answers: 1, 4, 5 (the simple present tense can replace *be going to* in these sentences because definite plans are being discussed)

5 Page 11.

Read the instructions and the example. Have students refer back to any notes they may have written in Activity 2, or a calendar/schedule they may have. As they ask and answer questions in pairs, go around the room and listen for any common mistakes or problems in form or pronunciation to go over as a class.

E. The Simple Past Tense

Elicit from students what they already know about how to form and when to use the simple past tense. Read the explanation above the chart. Have them read the examples and time expressions in the chart. Refer students to Appendices 2 and 3 for spelling rules and pronunciation of *-ed* endings, and Appendix 1 for irregular verbs. Most students at this level will feel comfortable choosing when to use the past tense, but may still need work on pronunciation and on reviewing irregular verbs.

6 Page 11.

Ask students if they have heard of Helen Keller and what they know about her accomplishments. Activities 7 and 8 are also about Helen Keller, so it may be worth spending some time on establishing a context for the exercises. Read the instructions. Have students complete the exercise individually or in pairs and check answers as a class by having students read them out loud. Listen for correct pronunciation of *-ed* endings and correct word order with adverbs.

Answers: 1. was 2. liked 3. developed 4. left 5. didn't learn, did 6. was 7. ignored 8. often got, refused 9. had, sat, stared 10. frequently refused, sometimes threw 11. thought 12. worried

F. The Habitual Past: *Would* + Simple Form and *Used To* + Simple Form

Read the explanation above the chart and have students read the examples and notes out loud. Emphasize the distinction between used to like and would like by eliciting additional examples of each type of sentence. Also point out the common error of using the *be* verb with *used to*, for example: *I am used to learning French. Be used to* means *be accustomed to*. Point out question and negative form with used to: *Did you use to study French? I didn't use to study French.* Point out how the final *-d* drops when the auxiliary *do* is used. Finally, point out that when past actions are described in several sentences, in order to avoid a repetitive style it is best to alternate *used to* and *would*, or use *used to* once and thereafter use *would*.

7 Page 12.

Read the instructions and the examples. Have students work individually or in pairs to go over their sentences from Activity 6 and determine which could be expressed with *used to* or *would*. Check answers as a class or in pairs. Encourage students to state why *used to* or *would* are not possible in certain sentences.

Answers

3. Helen developed a fever at 19 months old. (Neither *would* nor *used to* is possible.)
4. This fever left Helen permanently deaf and blind. (Neither *would* nor *used to* is possible.)
5. Helen didn't learn language as other children did. (Neither *would* nor *used to* is possible.)
6. Helen used to be difficult. (*Would* is not possible; the situation was continuous, not repetitive.)
7. She used to ignore / would ignore everyone for hours at a time.
8. Helen would often get frustrated and would refuse to cooperate. / Helen used to get frustrated often and used to refuse to cooperate.
9. Helen used to have a dog (*would* is not possible; continuous situation) and she would sit / used to sit for hours with her dog and stare into space.
10. She would frequently refuse to eat and sometimes would throw food on the floor. / She frequently used to refuse to eat and sometimes used to throw food on the floor.
11. Her family used to think that Helen was going to grow up to be like an animal. (*Would* is not possible; continuous situation.)
12. They used to worry / would worry that nothing could help her.

8 Page 13.

Read the instructions and the example. Have students work individually or in pairs and check answers in pairs or as a class. Point out that in some cases either *would* or *used to* may be possible, but they should read over the entire passage when they are done and check to make sure that these expressions are varied so that the writing style does not seem repetitive.

Answers: 1. met 2. was 3. moved 4. spent / would spend 5. tried / would try 6. often became / would often become 7. decided 8. used to put / would put 9. would spell 10. came 11. held 12. spelled 13. wrote 14. was 15. knew 16. was 17. opened 18. became 19. would eagerly work / used to work eagerly 20. went 21. graduated 22. died

9 Page 14.

Read the instructions and example. Have students work individually or in pairs. Correct answers as a class. Encourage students to explain the reasons behind the errors.

Answers (corrections are underlined): 1. I have a friend named Jack, who used to live a few houses away. 2. When I met him, Jack was determined to learn Spanish. 3. He used to buy lots of language tapes. 4. He used to live in Columbia. 5. Unfortunately, he never practiced speaking and listening to Spanish. 6. Now he reads and writes Spanish well... 7. He will speak Spanish well one day. (Note that students may be tempted to correct the sentence this way: *He is going to speak Spanish well one day*. Structurally, this is correct; however, will is the better choice because the context here is a prediction about the future, not a definite plan.) 8. He knows lots of people from Spanish-speaking countries.

Using What You've Learned

10 Page 15.

Read the instructions. Have students talk about their childhood in small groups. You might help them prepare for this activity by first allowing time to brainstorm specific childhood memories that illustrate obedience or disobedience. They can write a short paragraph to share with a group, or discuss the memory first and then write a paragraph about it. Students can exchange finished paragraphs in pairs to check for correct use of *would, used to*, and other tenses.

Part 3 The Continuous Tenses

Setting the Context

Write the word "grammar" on the board. Have students try to define what it really means and why it is important. (You can also prompt discussion by asking how people learn languages: do they memorize sentences? Or is there some other way?). Then have students read the passage individually.

Discussing Ideas

Have students discuss the passage in small groups and try to state how grammar works in their own words. (You might point out that this idea of restating something in your own words and sentence structures is called *paraphrasing*. It is often useful to try to paraphrase something without looking back at the original text).

A. The Continuous Tenses: An Overview

Note that students may also have learned these under the term *progressive tenses*. If they seem confused, point out that both terms mean the same thing. Elicit what they already know about continuous tenses: how they are formed and when they are used. Read the explanation above the chart. Have students read the examples in the chart. Go over question and negative form by having students make questions and negative statements from the examples in the chart. Point out that the auxiliary verb reflects changes in time, singular/plural, and third person singular. Elicit some additional examples of what things are in progress now, were in progress at a certain time in the past, and will be in progress in the future.

1 Page 16.

Read the instructions. Have students give the tense and time frame of the verbs in the first sentence in the reading passage. You might also have them identify the time expressions by circling them. Be sure that students understand the distinction between tense and time frame. As they should have noticed in the last section, a verb tense is merely a structure; different verb tenses can often be used in different time frames.

Answers: The sentence you are reading now (present continuous), the one you were reading a moment ago (past continuous), and the one you will be reading (future continuous) in a moment may be completely original.

B. The Present Continuous Tense

Read the information above the chart. Have students read the example in the chart out loud. Elicit additional examples for each use of the present continuous. Point out Appendix 2 page 409 which has spelling rules for *-ing* endings.

Optional Activity: Have students go around in the room in a chain asking and answering questions in the present continuous tense with time expressions. You can go around once for each time frame of the present continuous tense or, if students seem fairly comfortable with this structure, have them interchange the time frames.

2 Page 16.

Have students each choose someone they know in another country—perhaps a friend or family member, or even a famous person. Have them discuss that person using all three time frames of the present continuous tense. Encourage them to ask follow-up questions to make the activity more conversational. As they talk, go around the room and listen for common errors or problems to go over later as a class. Answers will vary.

3 Page 16.

Read the instructions and the example. Have students complete the exercise individually or in pairs. Check answers as a class, and encourage students to explain their choice of simple present or present continuous tense in the cases where both are possible.

Answers: 2. come 3. am studying 4. am living (or: live) 5. is 6. is 7. is 8. meet (or: am meeting) 9. is 10. wants 11. do 12. like 13. don't appreciate 14. seem 15. sounds 16. talks 17. become 18. don't understand 19. never seem 20. always have to (or: am always having to) 21. am working 22. believe 23. it beginning

4 Page 17.

Read the instructions. Have students work individually to write an additional paragraph to the essay in Activity 3, imagining Moshen's point of view. Then have them exchange paragraphs in pairs to check for correct use of verb tenses.

Optional Activity: Have students write a paragraph about their own thoughts on studying in North America and then exchange paragraphs in pairs to check for correct use of verb tenses.

Optional Activity: Have students write a letter to Moshen to reassure him and help him build confidence; encourage them to use the present continuous tense in all three time frames as much as possible, as well as the simple present tense where appropriate.

C. The Past Continuous Tense

Read the explanation above the chart. Point out in the second row of the chart that *while* is used with the past continuous tense, and the interrupting action, introduced with *when*, is used with the simple past tense. Elicit additional examples by asking students what they were doing when you first walked into the room, or what they were doing when a significant event in history happened.

5 Page 18.

Read the instructions and the example. Have students complete the exercise individually or in pairs. Check answers orally as a class.

Answers: 2. was walking 3. realized 4. was taking 5. thought 6. got 7. was introducing 8. upset 9. tiptoed 10. tried 11. was looking 12. directed 13. was saying 14. was 15. didn't understand 16. was trying 17. pointed 18. understood 19. sat

6 Page 18.

Read the instructions and the example. Have students complete the exercise individually or in pairs. Check answers orally as a class and encourage students to explain their choices for sentences where more than one verb tense is possible.

Answers: 2. was 3. was 4. can 5. asked 6. got up 7. walked 8. opened 9. saw 10. was about 11. felt 12. was bending down 13. let out 14. thought 15. can 16. knelt down 17. was 18. was 19. uncovered 20. couldn't believe 21. saw (or: was seeing) 22. was

7 Page 19.

Read the instructions. Have students write their interview questions individually and role play the interview in pairs. After student write up their incident reports (these should be no more than a paragraph long), have them exchange reports in pairs to check for correct verb tense usage.

Optional Activity: Have students find an incident in the news, either on TV or in the newspaper, involving a crime. Have them imagine they are a detective and interview one or more key witnesses, and then write up an incident report. You could expand this activity further by having students role play the interviews in front of the class.

8 Page 19.

Read the instructions. Have students complete the passage individually or in pairs. Have them compare answers in groups and explain their choices of verb tense for sentences where more than one verb tense is possible.

Answers: 2. decided 3. could speak 4. set up 5. were doing 6. were 7. arrived 8. was still waiting 9. was 10. wanted 11. was introducing 12. silently translated (or: was silently translating) 13. learned

Optional Activity: Have students write a paragraph about an embarrassing experience of their own. Have them exchange finished paragraphs with a partner to check for errors with verb tense usage. Or have them tell their stories in small groups.

D. The Future Continuous Tense

Read the explanation above the chart. Have students read the examples out loud. Emphasize the differences in tone. Elicit additional examples for both uses of the future continuous tense.

Optional Activity: Elicit more examples and work on the more conversational tone by having students go around the room in a chain asking and answering questions in the future continuous tense.

9 Page 20.

Read the instructions and the example. Have students role-play the conversation in pairs. Go around the room and listen for errors or common problems to go over later as a class.

10 Page 21.

Read the instructions and the examples. Have students write their future plans individually, using all of the future forms for each item.

Optional Activity: Expand Activity 10 by having students ask and answer questions about each other's future plans, in pairs or groups. Encourage follow-up questions to make the activity more conversational.

Optional Activity: For an alternative, fun version of Activity 10, have students answer the questions as if they were a celebrity. Student could also role play interviews for a TV talk show, using different forms of future statements and the time expressions listed in Activity 10.

11 Page 21.

Read the instructions and example. Have students work individually or in pairs. Correct answers as a class. Encourage students to explain the reasons behind the errors.

Answers (corrections are underlined):
1. correct 2. When he arrived in Florence, he immediately enrolled in a language school. 3. It has been three months, but when people are speaking to him, he still doesn't understand them. 4. Yesterday Mark went to the language lab. (or: Yesterday Mark was going to the language lab when he...) 5. When the class was over, Mark waved "good-bye" to his teacher. 6. At the same time she was motioning for him to come to the front of the class. 7. However, when Mark got to the front of the class, the teacher looked confused. 8. She said that she was simply waving "good-bye" to Mark. 9. Mark suddenly realized that the Italian "good-bye" gesture is (or was) very similar to the American "come here" gesture. 10. Mark will be studying for the next year in France. 11. correct 12. At least that is what he wants!

Using What You've Learned

12 Page 21.

Read the instructions and the example. To help students prepare, you could allow a few minutes of brainstorming time for them to write down miscommunication experiences they have had and then choose one to talk or write about. You can have students discuss the incident in groups and then write a paragraph about it, or vice versa.

Part 4 The Perfect and Perfect Continuous Tenses and Verb Tense Review

Setting the Context

Have students discuss the prereading question in groups or as a class. Then have them read the passage individually.

Discussing Ideas

Have students discuss the passage and the questions in groups. Then have them report to the class any other explanations for languages they have heard. Alternatively, have them create a mythical explanation for why we have multiple languages and present it to the class.

A. The Perfect Tenses: An Overview

Elicit from students what they already know about forming and using the perfect tenses. Then read the information above the chart and have them read the examples in the chart out loud.

Optional Activity: Have students create time lines for the present, past, and future perfect tenses to explain visually how times are discussed in relation to each other with the perfect tenses.

B. The Present Perfect Tense

Read the information above the chart and have students read the examples out loud. Point out that changes with singular/plural are seen in the auxiliary *have*, not in the main verb. Also point out that the two times being compared are any time in the past all the way up until the present.

Optional Activity: Have students go around the room in a chain asking and answering questions about language learning in the present perfect tense.

1 Page 23.

Read the instructions and example. Have students complete the exercise in pairs. Check answers as a class.

Answers: 1. *Now they have begun to do this* means that they began at an unstated point in the past, probably recently, and this action affects the present situation. *Now they are beginning to do this* means that they are just beginning at or around the present time.
2. *When we finish, they will have lost their one language* means that sometime between the present time and the future, before they are finished, the language will be lost. *When we finish, they will lose their one language* means that the language will not be lost until the moment that they are finished. 3. The Lord had made a babble of language first; the city was given the name after. The past perfect verb tense indicates the action that happened first.

2 Page 24.

Read the instructions and the example. Have students complete the exercise individually or in pairs. Encourage them to read the passages once for comprehension and to identify the time expressions. Go over the answers as a class.

Answers: 1. have wondered, have made, now know, go, do, live 2. have always had, have begun, helped, has helped 3. has been, did, have been 4. have always been, believed, has shown, was

C. The Perfect Continuous Tenses: An Overview

Elicit from students what they already know about forming and using the perfect continuous tenses. Then read the information above the chart and have them read the examples in the chart out loud. Point out that the perfect continuous tense is often chosen to emphasize the duration of the activity. Each of the examples in the chart could be expressed in a perfect tense without the continuous, but the emphasis would be on the activity itself rather than the length of time.

Optional Activity: Have students create time lines for the present, past, and future perfect continuous tenses to explain visually how times are discussed in relation to each other with the perfect tenses. If they made time lines for the overview of perfect tenses, they might add these timelines to the same piece of paper and talk about the differences in representation.

D. The Present Perfect Continuous and Present Perfect Tenses

Read the explanation above the chart. Have students read the examples in the chart. Point out the difference in emphasis: time/duration of the activity (present perfect continuous), versus the activity itself or the completion of the activity (present perfect).

3 Page 25.

Read the instructions and example. Have students work individually or in pairs. Correct answers as a class.

Answers: 1. have been communicating 2. have been teaching 3. has already learned 4. has been asking 5. has been practicing 6. has mastered 7. has combined 8. has not learned

E. The Past Perfect and Past Perfect Continuous Tenses

Read the explanation above the chart. Have students read the examples in the chart.

Optional Activity: For additional practice forming this tense, list pairs of past events on the board. (For example: *studied English in high school, moved to the U.S*). Have students form sentence, in writing or orally, combing the two events into one sentence. To do this, they must determine which event happened first. (For example: *Before I moved to the U.S., I had studied English in high school*). To make the activity easier, put the events in columns labeled "first event" and "second event." To make it more challenging, do not label first and second events.

4 Page 26.

Read the instructions and the example. Have students do the exercise individually or in pairs. Check answers as a class.

Answers: 1. had been sleeping, got up 2. had finished, arrived 3. had showered, (had) eaten 4. had closed, (had) locked 5. had been following 6. had been sitting 7. had just begun 8. hadn't forgotten 9. had been following 10. had already turned in, had been

5 Page 27.

Read the instructions and the example. Encourage them to read the passage once first for comprehension and identify the time words. Have students do the exercise in pairs and compare answers with another pair.

Answers: 1. was still, had completely rusted 2. found, was, had already passed away 3. walked, recognized, had seen, had died, (had) moved 4. looked, was, had grown, had almost disintegrated 5. found, moved

6 Page 28.

Read the instructions. Have students write their own Rip Van Winkle experiences individually and share them in groups. Groups should listen for and correct any errors in verb tenses.

F. The Future Perfect and Future Perfect Continuous Tenses

Read the explanation above the chart. Have students read the examples in the chart.

Optional Activity: For additional practice forming this tense, list future times and events on the board in pairs. (For example: *2003, receive an M.B.A*). Have students form sentences, in writing or orally, combing the two events into one sentence using the future perfect or future perfect continuous tenses. To do this, they must determine which event happened first. (For example: By 2003, *I will have received an M.B.A*).

7 Page 28.

Read the instructions and the example. Encourage them to read the passage once first for comprehension and identify the time words. Have students do the exercise in pairs and compare answers with another pair.

Answers: 1. will still be, will have rusted 2. will find, will be, will have already passed away 3. will walk, will recognize, will have seen, will have died, will have moved 4. will look, will be, will have grown, will have almost disintegrated 5. will find, will now be, will move

8 Page 29.

Read the instructions and the example. Have students complete the exercise individually. Have them check answers in pairs or as a class. Encourage them to explain their choices when more than one tense is possible, and the differences in meaning that might result.

Answers: 1. have discussed (or: have been discussing) 2. were discussing (or: discussed) 3. will probably still be discussing 4. discussed (or: have discussed) 5. discussed 6. will have been discussing 7. discuss (or: are discussing) 8. are discussing 9. had discussed (or: discussed) 10. will never discuss

Optional Activity: Have students choose a different verb (or give them one, such as *learn* or *read*) and write similar sentences as in Activity 8, using the verb in as many tenses as they can.

9 Page 29.
Read the instructions and the example. Have students complete the exercise individually and compare answers in pairs or groups, checking each other's sentences for errors. Encourage them to explain their choices when more than one tense is possible, and the differences in meaning that might result. Answers will vary

10 Page 30.
Read the instructions and example. Have students work individually or in pairs. Correct answers as a class. Encourage students to explain the reasons behind the errors.

Answers (corrections are underlined):
1. Before I studied English, I had thought it was an easy language. 2. Now I know that it isn't easy. 3. My language has only a little slang. 4. I have been studying English since April, and I have only begun to learn some of the common slang words. 5. I have been trying to learn more of these words every day. 6. Last night, for example, I studied (or: was studying) from 9:00 PM to midnight. 7. I had been studying for three hours when I finally quit. 8. I went to my teacher last Monday and she told me to see her after class. 9. But when I went to her classroom after school, she had already left. 10. It's now May 15; by the middle of June, I will have been studying English for three months. 11. On June 23, I will be studying German. 12. On June 30, I will have been studying German for one week.

11 Page 30.
Read the instructions and the example. Have students complete the exercise individually or in pairs and compare answers in pairs or groups. Encourage them to read the passage once for comprehension before they begin and to identify the time words that will help them to choose the best verb tenses. Encourage them to explain their choices when more than one tense is possible, and the differences in meaning that might result.

Answers: 1. has interested 2. began 3. called 4. means 5. was living (or: lived) 6. spoke 7. believed 8. were (or: are) 9. he had published 10. were learning 11. is 12. is 13. are 14. falls 15. has 16. was 17. were speaking 18. have written 19. has declined (or: has been declining) 20. is 21. think 22. will become 23. does not mean 24. will never be 25. has 27. also has 28. is rapidly growing 29. are 30. will speak (or: will be speaking) 31. predict 32. will have become

Using What You've Learned

12 Page 32.
Read the instructions and the examples. Have students work in groups or pairs to imagine that they are futurists discussing and predicting changes. You could assign each group/pair a context (such as technology, education, fashion, etc.) or have them choose any areas they like. Have them report their findings to the class and encourage further debate/discussion if time permits.

Part 5 Modal Auxiliaries

Setting the Context

Have students discuss the prereading questions in groups or as a class. Then have them read the passage individually.

Discussing Ideas

Have students discuss the passage and the question in groups. If possible, have students from different languages in each group so that they can compare examples.

A. Introduction to Modals

Elicit what students may already know about modals—examples, how they are formed, when they might be used. Read the information above the chart. Have students read the examples of modals and their multiword equivalents in the first row of the chart out loud. Elicit additional examples for each modal and related structure. Have them read the examples in the next part of the chart aloud. These more complex modal structures may be less familiar or comfortable to students. Explain that these will be discussed in greater detail in this chapter. Finally, model the pronunciation of rapid forms in the third part of the chart. Have students repeat them. Then give them examples of pronunciation of reduced forms in reduced sentences, or have them write their own and practice pronouncing them in rapid speech.

1 Page 34.

Read the instructions and the example. Have students work individually or in pairs to come up with alternative expressions. Check answers as a class, listening for correct pronunciation. In some cases, more than one answer is possible.

Sample Answers: 1. Deb isn't able to go out. 2. I can translate from Korean to English. 3. They are supposed to keep their promise. (or: they ought to) 4. You will enjoy that movie. 5. We couldn't help her. 6. He must (or: has got to) take ten courses in Spanish in order to major in it. 7. I don't feel good; I could (or: may) be getting a cold. 8. We should (or: ought to) review this chapter for the test.

B. Modals of Logical Probability

Read the explanation above the chart. Be sure that students understand that the term *inference* means *a guess based on evidence*.

2 Page 35.

Read the instructions and the example. Have students use a variety of modals and expressions from the chart to make guesses about reasons for the situations listed. They could do this individually and share their guesses in pairs or groups, or do the entire activity in groups, making as many theories as possible for each situation. Answers will vary.

Optional Activity: To expand Activity 2, have students exchange sentences in pairs and evaluate the degree of certainty of the writer for each sentence.

C. Expressing Predictions

Students should already be familiar with using the simple future to make predictions. However, there are degrees of certainty in making predictions that can be expressed with modals. Read the information above the chart and have students read the examples out loud, noting the degrees of certainty/probability in the third column.

Optional Activity: To expand Activity 2, have students exchange sentences in pairs and evaluate the degree of certainty of the writer for each sentence.

3 Page 36.

Read the instructions and the example. Have students use a variety of modals and expressions from the chart to comment on the predictions listed. They could do this individually and share their guesses in pairs or groups, or do the entire activity in groups, making as many comments as possible for each situation. Answers will vary.

Optional Activity: To expand Activity 3, have students exchange sentences in pairs and evaluate the writer's degree of certainty or probability in each sentence.

D. Modals of Social Interaction

Read the explanation above the chart. Have students read the examples and notes in the chart. Point out the different levels of formality among these modals. Ask students to give examples of situations in which each modal might be appropriate (for example: a conversation between an employer and an employee, a parent and child, etc.)

4 Page 37.
Read the instructions and the example. Students can discuss these situations and levels of formality in pairs or groups. Answers will vary.

5 Page 37.
Read the instructions and the example. Have students write modals individually first and decide to whom they are speaking if no indication is given. Have students evaluate each other's levels of formality and word choice in pairs. Answers will vary.

E. Other Modals and Their Uses

Have students read the examples and notes in the chart. Highlight the difference between *can* (present ability) and *could* (past ability that one no longer has). Elicit some additional example of students' past and present abilities. With *would rather*, point out the more common contraction: *I'd rather*. You may need to spend more time reviewing *must/must not/have to/don't have to*, as these distinctions can be confusing even to advanced students. Emphasize the fact that *must not* and *don't have to* do not have the same meaning, whereas in the affirmative they can be used interchangeably. Point out that *You don't have to smoke in here* does not have the same meaning as *You must not smoke*; the former sentence means it is not necessary to smoke. Similarly, *We don't have to leave* means it's not necessary to leave; on the other hand, *You must not leave* is a command or an expression of urgent need. Elicit additional examples with *must* and *not have to*, perhaps in the context of learning languages.

6 Page 38.
Read the instructions and the example. Have students complete the exercise individually and compare answers with a partner.

Answers: 2. must not 2. don't have to 3. don't have to 4. must not 5. must (or: have to) 6. must (or: have to) 7. must (or: have to) 8. doesn't have to

7 Page 39.
Read the instructions and the example. Have students complete the exercise individually and compare answers with a partner.

Answers: 1. Soldiers must (or: have to/have got to) call officers "sir." 2. Common soldiers must not call officers by their first names. 3. A common soldier doesn't have to bow to officers. 4. You must (or: have to/have got to) salute officers. 5. Many years ago, soldiers had to treat officers almost like gods. 6. Many years ago, officers didn't have to give the soldiers any rights at all. 7. Today, soldiers must (have to/have got to) respect their officers, but they don't have to be afraid of their officers.

Optional Activity: Have students write a list of rules of etiquette as in Activity 7 for another area that they are familiar with (such as their place of employment, American classrooms, etc.)

8 Page 39.
Read the instructions. Encourage students to read the conversation once for overall comprehension. Have students complete the conversation individually and then practice it out loud with a partner twice, changing roles.

Answers: 1. can't 2. could 3. would rather 4. can 5. can 6. can 7. can

Optional Activity: Have students work in pairs to write their own dialogues, modeled after the one in Activity 8, and perform them for the class. You can have them focus only on modals of ability, as in Activity 8, or have them combine all the types of modals in the chart at the beginning of the section (Section E). Students can listen for the different types of modals when they listen to their classmates' role plays and take notes.

Using What You've Learned

9 Page 39.
Read the instructions. Have students give examples of slogans they have seen or heard in North American culture and/or other cultures. Then have them find their own ads with slogans that use modals and explain them to the class.

Optional Activity: Have students find ads without explicit use of modals (or bring in some yourself) and have students write slogans for them that use modals.

10 Page 40.
Read the instructions. Have students work in pairs to perform a role play for each situation. They need not write the dialogue in advance.

11 Page 41.
Read the instructions and the example. To add a game element to this activity, set a time limit for groups to guess activities being pantomimed, or have groups compete to guess the action first.

12 Page 41.
Read the instructions. Have students discuss all of the questions and report their ideas to the class. It may help to have them elect a "secretary" to take notes during the discussion.

13 Page 41.
Read the instructions. Students can research actors' accent learning process individually or in pairs.

Video Activities: The School for Success

Before You Watch
Have students discuss the two questions in small groups. Encourage them to give reasons for their answers to question 1 and as many specific examples as they can think of in question 2.

Watch [on video]
Have students read the questions before having them watch the video. Play the video. Give students time to answer the questions. Play the video again, if necessary. Go over the answers as a class.

Answers: 1. The School of Success 2. parents and children 3. c 4. a, b, d

Watch Again [on video]
Have students read the questions. Play the video and have students answer the questions. Put them in pairs to check their answers. Replay the video, if necessary.

Answers: 1. a 2. c 3. b 4. a

After You Watch
Read the instructions. Have students complete the paragraph individually and compare answers with a partner.

Answers: "The School of Success" is based on the ideas of George Frasier. Frasier says that parents need to be involved in their children's education. He believes that parents should make sure that their children are given the kind of attention they need. When a good home life is combined with a structured learning environment, all children can succeed.

Introduction to Focus on Testing
Ask if students are familiar with or have taken standardized tests like the TOEFL or TOEIC and, if so, what they found easy or difficult about these tests. Read the explanation about the Focus on Testing sections that will appear in each chapter of this book.

Focus on Testing

Set a time limit for students to complete this test individually. Go over the answers as a class.

Answers:
Part 1: 1. a 2. c 3. c 4. d
Part 2: 1. c 2. b 3. a 4. c

Chapter 2

Danger and Daring

Goals

- **Review of nouns, pronouns, and possessive adjectives**
- **Indefinite articles and quantifiers**
- **The definite article with count and noncount nouns**
- **The definite article with proper nouns**
- **More on nouns and noun modifiers**

Introduction

This chapter reviews grammatical structures which students have most likely learned before but may need help remembering or using. You can use this introductory passage as a diagnostic by having students discuss it at length and listening carefully to common problems or errors they have in using these structures in their speaking. You can also create a writing diagnostic by having them write a paragraph summarizing and analyzing the passage, or writing a brief reaction, and looking specifically for these grammatical issues in their writing. These diagnostic measures can help you to determine what to focus more time on in this chapter.

Before having students read the passage, have a brief pre-reading discussion about exploration in general as a class or in small groups. Ask them what the word "exploration" brings to mind, and ask them to give examples of famous explorers and character traits necessary for explorers. Then have students read the passage individually.

Discussing Ideas

Have students discuss the question in small groups and report their ideas to the class.

Part 1 Review of Nouns, Pronouns, and Possessive Adjectives

Setting the Context

Have students discuss the prereading questions about Marco Polo in pairs or groups. Then have students read the passage individually.

Discussing Ideas

Have students discuss the passage and the questions in small groups or pairs.

Optional Activity: Expand the discussion of Marco Polo by having students do a little research on him in the library or on the Web. Have them find out one or two more facts about him and share them with the class. You might also have them share their research strategies with the class or in groups: where did they find information on him? What keywords did they use for Web searches?

A. Introduction to Nouns

Elicit from students a definition of a noun and different types of nouns. Then have them check what they already know about nouns by reading the explanation in Part A. Have them list a couple of examples of each type of noun.

B. Count Nouns

Read the explanation above the chart and have students read the examples and notes in the chart. You might add that count nouns can always be pluralized by adding *-s* or *-es*.

Optional Activity: Have students reread the passage on Marco Polo on Student Book pg. 47 and list examples of count nouns in their singular and plural forms.

1 Page 48.

Read the instructions and the example. Have students complete the exercise in pairs, groups, or as a class. When you check answers as a class, have students read the answers aloud and listen for correct pronunciation of *-s* endings. You may wish to review or present pronunciation rules for *-s* endings. After a voiced word ending, *-s* sounds like "z" (*valleys, knives, plays*). After a voiceless word ending, *-s* has a soft sound (*beliefs, monarchs*). For words ending with *-sh, -ch*, or *-tch*, the final *-es* has its own syllable and is pronounced "es." Also when you check answers, go over spelling rules, especially as many of the count nouns on the list do not follow the *-s* ending rule. You could have students circle those words which are irregular in the plural form.

Answers: 1. valleys 2. mice 3. indices 4. tables 5. churches 6. children 7. deer 8. babies 9. crises 10. curricula 11. heroes 12. analyses 13. beliefs 14. alumni 15. mosquitoes 16. stimuli 17. series 18. plays 19. teeth 20. knives 21. tomatoes 22. monarchs

2 Page 48.

Read the instructions and the example. Have students read the entire passage once for overall comprehension. Check answers as a class and listen for correct pronunciation of *-s* endings.

Answers: 1. women, hips, rubies 2. people, highlands, sheep, sheep 3. deserts, oases, valleys, gems, minerals 4. horsemen, plains 5. Families, yurts, tents, roofs 6. wives, homes, tapestries, shelves, dishes 7. journeys, oxen, wagons, possessions 8. possessions, boxes

Optional Activity: If you feel your students need further practice with pronunciation of plural nouns and identification of irregular plural forms, have them go back over the sentences in Activity 2 and list the plural nouns in four categories: "z" sound, "s" sound, "es" sound, and irregular. You could encourage them to add nouns to this list as they continue working through the chapter and have them practice pronunciation from this list periodically.

C. Noncount Nouns

Read the explanation above the chart. Have students take turns reading the examples and notes in the chart out loud. Elicit additional examples of mass and abstract nouns. Point out that units of measurement make mass nouns countable by limiting the noun; therefore, the articles *a* and *an* can be used.

Optional Activity: Have students reread the passage on Marco Polo on Student Book pg. 47 and list examples of noncount nouns.

D. Nouns That Are Both Count and Noncount

Read the explanation above the chart. Have students read the examples and notes in the chart.

Optional Activity: Have students reread the passage on Marco Polo on Student Book pg. 47 and look for examples of nouns that could be either count or noncount depending on the context. (For example: *adventure*)

3 Page 50.

Read the instructions and the example. Have students complete the exercise individually or in pairs. Check answers as a class.

Answers: 1. C 2. C 3. N 4. C 5. C 6. N 7. N 8. N 9. C 10. C 11. N 12. N 13. C 14. C 15. N 16. N, N 17. C, C 18. N

4 Page 51.

Read the instructions. If you have done the optional activities for the previous sections, which have students identify types of nouns used in the Marco Polo reading passage, you may wish to omit this exercise, as it involves a similar process. Or, you could have students do this for a review without looking back at the charts for explanations. Have students complete the exercise individually or in pairs; have students check answers in pairs.

Answers:
Noncount nouns in paragraph two: riches, sophistication, silk, brocade, porcelain, money, paper, adventure

Count nouns in paragraph two and their singular/plural forms: wonders (wonder), weavers (weaver), centuries (century), craftsmen (craftsman), techniques (technique), empire (empires), transactions (transaction), diary (diaries), travels (trip), tales (tales), record (records) century (centuries)

5 **Page 51.**
Read the instructions and the examples. Have students complete the exercise individually and compare answers in pairs.

Answers: 1. Milk was being dehydrated into powder. 2. Jewels were being traded throughout Asia. 3. Sophisticated cities were being constructed. 4. Canals were being built. 5. Weather was being studied. 6. Stars were being mapped. 7. Paper money was being used throughout the empire. 8. Eye glasses were being developed. 9. Ice cream was being perfected. 10. Spaghetti was being made. 11. Silk was being woven into beautiful brocade. 12. Gunpowder was being used. 13. Highways were being built. 14. Plumbing systems were being developed. 15. Astrology was being practiced.

E. Personal Pronouns and Possessive Adjectives

Elicit from students what a pronoun is and what examples of pronouns they know. They may or may not be able to classify pronouns into types. Have them read the information above the chart and the examples in the chart. Elicit examples sentences using the different types of pronouns. (For example: *I own this pen; This pen belongs to me; My pen is this one; This pen is mine; I bought this pen myself*).

6 **Page 52.**
Have students work individually or in pairs to complete this exercise. Check answers as a class and have students state what types of pronouns are used in each sentence (subject, object, etc.)

Answers: 1. themselves 2. their 3. their, they 4. his 5. its, its 6. his, he, himself, he 7. our 8. its

Using What You've Learned

7 **Page 52.**
Read the instructions. You can help students prepare for this activity by allowing some time for brainstorming unusual experiences and sights they have had. Then have them select the most interesting subject and brainstorm ideas to include in the presentation.

Optional Activity: Have students write their notes for their presentation into the form of a paragraph or a short essay.

Focus on Testing

Set a time limit for this practice test and have students complete it individually. Then check answers as a class and review any points about pronouns or possessive adjectives if necessary.

Answers:
Part 1: 1. a 2. c 3. c 4. d
Part 2: 1. d 2. c 3. d 4. d

Part 2 Quantifiers: Indefinite Articles and Quantifiers

Setting the Context

Have students discuss the prereading questions in groups or as a class. Then have students read the passage individually.

Discussing Ideas

Have students discuss the passage in pairs or small groups and discuss the questions. Encourage students to visit the web site mentioned in the Student Book for more information, and to try to find other sources of information on the Polynesians to share with the class.

A. Indefinite Articles

Ask students to tell you what they know about indefinite articles—what they are and when to use them. Then read the information above the chart and have students read the chart individually. Give them (or elicit) some examples of incorrect use of indefinite articles for contrast (for example: *a island, an adventures, an advice*).

1 Page 55.

Read the instructions. Encourage students to read the passage once first for overall comprehension. Students can complete this exercise individually and check answers in pairs or as a class.

Answers: 1. X 2. X 3. X 4. a 5. an 6. X 7. X 8. X 9. X 10. X 11. an 12. an

2 Page 56.

Read the instructions. Encourage students to read the passage once first for overall comprehension. Students can complete this exercise individually and check answers in pairs or as a class.

Answers: 1. X 2. X 3. a 4. a 5. X 6. X 7. an 8. a 9. X 10. X 11. X 12. X 13. X 14. X 15. X 16. X 17. X 18. X 19. X 20. X 21. X 22. a 23. X 24. X 25. X 26. a 27. X 28. X 29. X 30. a 31. X 32. a 33. an 34. a

3 Page 57.

Read the instructions and the example. Students can complete this exercise individually and check answers in pairs or as a class.

Answers: 1. A Navigator had to notice and understand... 2. Ocean waves near islands have a particular appearance... 3. Good navigators could tell the difference... 4. A Polynesian navigator could also use a start to guide him or her during a voyage.
5. Navigators watched stars that rose or set over particular islands. 6. They would only use stars that were near the horizon. 7. To plan the course or direction, he or she would use a zenith star. 8. A zenith star points down to a specific island, and it helped a navigator determine location. 9. By the mid 1700s, sextants were generally used to determine the location of ships. 10. A sextant can determine latitude and longitude.

4 Page 57.

Read the instructions and the example. Have students work in pairs to ask and answer questions about equipment for various occupations. Encourage them to list as many different kind of equipment for each profession as they can think of. They may need to use a dictionary to locate specific words. You may wish to point out that the equipment they list will most likely be count nouns; they can state them in the singular form in order to practice using indefinite articles. Encourage them to think of five additional professions and ask and answer questions about those. Alternatively, they could think of five other professions and give the list to another pair to ask and answer questions about. Answers will vary.

Sample Answers: 1. A radiologist uses an ultrasound machine, a camera, an examination table, and a computer. 2. A secretary uses a telephone, a computer, a photocopier, a fax machine. 3. A gardener uses a trowel, a shovel, a watering can, a hose. 4. A cowboy uses a lariat (or lasso), a saddle, and a bridle. 5. A hunter uses a rifle.

B. Units of Measurement

Read the explanation above the chart. Have students read the examples and units of measurement in the chart.

5 Page 58.

Read the instructions. Have students work individually or in pairs to use the units of measurement listed in the chart to label the pictured items. Explain that in some cases more than one answer may be possible. Check answers as a class.

Answers: 1. a loaf of bread 2. a box of oranges 3. a jar of jam 4. a gallon (or bottle) of water 5. a bar of soap 6. a bunch of bananas 7. a dozen eggs (or: a carton of eggs) 8. a bag of rice (or: five pounds of rice, a package of rice) 9. a tube of toothpaste 10. a six-pack of soda pop 11. a bag of chips (or: a package of chips) 12. a roll of paper towels

Optional Activity: Have students use the units of measurement listed in the chart to plan a shopping list for a class party, or to list typical things that they buy at the grocery store.

Optional Activity: For oral practice with units of measurement, have students go around in a chain—without looking back at the chart—and stating one item that they typically buy at the grocery store. This can be done as a memory game, with students repeating all the items that the students before them have stated.

C. Indefinite Adjectives and Pronouns

Read the explanation above the chart. Have students take turns reading the examples in the chart out loud. Go over the notes together, eliciting additional examples of nouns to go with each type of quantity word. Point out that the quantity word *much* is generally not used in affirmative statements, only in questions and negative statements. (It would be odd, for example, to say "I have much time.") Instead, we usually use "a great deal of" or "a lot of" to express the idea of a large quantity in affirmative statements.

Point out the fact that these same expressions of quantity can be used as different parts of speech: as both adjectives and pronouns. If students have difficulty with this concept or with determining which parts of speech these words are functioning as, encourage them to label the parts of speech in any given sentence and see how the quantity expression functions.

Students may need extra review/ explanation of the distinction between few/ a few and little/ a little mentioned in the note at the bottom of the chart. Another way to think of this distinction that the indefinite article makes with these quantity words is to remember that, in general, the article makes the concept seem positive. (I have *a few* friends means "some friends," so one probably feels positively about that fact; on the other hand, I have *few* friends means "almost no friends," which expresses a negative idea. The quantity remains the same. In this example, perhaps the person has four friends. What changes is the way that the speaker *feels* about this quantity).

6 Page 59.

Read the instructions and the example, or demonstrate chaining questions and answers by modeling the first few exchanges with several students. Point out that this exercise is designed to practice negative responses with quantity words; even if they feel they should answer positively, they should practice using the negative answers for now. They are free to use either *any* or *some* in forming their questions.

Answers: 1. Do you have any (some) free time? Not much. 2. Do you have any (some) homework? Not much. 3. Do you have any (some) e-mail messages to send? (Not many) 4. Do you have any (some) quarters? Not many. 5. Do you have any (some) good food at home? Not much. 6. Do you have any (some) snacks with you? Not many. 7. Do you have any (some) homework assignments? Not many. 8. Do you have any (some) blank paper? Not much. 9. Do you have any (some) good magazines? Not many. 10. Do you have any (some) gas in your car? Not much. 11. Do you have any (some) change? Not much. 12. Do you have any (some) good advice for me? Not much. 13. Do you have any (some) news from home? Not much. 14. Do you have any (some) information about good Websites? Not much. 15. Do you have any (some) time for a cup of coffee? Not much.

7 Page 60.

This activity uses the same prompts and questions as Activity 6, but asks students to use quantity words in affirmative answers. Read the instructions and the example, or model the first few exchanges of the chain with several students.

Answers (of responses only): 1. Sure, I have a little. 2. Sure, I have a little. 3. Sure, I have a few. 4. Sure, I have a few. 5. Sure, I have a little. 6. Sure, I have a few. 7. Sure, I have a few. 8. Sure, I have a little. 9. Sure, I have a few. 10. Sure, I have a little. 11. Sure, I have a little. 12. Sure, I have a little. 13. Sure, I have a little. 14. Sure, I have a little. 15. Sure, I have a little.

Optional Activity: Use the prompts from Activities 6 and 7 to do one more chain of questions and answers. This time, however, do a less controlled version by having students give honest answers using much, many, a lot of, a few, few, a little, little, as the situation requires.

8 Page 60.
Read the instructions and the example. Have students work in pairs to plan supplies for their sailing trips. Have pairs report their lists to the class, and have the rest of the students listen for any errors with quantity expressions as pronouns and indefinite adjectives. Alternatively, have students trade lists with other pairs and identify quantity expressions used as indefinite adjectives versus pronouns. Answers will vary

Optional Activity: For a fun twist on Activity 8, have students work in groups to list ten items they would take if they were to be exiled on a deserted island. You could also write out a list of items and have them choose ten from that list, thinking about their priorities as they choose.

9 Page 60.
Read the instructions and the example. Point out how the word *only* modifies *a little* so that it has a negative feeling rather than a positive feeling about the quantity. Have students work in pairs to complete the passages and have them check answers as a class or with other pairs.

Answers: 1. A. a little B. only a little 2. B. a little 3. A. a few B. only a little, a few 4. A. a little B. a few 5. A. a little B. only a little

Optional Activity: Have students expand any or all of the short dialogues in Activity 9 into a longer role-play, using quantity expressions as indefinite adjectives and pronouns. Have them perform them for the class.

Using What You've Learned

10 Page 61.
Read the instructions and the example. If you have students discuss this topic in pairs, go around and listen for common problems or errors to review later as a class. Alternatively, this activity could be done as a memory chain activity if you did not already do it as an optional activity previously.

11 Page 61.
Read the instructions. Allow plenty of time for students to list possible items for each category and to think of reasons for their choices. When students report their lists to the class, have the other students listen for any errors with quantity expressions, or have groups exchange and proofread each others' lists before they present them to the class.

Part 3 The Definite Article with Count and Noncount Nouns

Setting the Context

Have students discuss the prereading questions about the Age of Discovery in groups or as a class. Then have students read the passage individually. Check vocabulary comprehension, as their may be some new words or expressions in this passage.

Discussing Ideas

Have students discuss the passage and the questions in small groups. Encourage them to paraphrase the ideas in their own words. If time permits, you could also have students do a little extra research on the Web or in the library to find some additional information on this topic to share with the class.

A. The Definite Article with Count Nouns

B. The Definite Article with Noncount Nouns

Elicit from students what they already know about the definite article: what it is and when it is used. Read the explanation above the chart. Have students read the examples in the chart out loud and go over the notes as a class. Note that students may wonder why commas are not necessary in the fourth example. (*The merchants that paid for explorations wanted to become rich*).The clause *that paid for explorations* does not need commas because it provides necessary information that explains who the merchants are. More information on restrictive and nonrestrictive clauses, and their associated comma rules, will be covered in Chapter 4.

1 Page 63.

Read the instructions. Students can do this identification activity individually or in pairs. Check answers as a class.

Answers:

1. Pattern one: the first part (count noun) of the fifteenth century (line 1); the most dramatic period (count noun) of change (lines 1–2); the societies (count noun) of Europe (line 3); the population (count noun) of Europe (lines 3–4); the cultivation (noncount noun) of new land (line 4); a new class (count noun) of merchants (line 5); their knowledge (noncount noun) of the East (line 7); the course (noncount noun) of history (line 10); the discovery (count noun) of the "New World" (line 11).
2. Pattern two: the recent, tremendous growth (noncount noun) in the population (lines 3–4); the demand (count noun) for new products (lines 4–5); the search (count noun) for new sea routes (lines 8–9); the European search (count noun) for new trade markets and products (line 9)

2 Page 63.

Read the instructions and the example, or model the first few exchanges of the chain questions and answers with several students. Students can go around the room following the list in alphabetical order, modifying the nouns with any information that they like. Or, to make this activity more challenging by adding the element of surprise, each student could state their own phrase or clause and then choose a noun to give to the next student to build off of.Answers will vary.

3 Page 64.

Read the instructions and the example, or model the first few exchanges of the chain questions and answers with several students.As with Activity 2, students can go around the room following the list in alphabetical order, modifying the nouns with any information that they like. Or, to make this activity more challenging by adding the element of surprise, each student could state their own phrase or clause and then choose a noun to give to the next student to build off of.Answers will vary.

4 Page 64.

Read the instructions and the example. Encourage students to read the sentences once first for overall comprehension, as the content is linked to form a short passage. Students can work individually or in pairs. Check answers as a class.

Answers: 1. X, X 2. the, X 3. The (or X) , the, the (or X) 4. The, X, X, X, X 5. The, the 6. X, X 7. The (or X), X 8. X

C. *The* with Quantifiers

Read the information above the chart. Have students read the examples in the chart out loud. Give some examples of incorrect sentences for contrast: *All of passengers are on board, Most of luggage is on board*. Elicit additional examples for each quantifier.

5 Page 65.

Read the instructions and example. Point out that some sentences may be correct. Have students work individually or in pairs. Correct answers as a class. Encourage students to explain the reasons behind the errors.

Answers (corrections are underlined):
1. Some of the world's greatest explorers...
2. correct 3. correct 4. Many of the explorers were financed by monarchs of different European kingdoms 5. Most of the exploring was in search of faster routes... 6. correct
7. Most of the pepper came from India.
8. Some of the other spices valuable in 15th century Europe...

D. Quantifiers and Subject/Verb Agreement

Read the explanation above the chart and have students read the examples and notes. It may be useful to write the example sentences on the board and have students identify the prepositional phrases. Underline the prepositional phrases, double-underline the quantifiers, and circle the count or noncount nouns at the end of each phrase. Then have students note how the count or noncount noun determines the form of the verb (singular or plural). Give some examples of incorrect sentences for contrast: *All of the money were from Spain; half of the food have been eaten*. For additional practice with subject/verb agreement, you could erase the endings of each sentence on the board, leaving only the prepositional phrases, and have students complete the sentences with new information. You could also write new quantifiers with prepositional phrases on the board and have students complete the sentences in their own words after identifying the count/noncount nouns in each phrase.

For the last example in the chart, point out that students may hear a plural verb used with *none* in conversational English (for example: *None of the sailors were experienced*). However, it is correct to use the singular verb in formal English. A good way to remember this rule is to think of *none as a word that is formed from* no one. *The word one* can be used to remember that this quantifier takes a singular verb regardless of the kind of noun that follows.

6 Page 66.

Read the instructions and the example. Have students complete the exercise individually or in pairs. Check answers as a class.

Answers: 1. exploring was (or: explorations were) 2. people were 3. ruler of Europe was interested 4. leaders were told 5. knowledge of the earth was based 6. calculations of distance were 7. guesses were 8. monarchs of Europe was 9. money was 10. crew with Columbus was 11. sailors were ready 12. ideas about the shape and size of the earth were

E. *The Number of* Versus *A Number of*: Subject/Verb Agreement

Read the explanation above the chart. Have students read the examples out loud. Give incorrect examples for contrast: The number of ships were quite high; A number of ships was built. Elicit some additional examples of sentences using *a number of* and *the number of*.

7 Page 67.

Read the instructions and the example. Have students work individually or in pairs. Check answers as a class.

Answers: 1. were 2. were 3. was 4. were 5. were 6. was

F. Two-Part Subjects: Subject/Verb Agreement

Read the information above the chart. Have students read the examples in the chart out loud and go over the notes together. (Alternatively, you could see how much students may already know about this subject by writing some of the example sentences on the board with the verb left blank and ask them what form of the *be* verb to use and how they know). Have students circle the nouns in each sentence that are used to determine the form of the verb.

8 Page 68.

Read the instructions. Have students work individually or in pairs. Encourage students to first underline the words or expressions used to introduce phrases (for example: *both, and, either, or, along with*, etc.) and circle the nouns that will be used to determine the form of the verb. They could even label the nouns "S" for singular or "P" for plural; the verb will agree accordingly. Check answers as a class.

Answers: 1. were 2. were 3. was 4. was 5. was 6. was 7. was 8. was 9. were 10. were

Using What You've Learned

9 **Page 69.**
Read the instructions and the example. You may need to allow ample time for students to do a little research in the library or on the Web. Encourage them to bring in maps or other visual aids for their presentations.

Optional Activity: Have students write up their presentation notes for Activity 9 into a short report. Have students exchange essays in pairs to proofread for errors, particularly for errors involving quantifiers.

10 **Page 69.**
Read the instructions and the example. Allow time for students to list their questions and answers first. Collect these and check them; have students make any necessary corrections. Then play the game by asking each team the other team's questions. (Note: you can play "host" yourself or have a student do this if you have an odd number). A good way to play this game is "Family Feud" style, having the teams sit in two rows and going down the line to take turns answering questions. This will ensure that everyone participates equally.

Part 4 The Definite Article with Proper Nouns

Setting the Context

Have students discuss the prereading question in groups or as a class. Then have them read the passage individually.

Discussing Ideas

Have students discuss the passage and the questions in groups. Encourage them to paraphrase the ideas in their own words, perhaps without looking back at the text. If time permits, have students do a little research on the Web or in the library to find one or two additional facts on this topic to share with the class.

A. *The* with Proper Nouns and Other Expressions

Be sure that everyone by now is familiar with the distinction between proper nouns (names of people, places, institutions) versus common nouns (things and ideas). Then read the explanation in section A of when to use the definite article.

1 **Page 71.**
Read the instructions. Have students complete the exercise in individually or in pairs. Check answers as a class.

Answers: 1. proper nouns in the passage (and other expressions) and article usage: the sixteenth century, Spain, Portugal, Asia, the northern nations, Europe, the Arctic, China, Siberia, North America, the following two centuries, Britain, Russia, the North Atlantic (ocean), the North Pacific ocean, the eighteenth century, the British commander James Cook, Cook, the Antarctic Circle, 1773, 1778, the Bering Strait 2. Names of countries (Spain, Russia, China, etc.) are not usually preceded by *the*. Exception: The United States. 3. The names of oceans and seas are usually preceded by *the*. Examples: The North Atlantic Ocean, the Bering Strait.

Optional Activity: For questions 2 and 3 in Activity 1, have students list other examples of countries and bodies of water with and without articles.

2 **Page 71.**
Read the instructions and the example. Have students complete the exercise individually or in pairs. Go over the answers as a class.

Answers: 1. X 2. the 3. X 4. X 5. the 6. X 7. X 8. the 9. the 10. X 11. the 12. X 13. the 14. the 15. X 16. X 17. the 18. X 19. the 20. the

Optional Activity: Have students use the information in Activity 2 to make a list of rules (and examples) about when to use the definite article. Encourage them to add additional examples for each rule.

3 Page 71.
Read the instructions and example. Have students work individually or in pairs and correct answers with other pairs. Encourage them to read the entire passage once first for overall comprehension.

Answers: 1. X, the 2. X, X, the, the, the 3. the, X, X, the, X 4. the, X, the, X 5. the, X, X, the, X 6. the, X, the, X 7. X, the, X, the, X, the, X 8. X, X, X 9. the, the, X, the 10. the, X 11. X, the, the 12. X, X, the, the, the 13. the, the 14. X, the, X, the, the, the (or X), X 15. X, X

4 Page 74.
Read the instructions. Have students do the exercise individually or in pairs and correct answers with other pairs. Encourage them to read the entire passage once first for overall comprehension. Remind them that for this exercise they may also use *a* or *an*.

Answers: 1. X, X 2. The, the, the, the 3. X, a, X 4. the, X, a, the, X, the 5. the, X, the 6. X, a, the 7. The, the, the, X, the 8. X, a, X, an, the, the, the 9. X, an, the, an, the, an, X, the 10. X, a, X, the, X, the

5 Page 74.
Read the instructions and the example. Have students do the exercise individually or in pairs and correct answers with other pairs. Encourage them to read the entire passage once first for overall comprehension. Remind them that for this exercise they may also use *a* or *an*.

Answers: 1. the 2. the 3. the 4. the 5. the 6. X 7. X 8. X 9. X 10. X 11. The 12. the 13. X 14. X 15. X 16. the 17. X 18. X 19. the 20. X 21. the 22. the 23. X 24. the 25. the 26. X 27. The 28. the 29. the 30. the 31. the 32. the 33. The 34. an 35. X 36. X 37. X 38. the 39. the 40. X 41. the 42. the 43. the 44. the 45. A 46. the 47. the 48. the 49. X 50. X 51. X 52. The 53. the 54. X 55. the 56. the 57. X

Using What You've Learned

6 Page 76.
Read the instructions. To help students prepare, allow some time for brainstorming ideas. Have them list possible places they could describe and then choose the one that seems the most interesting to them. Then allow them time to list information they could include in their presentation. They should note basic information, such as where the place is, when they go there, who else goes there, and why they like to go there. They could also get details to include in their presentation by listing information for the five senses: what do they see there? Hear? Smell? Taste? Touch? Feel (emotionally).

Optional Activity: After students have given their presentations from Activity 6, have them use their notes to write a paragraph or page-long description of the place. Or, assign this writing task as an alternative to the presentation if you feel your students need more practice with writing and you are limited on time.

Part 5 More on Nouns and Noun Modifiers

Setting the Context

Have students discuss the prereading questions in groups or as a class. Have them share any information they may know about Mt. Everest. Then have them read the passage individually.

Discussing Ideas

Have students discuss the passage and the question in groups.

A. Word Order with Noun Modifiers

Remind students that modifiers are words, phrases, or clauses that give additional information about a noun, and that when there are more than one of them, they follow a set order. Have students read the information and examples in the chart. An alternative way to present the material in the chart (which involves some preparation time) is to give the students the four examples sentences scrambled. (You can write out the different words on index cards or type of the sentences with the words scrambled in each). Have students try to unscramble them either before or after they look at the chart. If they unscramble them before, the activity serves as a diagnostic/review; if they unscramble them after or while they read the chart, the activity becomes a hands-on way to understand the information in the chart.

Optional Activity: Scramble all the words or phrases of the sentences in activity 1 (below) on index cards, keeping the cards for each sentence separate, and have students compete in teams or pairs to unscramble them quickly and correctly.

1 Page 77.

Read the instructions and the example. Have students work individually or in pairs to come up with alternative expressions. Check answers as a class.

Answers: 1. The Himalayas are the highest range of mountains in the world. 2. According to a clerk at the trigonometric Survey of India, Peak XV was the highest mountain in the world. 3. This peak, Peak XV, was the highest peak that had ever been recorded. 4. A careful check of his calculations confirmed his claim. 5. The elevation of the top of Peak XV was set at 29,002 feet. 6. More careful, modern observations have established an elevation of 29,028. 7. Early surveyors did not know that Tibetans had long ago recognized Peak XV as the world's greatest mountain. 8. For many centuries, the Tibetans had called it Chomolongma, which means mother goddess of the world.

B. Collective Nouns: Agreement with Verbs and Pronouns

Read the explanation above the chart. Have students read the examples and common collective nouns out loud. Be sure that they understand that American English tends to treat collective nouns as singular. British English typically treats them as plural because they focus more on the individual members of the unit, rather than the unit as a whole.

2 Page 78.

Read the instructions and the example. Students can complete this exercise individually or in pairs, and check answers in groups.

Answers: 1. was, They 2. was, was 3. it 4. it, was 5. was, its 6. were 7. its 8. was, its 9. was 10. was

Optional Activity: To expand Activity 2, have students write a paragraph using as many collective nouns as possible (modeled after the sentences in Activity 2). They could write about another team that did something requiring great courage (perhaps a sports team or other explorers they know of). Alternatively, students could work in groups or pairs and write up the event as a news report, then perform it for the class. The class can listen closely for the collective nouns used by each group.

C. Subject/Verb Word Order with "Negative" Adverbs

Read the information above the chart and have students read the examples out loud. Ask students to label the parts of speech in each example sentence and to notice the inverted word order when the adverb begins the sentence (when it precedes the subject). Give them (or elicit) some incorrect examples for contrast: *Scarcely he was able to breathe; He scarcely was able to breathe.*

3 Page 79.

Read the instructions and the example. Have students work individually and compare answers with a partner.

Answers: 1. Never had a man succeeded in reaching the summit. / A man had never succeeded in reaching the summit. 2. Seldom had men climbed to such heights without needing medical assistance. / Men had seldom climbed to such heights... 3. Rarely are there calm days on Mt. Everest. / There are rarely calm days on Mt. Everest. 4. Barely had they reached the summit when they embraced and Hillary took Norkay's picture. / They had barely reached the summit when... 5. Rarely do human beings endure so much hardship and yet succeed. / Human beings rarely endure so much...

Optional Activity: Have students use negative adverbs to write sentences about themselves.

D. Parallel Structure with Nouns and Noun Modifers

Read the explanation above the chart. Have students read the examples and notes in the chart. Have them label the parts of speech in each example sentence (both the correct and the incorrect ones) in order to highlight the parallel structures (or lack thereof). Tell them that labeling the parts of speech is a good way to check their own writing for parallel structure.

4 Page 80.

Read the instructions and example. Point out that some sentences may be correct. Have students work individually or in pairs. Correct answers as a class. Encourage students to explain the reasons behind the errors, and to state the parts of speech of the parallel structures.

Answers (corrections are underlined):
1. After 1953, different climbing teams established routes <u>on the northeast ridge and the southern ridge of Mt. Everest</u>. (OR...on the northeast and southern ridges of Mt. Everest)
2. None of these expeditions attempted the west ridge, which was considered to be <u>an extremely difficult and dangerous route</u>. 3. Correct
4. Correct 5. The south ridge of the mountain was quite well known to the climbers, but the west ridge of the mountain <u>was completely unknown</u>. 6. On February 20, 1963, an army of a thousand, including <u>climbers</u>, Sherpas, and porters, began the 185-mile hike to Mt. Everest.
7. Correct 8. Three weeks later, on May 22, Luther Jerstand and Barry Bishop, climbing the south ridge, and Thomas Hornbein and William Unsoeld, <u>climbing</u> the west ridge, reached the top of Mt. Everest.

Using What You've Learned

5 Page 81.

Read the instructions. Have students read the quotation by Mallory individually and discuss the quotation in groups.

Optional Activity: After students discuss Activity 5, have them write up their analysis/opinion of the quotation by George Mallory. Have students proofread each other's writing in pairs, checking in particular for correct use of the structures presented in this chapter.

Video Activities: Extreme Sports

Before You Watch

Have students discuss the questions in small groups. To facilitate conversation, you might bring in some pictures of hang gliders and/or paragliders.

Watch [on video]

Have students read the questions before having them watch the video. Play the video. Give students time to answer the questions. Play the video again, if necessary. Go over the answers as a class.

Answers: 1. a 2. c 3. b

Watch Again [on video]

Have students read the questions. Play the video and have students answer the questions. Put them in pairs to check their answers. Replay the video, if necessary.

Answers: 1. Torrey Pines 2. a. *It* is hang gliding and paragliding. b. people who have done the sport many times c. frightening, threatening d. peaceful, serene 3. a, c, e

After You Watch

Read the instructions.

Answers: 1. a 2. an 3. The 4. the 5. The, the 6. a 7. The

Focus on Testing

Set a time limit for students to complete this test individually. Go over the answers as a class.

Answers:
Part 1: 1. b 2. c 3. b 4. a
Part 2: 1. c 2. c 3. c 4. a

Sex and Gender

Goals

- Commands and exclamations
- Compound sentences
- Transitions
- Complex sentences
- Sentence problems

Introduction

This chapter covers grammatical structures that are often more of an issue in formal written English, though many of them will apply to students' speaking as well. You can use this introductory passage as a diagnostic by having students discuss it at length and then write a paragraph summarizing and analyzing the passage, or writing a brief reaction. Look specifically for these grammatical issues in their writing.

Before having students read the passage, have a brief pre-reading discussion as a class or in small groups. Then have students read the passage individually.

Discussing Ideas

Have students discuss the question in small groups and report their ideas, with specific examples, to the class. You could also encourage students to think of this issue cross-culturally, perhaps comparing their impressions of gender differences in North America compared with other countries.

Part 1 Commands and Explanations

Setting the Context

Have students discuss the prereading questions and the nursery rhyme in pairs or groups. Then have students read the passage individually.

Discussing Ideas

Have students discuss the passage and the questions in small groups or pairs. Ask them if they can think of examples of gender role conditioning in other cultures. You can also encourage them to debate the issue by pairing people who feel gender roles are learned with those who feel they are innate.

Optional Activity: If you have students debate the innate versus learned behavior issue, and if time permits, have them do a little research on the Web or in the library to find some examples to support their views.

A. Commands

Elicit from students a definition of a noun and different types of nouns. Then have them check what they already know about nouns by reading the explanation in Part A. Have them list a couple of examples of each type of noun.

B. Count Nouns

Students may have learned this structure under the term *imperatives*. Have them read the examples in the chart. Point out that the subject *you* is implied. You might also model appropriate tone of voice for commands and suggest the use of *please* to soften a command.

1 Page 87.

Read the instructions. Have students complete the exercise in individually, in pairs, or as a class. Check answers as a class.

Answers: The verb for each of the commands is *be*. The subject is *you;* it is implied.

2 Page 87.

Read the instructions and the example. Have students complete the exercise individually and compare their answers in groups. Encourage them to debate over whether or not these commands are most likely directed at girls or boys, as these stereotypes may be changing or may vary from culture to culture.

Answers: 1. Get some exercise. 2. Go on a diet. 3. Eat all your food so you can be strong. 4. Don't go around with those types of people. 5. Think about your reputation. 6. Have a good time before you're too old.

Optional Activity: Have students use their discussion of the commands in Activity 2 to list stereotypical traits of males and females. You can expand this activity even more by having students use both their discussions and their lists to write a short paragraph on the topic of stereotypical gender behaviors, incorporating commands when possible.

3 Page 87.
Read the instructions and the example. Have students complete the exercise individually and compare their commands with a partner.

Answers: 1. Don't eat 2. Cut 3. Comb (or brush) 4. Wear (or use) 5. Wear (or use) 6. Wash

Optional Activity: Put students into pairs or groups. Have them incorporate the commands from Activities 2 and 3 into a short skit about gender behavior. If students are in pairs, they could write and perform dialogues between a parent and a son or daughter. If they are in groups of three, they could perform conversations between two parents and a son or daughter, or one parent and a son and daughter.

4 Page 88.
Read the instructions. You can have them do this activity in groups or as a class; encourage them to label the parts of speech in the two exclamations and state a rule about using *why* and *how*.

Answers: *What* is used before a noun. *How* is used before an adjective (or an adverb, though the example passage does not show an example of *how* + adverb). (Point out that although *what* and *how* are question words, question word order is not used for exclamations that use these words. *How pretty is he* is not correct).

5 Page 88.
Read the instructions and the examples. Have students work individually or in pairs to form exclamations from the statements.

Answers: 1. How tired Bill looks. 2. What a tired expression Bill has. 3. What a large nose Pinocchio had. 4. How large Pinocchio's nose was. 5. What a warm smile Mary has. 6. How warmly Mary is smiling. 7. How rich Tim is. 8. What an awful lot of money Tim has.

Optional Activity: Have students walk around the room and give each other compliments, using both *what* and *how*.

Using What You've Learned

6 Page 88.
Read the instructions. Allow ample time for students to practice their presentations. They should plan their affirmative and negative commands in advance, but need not write out the entire dialogue. To encourage careful listening when the role-plays are being performed, tell the other students to listen carefully for examples of commands and to write down what they hear.

Optional Activity: For more practice using commands (and perhaps weaving in exclamations as well), have students do a similar role-play to the one they performed in Activity 6, but between a parent and an older child—a teenager. Are there different rules? (If time does not allow this expansion, you could also have students discuss how the role-plays might change if a teenager was involved).

7 Page 88.
Read the instructions and the example. Allow students some preparation time to choose a student and to write out some exclamations. To ensure that every student gets discussed, you could put everyone's name in a hat and have students draw a name of someone to write about. (If they draw their own name they should put it back and draw again).

8 Page 88.
Read the instructions and the example. Be sure to read the example melodramatically. Explain the meaning of *melodramatic* (exaggerated, overly emotional) or see if students can definite it from context after reading the instructions and the example.

9 Page 89.
Read the instructions. Make sure that everyone is familiar with the story of Little Red Riding Hood. If not, you may wish to distribute a copy of it (a simplified children's version would do, just to give them the basic story elements). Be sure that they incorporate exclamations; they could also try to incorporate commands.

Part 2 Compound Sentences

Setting the Context

Have students discuss the prereading questions in groups or as a class. Then have students read the passage individually.

Discussing Ideas

Have students discuss the passage in pairs or small groups and discuss the questions. You might also encourage students to discuss IQ tests in general—what do they know about them? Do they think they are accurate? What are their advantages and disadvantages? They can even look for some examples of IQ tests on the Web.

A. Coordinating Conjunctions with Clauses

Read the explanation of coordinating conjunctions.

1 Page 90.
Students can complete this exercise individually or do it together as a class. If you do it as a class, read the passage aloud while students read along and look for the coordinating conjunctions.

Answers: The sentences with the connecting words *for* and *but* are the last two sentences of the passage. *For* expresses a cause-effect relationship. *But* expresses a contrasting ideas relationship. The sentences are punctuated in the same way; a comma appears before the conjunction.

2 Page 90.
Read the instructions. Encourage students first to determine the relationship between the sentences in each number, and then to add the appropriate conjunction. Students can complete this exercise individually and check answers in pairs or as a class. Point out that in some cases there may be more than one possibility, and that for all of them the punctuation will be the same (a comma before the conjunction)

Answers: 1. but (yet) 2. for 3. and 4. and (so) 5. but (yet) 6. or

Optional Activity: Have students write out a key to the meaning of each of the coordinating conjunctions, based on the passage, Activities 1 and 2, and their own knowledge. Answers: and = additional information, but = contrasting information, yet = contrasting information, for = cause/effect, or = choice, so = logical conclusion

3 Page 90.
Read the instructions and the example. Students can complete this exercise individually and share their answers in groups or with the class, since they are using their classmates for subject matter. Answers will vary.

4 Page 91.
Read the instructions and the example. Students can complete this exercise individually and share their answers in groups. Answers will vary.

B. Coordinating Conjunctions with Words and Phrases

Read the explanation above the chart. Have students read the examples and units of measurement in the chart. Emphasize the fact that the structures used on either side of a conjunction must be parallel (the same part of speech, or two phrases, or two clauses). Give some incorrect examples for contrast: *We were tired but happiness; The clerk spoke rapidly yet clear.* Tell them that a good way to check their own writing for parallel structure is to circle each coordinating conjunction and label the parts of speech on either side of it.

5 Page 91.

Read the instructions. Have students work individually or in pairs. You may wish to point out that the first section, under the heading *Julie*, is merely to establish a context for the sentences to come; they need not do anything with this sentence but read it.

Answers: 1. Julie's face seemed, at times, childlike, but on closer inspection was wizened, for she had been through a lot in her life. 2. Julie was born in the Philippines and grew up in China during the ten-year Cultural Revolution, so she is no stranger to hard times. 3. Some of her family starved during the Cultural Revolution, for there was no food to buy or borrow. 4. Julie was able to stay alive by moving to a communal farm, but she became ill with hepatitis there and almost died. 5. Eventually, the situation in China improved, so Julie moved back to the city and got married. 6. She had a husband, a child, and a relatively well-paying job, but she left them all to come to the United States. 7. She worked and studied in Santa Barbara, California, and she didn't see her son or husband for several years. 8. Leaving China was a big sacrifice for her and her family, but it was an opportunity that comes once in a lifetime. 9. Julie finally left California for China, for she wanted to see her son and husband, and she planned to return to Santa Barbara to finish her degree. 10. Life gave Julie a very special opportunity and forced her to make difficult choices between family and education.

Optional Activity: Have students write a paragraph about someone else they know who has done something that does not conform to traditional expectations of gender roles. They can use the sentences about Julie in Activity 5 as models, and pay particular attention to the correct use of coordinating conjunctions and parallel structure.

C. Correlative Conjunctions

Read the explanation above the chart. Have students take turns reading the examples in the chart out loud. Encourage them to label the parts of speech in the boxed sections of each example sentence. Go over the notes together, eliciting additional examples of sentences with each type of correlative conjunctions. Emphasize the fact that concise writing is favored in American English; read the note to this effect at the bottom of the chart.

6 Page 93.

Read the instructions and the example. Have students work individually or in pairs. Check answers as a class.

Answers: 1. Not only did Jassem love the idea of studying in the United States, but also he wanted a break from his job. / Jassem loved idea not only of studying in the United States but also the idea of taking a break from his job. 2. Either he could study at Columbia University or he could study at Michigan State University. / He could study at either Columbia University or Michigan State University. 3. Both his colleagues and his family encouraged him to go. 4. However, his wife could neither accompany nor visit him for at least six months.

7 Page 94.

Read the instructions and the example. Have students find repetitions and combine sentences individually or in pairs.

Answers (of combined sets): 1. He had never been either far away from his family or outside of Kuwait. (OR: He had been neither far away from his family nor outside of Kuwait). 2. Both the language and the food, climate, and culture were new to him. 3. Neither his fellow students nor his friends from Kuwait could help him.

4. In the following months, both Jassem's homesickness and his telephone bill grew.
5. Either he would call his wife every morning and afternoon, or she would think that something was wrong.

8 Page 95.
Read the instructions and the example. Have students work individually or in pairs to complete Jassem's complaints.

Sample Answers: 1. I want to see both my wife and my kids. 2. Either send my family to the United States or permit them to visit me.
3. I am not only bored but also lonely.
4. Living alone is neither convenient nor happy.
5. I wish I knew someone who was both rich and important. 6. Neither my son nor my daughter know how difficult this separation is.
7. Not only are my children intelligent but also they are beautiful. 8. Either my children will study at Berkeley or they will study at UC Davis.

9 Page 95.
Read the instructions and example. Point out that some sentences may be correct. Have students work individually or in pairs. Correct answers as a class. Encourage students to explain the reasons behind the errors.

Answers (corrections are underlined):
1. Julie survived not only the Cultural Revolution but also life without her mother.
2. She didn't stop working or studying. (OR: She stopped neither working nor studying).
3. Correct 4. Jassem had to either pay the phone bill or lose his phone. 5. Not only was Jassem unhappy, but also his wife was unhappy. 6. Correct

Using What You've Learned

10 Page 95.
Read the instructions and the example. If you have students discuss this topic in pairs, go around and listen for common problems or errors to review later as a class. Alternatively, this activity could be done as a memory chain activity if you did not already do it as an optional activity previously.

11 Page 95.
Read the instructions. Allow plenty of time for students to do a little research on the Web or in the library if necessary. Students could also make this a more challenging presentation by comparing marriage customs between two cultures.

Optional Activity: Have students use their presentation notes from Activity 11 to write a brief report about marriage customs in another culture.

Part 3 Transitions

Setting the Context

Have students discuss the prereading questions in groups or as a class. Then have them read the passage individually.

Discussing Ideas

Have students discuss the passage and the questions in small groups. Encourage them to paraphrase the ideas in their own words. If time permits, you could also have students do a little extra research on the Web or in the library to find some additional information on this topic to share with the class.

A. Transitions

Elicit from students what they already know about transitions: what some examples are and when they are used. Read the explanation above the chart. You may wish to add that transitions can link ideas between sentences or between paragraphs. They help aid coherence, or the sense that ideas "flow" in a written work. Have students read the examples in the chart out loud and go over the notes as a class. It may be useful to point out that an alternative term for transitions that come between two independent clauses (clauses with a subject and a verb that can stand on their own as a complete sentence) is *conjunctive adverbs*. Point out that either a semicolon or a period can come before one of these types of transitions (they can come in the middle or at the beginning of a sentence), but a comma must always follow the transition. Write some incorrect examples on the board for contrast and have students correct them: *The dinner was delicious, nevertheless we felt that it was overpriced. The main course was superb; however, not the dessert.* (Note that in the second incorrect example, the problem is that an independent clause does not follow this transition word; there is no verb).

1 **Page 97.**

Read the instructions and the example. Students can do this identification activity individually or in pairs. Point out that this is both an exercise and a reference list of types of transitions and their uses. Answers may vary within each section (that is, transitions of additional information could be used interchangeable, as could those of contrast, result, etc.) Check answers as a class. Note that there are only two choices for correct punctuation: beginning a sentence with the transition word (which must begin with a capital letter and be followed by a comma), or having the transition word in the middle, with a semicolon and a comma on either side. Also note that the transition *otherwise*, which indicates negative condition, may be unfamiliar or confusing for some students. When you check answers, explain that another way to think of this word is *if this were not true, something else would be the result.* You could have students "translate" the negative conditions in numbers 13–16 as affirmative conditions to underscore this point.

Answers: 1. At birth, boys are, on average, one-half inch taller than girls; moreover, boys weigh slightly more. OR: At birth, boys are, on average, one-half inch taller than girls. Moreover, boys weigh slightly more. (for each of the sentences, either structure is possible). 2. Girls develop faster physically than boys; furthermore, girls mature more quickly intellectually. 3. Female babies suffer from fewer birth defects; in addition, as they mature, women contract fewer diseases. 4. Later in life, men are more prone to hepatitis; also, they are more susceptible to heart disease, tuberculosis, and asthma. 5. The Y chromosome brings more males into the world; however, it does not make things easier for them when they arrive. 6. By the age of 20, the number of surviving males and females is about equal; nevertheless, by the age of 30, women are clearly ahead. 7. A great number of diseases are more likely to trouble men; however, only genital cancer and diabetes more often strike women. 8. Women have a higher rate of genital cancer; nevertheless, when all types of cancer are included, men suffer in greater numbers. 9. Men's bodies are generally bigger than women's; thus, men have heavier brains and hearts. 10. A man's lungs are larger than a woman's; therefore, he takes four to six fewer breaths per minute. 11. Women's hips are larger than men's; hence, when women walk, their hips sway, and they run more slowly. 12. Women have less water in their bodies; consequently, women become drunk more easily. 13. Scientists have done a great deal of genetic research; otherwise, we wouldn't know the role of genes and chromosomes in reproduction and illness. 14. The Y chromosome weakens males; otherwise, men would live as long as women. 15. Men have more water in their bodies; otherwise, they would get drunk just as easily as women. 16. Women have larger hips; otherwise, they might be able to run faster than men. 17. Women are stronger than most people thin; in fact, a woman can often lift and carry a larger percentage of her body weight than a man can of his. 18. Women float in water more easily than men; as a matter of fact, women are on average 10 percent more buoyant. 19. Women often have a great endurance for extremely low temperatures; in fact, they can survive in very cold conditions much longer than men can. 20. Men tend to have a lower percentage of fat than women; as a matter of fact, adult males average 20 percent fat, whereas adult women commonly have over 25 percent.

Optional Activity: Have students go back to a piece of writing they did earlier in this unit and add a variety of these transition words where appropriate.

2 Page 98.

Read the instructions. Read the paragraph aloud while students follow along and look for errors in punctuation; your voice inflection may help them to discover the errors with more ease.

Answers (corrections are underlined):

The sex of a child is determined at conception; <u>however</u>, no differences begin to show in the fetus until six to eight weeks later. At that point, androgens, the male hormones, come into play. Interestingly, these male hormones (or their absence) affect both sexes. Androgens are produced within the XY fetus; <u>as a result</u>, a boy beings to develop. These androgens are absent in the XX fetus; thus, the latter starts to take on female characteristics.

How important are these androgens to the development of the male child? As a matter of <u>fact, they</u> are essential. For the boy to develop, the male hormones must be present; <u>otherwise</u>, "he" will be born with the anatomy of a girl.

(Note that for each sentence above where the transition word appears in the middle of the sentence, an alternative would be beginning a new sentence with the transition word (capitalized) followed by a comma.

3 Page 98.

Read the instructions. Be sure students understand that they are to summarize the content of the passage, not the grammar rule they just practiced in Activity 2. Have pairs exchange completed summaries to check for correct use of transition words. Answers will vary.

4 Page 98.

Read the instructions. Encourage students to read the passage once first for overall comprehension. Students can work individually or in pairs. Check answers as a class. Note that for each of the sample answers given below, any transition word within each category of transition could be substituted. Therefore, answers may vary. The important thing is that they choose the correct category of transition to express the relationship of the ideas.

Sample Answers: 1. therefore
2. ; however, 3. Furthermore,
4. ; nevertheless, 5. . However, 6. In fact,
7. ; moreover, (or: ; as a matter of fact,)
8. ; otherwise, 9. ; nevertheless, 10. . Thus,

5 Page 99.

Read the instructions and example. Have students work individually or in pairs to complete the sentences in their own words.

Sample Answers: 1. Women are smaller than men; nevertheless, they present a strong competition to them in many sports. 2. In the past, women rarely exercised; consequently, many older women may not understand today's emphasis on fitness for women.
3. Women suffer from fewer diseases; as a result, they live longer than men. 4. Men have historically dominated women; in fact, some people say that it is men who write history.
5. Boys are believed to be better at math; however, test results show that this is not really true. 6. We should finish this exercise; otherwise, we will be here all day.

Optional Activity: Have students write sentences with an alternative form of punctuation for each of the sentences in Activity 5. (In other words, if they wrote sentences with a transition in the middle, have them write the same sentence with a transition beginning a sentence, and change the punctuation accordingly).

Using What You've Learned

6 Page 100.

Read the instructions. Go over guidelines for formal debates, and allow plenty of time for students to come up with reasons to support their opinions. Note that this debate could also be conducted in teams; you could have small groups where the women debate with the men, on separate teams.

Optional Activity: Have students write up their discussion notes for Activity 6 into a short argumentative essay. Have students exchange essays in pairs to proofread for errors and to give feedback on the overall organization and ideas. Allow time for revisions.

Part 4 Complex Sentences

Setting the Context

Have students discuss the prereading question in groups or as a class. Then have them read the passage individually.

Discussing Ideas

Have students discuss the passage and the questions in groups. If possible, have students from different languages in each group so that they can share their knowledge of gender communication differences in their own languages.

A. Complex Sentences: An Overview

By now students may be familiar with the terms independent clause and dependent clause, as you may have touched on them in earlier sections. This section, however, describes the three different classes of dependent clauses (adjective, adverb, and noun) and presents various types of connecting words to use with them. Elicit from students what they already know about independent and dependent clauses, for review, and then read the explanation above the charts. Have students read the examples in the chart. Point out in the examples how dependent clauses, although they have a subject and a verb, cannot stand on their own as a complete sentence.

Optional Activity: For more practice with connecting words and various types of dependent clauses, write some independent clauses on the board (or elicit some from students) and have students make complex sentences by adding dependent clauses and connecting words.

2 Page 102.

Read the instructions. Have students complete the exercise in individually or in pairs. Check answers as a class. Encourage students to state the function of each clause (for example: to express manner, place, time, etc.)

Answers (connecting words are boldfaced; dependent clauses are underlined):

1. Researchers in Madagascar have found **that** the most aggressive buyers and sellers are women. (noun clause)
2. **Although** women often bargain in the marketplace, men only buy and sell goods that have a fixed price. (adverb clause)
3. Social scientists who have studied Madagascar aren't sure **why** the women dominate confrontations. (noun clause)
4. no dependent clause (note that students may mistake In most other cultures for a dependent clause; in fact, it is a prepositional phrase. There is no verb, so it cannot be a clause).
5. No dependent clause (this is a compound sentence, with two independent clauses joined by the coordinating conjunction *but*)
6. **When** a male uses *yo*, it means something similar to, "You had better believe me!" (adverb clause)
7. **If** a female says *yo*, it often has a softer meaning. (adverb clause)
8. Sex differences in the English language were much greater in the past **because** men and women socialized together very little. (adverb clause)
9. In Victorian England (1837-1901), the difference between male and female language was **so great that** women couldn't use or listen to a large number of "male" words. (adverb clause)
10. For example, leg was considered **such an offensive word that** it was never used in the presence of a woman. (adverb clause)
11. Even the legs of furniture were covered **so that** women would not be shocked. (adverb clause)

3 Page 104.
Read the instructions and the example. Have students complete the exercise individually or in pairs and compare answers in groups.

Answers (connecting words are boldfaced; dependent clauses are underlined):

1. **Since** Victoria ruled Britain, the language of males and females has become quite similar.
2. Linguists have proved **that** differences still exist in the way men and women speak English.
3. The differences **that/which** remain are more subtle, however.
4. **Although/even though/despite the fact that/in spite of the fact that** some "offensive words" are more common among males, women are using these words more and more.
5. Still, women tend to speak a more refined form of the language than men **who/that** are in the same social class.
6. In most languages, the voice quality of males and females is **so different that** the sex of a speaker is recognized immediately.
7. In fact, there is **such a big difference that** one sex has trouble imitating the other.
8. **When** an American woman imitates a man, she separates the syllables more clearly and lowers the pitch.
9. However, **if** an American male wants to sound like a female, he uses more "breathiness" in his voice, blends the stressed syllables, and raises the pitch.
10. By contrast, a male Mohave Indian needs only to use words typical of a woman **so that** he can sound like one.

B. Complex Sentences: Focus

Read the explanation above the chart. Have students read the examples in the chart out loud. For a more hands-on approach, you could have them cover up the "focus" column while they read the example sentences and have them try to determine the focus of the sentence—and how one determines it—before checking the explanation in the focus column.

4 Page 105.
Read the instructions. Have students do the exercise individually or in pairs and correct answers with other pairs. Encourage them to read the sentences once first for overall comprehension.

Answers: (main clause is underlined in each sentence):

1. The Iroquois Indians, who probably came as close to having a matriarchal society as any people, lived in North America. (Focus is on where the Iroquois lived). The Iroquois Indians, who lived in North America, probably came as close to having a matriarchal society as any people. (Focus is on the Iroquois' matriarchal society)
2. In this society, even though the women played a central role in the election of new leaders, these leaders were always men. (Focus is on male leaders in this society). In this society, even though the leaders were always men, women played a central role in the elections of these leaders. (Focus is on women's roles in the elections).
3. In the last century, Great Britain and the Philippines each gave the highest governmental position to a woman; thus, these might at first glance appear to have been matriarchal societies. (Focus is equally on these two societies' treatment of women, and how the treatment suggests these were matriarchal societies). Because Great Britain and the Philippines each gave the highest governmental position to a woman, they might appear at first glance to have been matriarchal societies. (Focus is on how these two countries might appear to have been matriarchal societies).
4. While the leaders of both countries were female, the governments actually were dominated by males. (Focus is on male-

dominated governments). The leaders of both countries were female in spite of the fact that the governments actually were dominated by males. (Focus is on the female leaders).

5. Margaret Thatcher became Prime Minister of Great Britain when her Conservative Party defeated the Labor Party in 1979. (Focus is on Margaret Thatcher's election to the position of Prime Minister). When Margaret Thatcher became Prime Minister of Great Britain in 1979, it was due to the victory of the Conservative Party over the Labor Party. (Focus is on the Conservative Party's victory over Labor)
6. It was a revolution in 1985 that brought Corazon Aquino to power in the Philippines. (Focus is on the revolution of 1985). Corazon Aquino came to power in the Philippines because of the revolution that broke out in 1985. (Focus is on Corazon Aquino's coming to power in the Philippines).

5 Page 106.

Read the instructions. Have students do the exercise individually or in pairs and compare answers in groups.

Sample Answers (may vary): 1. The Iroquois Indians lived in North America, and they probably came as close to having a matriarchal society as any people. 2. In this society, these new leaders were always men; however, the women played a central role in the election of new leaders. 3. In the last century, Great Britain and the Philippines each gave the highest governmental position to a woman, so these might at first glance appear to have been matriarchal societies. 4. The leaders of both countries were female, yet the governments actually were dominated by males. 5. The Conservative Party defeated the Labor Party in 1979; consequently, Margaret Thatcher became Prime Minister of Great Britain. 6. There was a revolution in the Philippines in 1985; as a result, Corazon Aquino to power.

Using What You've Learned

6 Page 106.

Read the instructions. Have students write up these questions in survey form, with room to take notes, and encourage them to think of some additional questions of their own. Point out that this activity is not a debate, but an information-gathering exercise to learn cross-cultural perspectives on gender roles.

Optional Activity: To expand Activity 6, students could interview more than one person—perhaps someone from North American culture and another culture, or two different cultures—and structure their presentation as a comparison of perspectives.

Optional Activity: Have students write their notes from Activity 6 into a short report.

Part 5 Sentence Problems

Setting the Context

Have students discuss the prereading questions in groups or as a class. Then have them read the passage individually.

Discussing Ideas

Have students discuss the passage and the question in groups.

Optional Activity: To expand the Discussing Ideas section above, have students debate the advantages and disadvantages of stay-at-home dads. Or have students write their views into a paragraph. You could use the paragraph as a diagnostic tool to help determine what areas of this last section to focus on the most, or use it for students to return to at the end of the section and edit for errors.

A. Comma Splices and Run-On Sentences

Read the explanation above the charts. Have students read the information and examples in the chart. Have students state (orally or in writing) the punctuation rules for each type of sentence based on their analysis of the examples. Elicit some additional examples and give them some incorrect examples for contrast.

1 Page 107.

Read the instructions and example. Point out that some sentences may be correct, and that there may be several ways to correct the errors. Have students work individually or in pairs. Have students compare their corrections in groups (to stress how a variety of options may be available). Encourage students to explain the reasons behind the errors.

Sample Answers (corrections are underlined): 1. Although they live in a traditional society, Jean and Francoise have a modern marriage. 2. Jean is a well-known political cartoonist and works at home; his wife, on the other hand, teaches linguistics at a university and spends most of her day on campus. 3. Since Jean is at home more, he does more of the housework and helps care for the children. On the other hand, Francoise does the rest of the cleaning and all of the sewing. 4. Whereas Francoise fills out the tax forms, Jean does the shopping and most of the cooking. The relationship is not perfect, but it works. 5. They are delighted to have three daughters. Each of the marriage partners disciplines the children, but Jean is more successful at it. 6. Correct

Optional Activity: Have students review a piece of their own writing that they did earlier in this chapter or the book (if you assigned a short paragraph at the beginning of Part 5, it would work well for this task) and look for comma splices.

B. Fragments

Read the explanation above the chart. Have students read the examples and corrections out loud. For additional practice, have groups write out some sentence fragments and then give them to other groups to correct by adding independent clauses or by completing the clauses however they like.

2 Page 108.

Read the instructions and example. Point out that there may be several ways to correct the errors. Have students work individually or in pairs. Have students compare their corrections in groups (to stress how a variety of options may be available).

Sample Answers (corrections are underlined): 1. Many other types of marriage have been tried in different cultures. For example, polygamy has been tried in some cultures. 2. Polygamy, which is another marital variation, involves the marriage of several women to one man. 3. Polygamy is still practiced in a few societies, particularly where there are large numbers of Muslims. 4. Although most Muslims have monogamous marriages, the Koran, the holy book of Islam, allows a man to be married to four wives at one time. 5. Ibn Saud, who founded the Kingdom of Saudi Arabia, had hundreds of wives in his lifetime, but never more than four at one time. 6. The marriage of several men to one woman is called polyandry. 7. Polyandry is uncommon today, despite the fact that it was practiced in India, Ceylon, Tibet, and the South Pacific.

3 Page 109.

Read the instructions. You could read the short passage aloud while students follow along and look for errors; the tone of your voice may help students find the errors. Correct answers as a class. Encourage students to explain the reasons behind the errors. Point out that there may be more than one way to correct some of these errors.

Sample Answers (corrections are underlined):

The marriage of one group of males to another group of females is not practiced today; however, "group marriage" has been tried at different times in the past. The Oneida community in upstate New York was the most successful of these efforts. Oneida, which was founded in 1848 with some 58 adults and their children, was perhaps the most radical social experiment in the history of the United States.

Oneidans believed that romantic love produced selfishness and jealousy. In its place, the members adopted a policy of "free love." Under this policy, all adults were considered married to all adults of the opposite sex. Any male could mate with any female, though both parties had to agree. Later, in 1869, Oneida began the world's first large-scale experiments in eugenics. At that time, certain males and females were scientifically selected to be mates, so that the strongest and most intelligent children would be born.

Optional Activity: Have students review a piece of their own writing that they did earlier in this chapter or the book (if you assigned a short paragraph at the beginning of Part 5, it would work well for this task) and look for fragments.

Using What You've Learned

4 **Page 109.**
Read the instructions and the poem. Have students "translate" the poem into grammatically correct prose and compare their results with a partner.

Optional Activity: Have students write their own poem (perhaps in tribute to a man or a woman) modeled after the John Benites poem. Then have them rewrite it in grammatically correct prose form, or exchange and rewrite them in pairs. Have students discuss as a class or in groups the differences in style and effects in poetry versus prose.

Video Activities: Seeking Love

Before You Watch
Have students discuss the questions in small groups. To spark conversation, you might bring in copies of personal ads from a newspaper.

Watch [on video]
Have students read the questions before having them watch the video. Play the video. Give students time to answer the questions. Play the video again, if necessary. Go over the answers as a class.

Answers: 1. love 2. a, b, c 3. a. should do b. should do c. should not do d. should not do

Watch Again [on video]
Have students read the questions. Play the video and have students answer the questions. Put them in pairs to check their answers. Replay the video, if necessary.

Answers: 1. a 2. d 3. b, c, e 4. b 5. b 6. a

After You Watch
Read the instructions. Have students complete the sentences individually and then share answers with a partner, checking for correct parallel structure.

Sample Answers: 1. I want to have both a career and a family. 2. Either call me on Tuesday or on Wednesday. 3. I am not only lonely but also miserable. 4. Living alone is neither economical nor exciting. 5. I wish I could meet a person who was both intelligent and good-looking. 6. Neither my friends nor my family has been able to help me find someone who is right for me.

Focus on Testing

Set a time limit for students to complete this test individually. Go over the answers as a class.

Answers:
Part 1: 1. c 2. b 3. a 4. b
Part 2: 1. c 2. c 3. b 4. c

Mysteries Past and Present

Goals

- Adjective clauses: restrictive versus nonrestrictive
- Adjective clauses: replacement of subjects
- Adjective clauses: replacement of objects
- Other adjective clause constructions
- Review of chapters 1 to 4

Introduction

You can use this introductory passage as not only a way to introduce the theme of the chapter but also as a diagnostic. Have the students discuss it at length and then write a paragraph summarizing and analyzing the passage, or writing a brief reaction. Look specifically for the presence and/or correct use of adjective clauses in their writing.

Before having students read the passage, have a brief pre-reading discussion as a class or in small groups. Then have students read the passage individually.

Discussing Ideas

Have students discuss the passage and the questions in small groups. If time permits, students could do a little research on the Web or in the library and present a few facts about other ancient societies to the class.

Part 1 Adjective Clauses: Restrictive Versus Nonrestrictive

Setting the Context

Have students discuss the prereading questions in pairs or groups. Have them discuss the title, "Enigma", and see if anyone knows what that word means or can guess at the meaning. Then have students read the passage individually.

Discussing Ideas

Have students discuss the passage and the questions in small groups or pairs. Ask them if they can define the word *enigma* from the context, or think of synonyms (for example: *mystery, puzzle, riddle*). Encourage them to think of a number of theories for why the Great Pyramid was built and report one or two of them to the class.

Optional Activity: If time permits, have students do a little research on the Web or in the library to find more information about the Great Pyramid.

A. Introduction to Adjective Clauses

Read the explanation above the chart. Have students read the examples in the chart out loud. You might emphasize the fact that adjective clauses (also called relative clauses) give more information about a noun, pronoun, or entire sentence by having students also read the example sentences without the adjective clauses. Discuss the differences in meaning. You might also have them circle the relative pronoun in each sentence (*that, which, whose, when, one of which*).

B. Restrictive Versus Nonrestrictive Adjective Clauses

Read the information above the chart. Have students read the examples in the chart. In the first chart, have students also read the examples sentences without the relative clauses and discuss the differences in meaning. Have them note how the sentences without restrictive adjective clauses lead one to ask questions like *What men? Which tombs?* With these sentences, the restrictive clauses are necessary to answer those questions and give us essential information about the subjects. The other sentences, however, still make sense when the adjective clauses are removed — we still get enough basic information to understand the meaning. The information in the clause is nonessential or extra. This distinction is further highlighted in the second set of charts, when the author's point of view or a certain context will determine the choice of the type of clause. Read those sentences aloud, pausing before and after the clause in the second example, so that students can hear the difference between essential and extra information.

1 Page 116.

Read the instructions. Have students complete the exercise in individually, in pairs, or as a class. Check answers as a class and encourage them to state whether each adjective clause is restrictive or nonrestrictive, and how they know.

Answers (adjective clauses are underlined; the nouns they modify are boldfaced):

1. In all, ten pyramids of varying sizes stand on Giza, but **the one** which archaeologists have studied the most is the great pyramid. (restrictive)
2. This pyramid was named after **the pharaoh Cheops**, who supposedly ordered it built. (nonrestrictive)
3. **The Great Pyramid**, which is as tall as a 40-story modern skyscraper, is made up of more than two and a half million blocks of limestone and granite. (nonrestrictive)
4. **These blocks**, which came from an area about 20 miles to the east, weigh from 2 to 20 tons apiece. (nonrestrictive)
5. The Great Pyramid contains more stone than **all the cathedrals, churches, and chapels** that have been built in England since the time of Christ. (restrictive)
6. **The Great Pyramid's base**, which is perhaps the most impressive feature, would cover 13 acres or seven blocks in New York City. (nonrestrictive)
7. The **huge piece of land** on which the pyramid sits was made level to within a fraction of an inch. (restrictive)
8. Modern engineers who have studied the structure are astounded by **the problems** which were involved in building the pyramid. (restrictive)

2 Page 117.

Read the instructions and the example. Have students complete the exercise individually and compare their answers in groups.

Answers:

1. The place where the pyramid stands is almost perfectly level. / The plateau of Giza, where the pyramid stands, is almost perfectly level.
2. My brother, who majored in Egyptian architecture in college, visited Giza in 1985. / My brother who majored in Egyptian architecture in college visited Giza in 1985.
3. The famous Temple of Karnak is located near a town whose ancient name was Thebes. / The famous Temple of Karnak is located in Luxor, whose ancient name was Thebes.
4. In 1922, Howard Carter, who was to become the world's most famous archaeologist, uncovered the tomb of Tutankhamen across the Nile from Karnak. / In 1922, the man who was to become the world's most famous archaeologist uncovered the tomb of Tutankhamen across the Nile from Karnak.
5. While Carter and his men were opening this tomb, they came upon a curse which warned "Death will slay with his wings anyone disturbing the pharaoh." / While Carter and his men were opening this tomb, they came upon the curse of Tutankhamen, which warned "Death will slay with his wings anyone disturbing the pharaoh."

6. Not one of Carter's 20 men, who were present at the tomb's opening, believe that his life was in danger. / Not one of the 20 men who were present at the tomb's opening believed that his life was in danger.

3 **Page 119.**

Read the instructions. Have students read the passage and identify and edit the adjective clauses individually. Then read it aloud (being sure to emphasize pauses before and after nonrestrictive clauses) while students try to check their answers. Finally, go over the answers as a class. Encourage students to read the passage aloud, with the appropriate pauses.

Answers (adjective clauses are underlined; commas are added before and after the nonrestrictive clauses):

In 1798, Egypt was invaded by Napoleon, who wanted to cut off the British trade route to India. With him, Napoleon brought 35,000 troops and a collection of "savants" whose job was to gather knowledge about Egyptian artifacts. The French advanced to Giza, where they were confronted by the Mamluks, who ruled Egypt in the name of the Ottoman Empire.

In the Battle of the Pyramids, the Mamluks, who fought with swords and knives, were easily defeated. Napoleon's troops, whose weapons included cannons and rifles, killed 2,000 Mamluks while losing only 40 of their own. Soon afterward, the Mamluks surrendered to Napoleon, whose savants were then free to explore the pyramids in great detail.

Napoleon's savants, who surveyed the pyramid, were astonished at the geological positioning of the pyramid. First, they discovered that the pyramid was precisely aligned north, south, east, and west. Even more amazing, diagonals that were drawn through the pyramid at right angles outlined the entire Delta of the Nile. Obviously, the structure could not have been located at random. The structure's orientation is a perfect geographic marker. And just as surely, the ancient Egyptians who built the pyramid had a knowledge of astronomy and geography that was not equaled for thousand of years.

Using What You've Learned

4 **Page 120.**

Read the instructions. Students can compare cultural superstitions in groups of people from different cultures, or groups of people from the same or similar cultures. With the first type of grouping, the group presentation could focus on comparing and contrasting things associated with good or bad luck across cultures; with the second type, the presentation could be more informative, educating the class about a particular culture's beliefs.

Optional Activity: Expand Activity 4 into a writing task by having students write a paragraph or a short report about cross-cultural superstitions, incorporating restrictive and nonrestrictive adjective clauses wherever possible. Have students exchange finished paragraphs or reports and check for errors, particularly errors with adjective clauses.

Part 2 Adjective Clauses: Replacement of Subjects

Setting the Context

Have students discuss the prereading questions in groups or as a class. Then have students read the passage individually. You could also have them take turns reading each paragraph out loud, as a class (five people would read) or in groups.

Discussing Ideas

Have students discuss the passage in pairs or small groups and discuss the questions. If time permits, you could have them do some brief research on the Web or in the library to find information about collapsed civilizations to share with the class.

A. Clauses with *Who, Which,* or *That*

Ask students to state what they remember about the function of a pronoun in a sentence. (It replaces a noun). Ask them to give examples of some types of pronouns (for example subject, object, reflective, possessive). Explain that there is a special type of pronoun used in relative clauses, called a *relative pronoun*. It is used to link the relative (adjective) clause to the main clause, and it always has a referent (something it refers to) in the main clause. Read the explanation above the chart. Have students read the examples in the chart out loud. Point out that using relative clauses is a way to combine shorter sentences and make one's writing more varied and interesting. To emphasize the fact that some relative pronouns cannot be used with certain clauses, give them some incorrect examples and state what is wrong with them and how to correct them. (For example: *The man which found the ruins was named Stephens. / The Pyramid who is the most famous is El Castillo. We visited El Castillo, that is at Chichen Itza.*)

1 Page 122.

Read the instructions and the example. Do the first one together as a class. Students can complete this exercise individually or in pairs. You might have them first go through all the sentences and underline the repeated words or ideas (in the example, they would underline <u>Mayan ruins</u> in each sentence). This will help them to choose the correct relative pronoun when they join the sentences. Check answers as a class. Encourage students to state whether each clause is restrictive or nonrestrictive, and what other choices for relative pronouns there are.

Answers: 1. John Lloyd Stephens was an American lawyer and explorer who (that) came across the ruins of Copan in the 1840s. (restrictive; no commas) 2. The famous Pyramid of Kukulcan, which is also known as *El Castillo*, is located at Chichen Itza, which was the capital of the Mayas of the Yucatan. (nonrestrictive; commas) 3. Palenque, which is in the Chiapas highlands of southern Mexico, was built as a gateway to the Underworld. (nonrestrictive; commas) 4. Small windows in the observatory tower at Palenque frame the rising of the Planet Venus, which was use to determine where to begin war. (nonrestrictive; commas) 5. War was declared by kings, who used the stars and planets such as Venus to decide when to fight. (nonrestrictive; commas) 6. Tikal is located in the Tikal National Park, which is a 575- square- kilometer preserve with thousands of ruins. (nonrestrictive; commas) 7. The central city of Tikal, which was about 16 square kilometers, had about 3,000 buildings. (nonrestrictive; commas) 8. Tikal was first explored in 1881 by Alfred Maudslay, who was an English archaeologist. (nonrestrictive; commas) 9. Tulum was a fortresslike port that (which) was established by the Maya for its vast trading network. (restrictive; no commas) 10. The temple at Tulum has a small artch that (which) frames the rising sun at dawn on the winter solstice. (restrictive; no commas) 11. Copan, which was one of the largest Mayan cities, has the best- preserved court of the ancient ball courts. (nonrestrictive; commas) 12. Copan has amazing examples of Mayan hieroglyphs, which include the longest stone inscription in the Western hemisphere. (nonrestrictive; commas)

B. Clauses with *Whose*

Read the explanation above the chart. Have students read the examples in the chart.

2 Page 123.

Read the instructions. Have students work individually or in pairs. Encourage students to state whether each clause is restrictive or nonrestrictive

Answers: 1. A great accomplishment of the Mayans was their writing system, whose inscriptions were in the form of hieroglyphics. (nonrestrictive) 2. The Mayans developed a complex system of books whose primary purpose was to record the transition of power from king to king. (restrictive) 3. Archaeologists found several "codexes" of the Mayans, whose history was recorded in these books.

(nonrestrictive) 4. Many Mayan books did not survive the Spanish Conquest, whose goal was to convert native populations to Christianity. (nonrestrictive) 5. Most of the Mayan books did not survive the humid weather of the tropics or the zealousness of the Spanish conquerors, whose priests burned most of the Mayan books. (nonrestrictive) 6. Explorers found four books, whose names are the Dresden Codex, the Madud Codex, the Paris Codex, and the Grolier Codex. (nonrestrictive) 7. The bark of fig trees was used to make these books, whose pages were inscribed and then folded together and placed in royal tombs. (nonrestrictive) 8. Today many of the Mayan pyramids are still covered by the jungle, whose humid climate continues to deteriorate the ruins. (nonrestrictive)

3 Page 124.

Read the instructions and the example. Explain that definitions are commonly made with the use of adjective clauses. Have students combine the information in the two columns to form definition sentences. Be sure to point out that this is not a matching activity. 1 and a should be combined, 2 and b, and so on.

Answers:
Section 1: b. The caiman is a fierce crocodile that (which) lives in tropical areas in the Americas. c. The coral snake is a snake that (which) is small and highly poisonous. d. The jaguar is a spotted feline whose size and ferocity make it feared throughout the region. e. The ocelot is a spotted leopardlike cat whose habitat extends from Texas through South America.

Section 2: a. The agouti is a rodent that (which) is short-haired, short eared, and similar to a rabbit. b. A peccary is a hoofed mammal that (which) looks somewhat like a pig. c. The rabbit is a small, long-eared rodent that (which) lives in burrows. d. The tapir is a large, stout mammal whose snout is flexible.

Section 3: a. The black howler is a monkey that is one of the largest primates in the Americas. b. The spider monkey is a golden brown monkey whose tail is often longer than its body. c. The quetzal is a large tropical bird whose bright red, green, and white feathers gave Mexico its national colors.

Optional Activity: Have students select five terms that are important to their own culture, or to an activity that they enjoy doing. Have them write definitions using adjective clauses with *that*, *which*, and *whose*.

C. Anticipatory *It* with Adjective Clauses

Read the explanation above the chart. Have students read the examples in the chart.

4 Page 125.

Read the instructions and the example. Have students work individually or in pairs. Check answers as a class.

Answers: 1. It was European diseases that (which) killed thousands of Mayans. 2. It was Catholic missionaries who (that) prohibited the Maya religion. 3. It was Catholic missionaries who (that) burned all but four of the sacred Maya bark- paper books. 4. Was it drought or overpopulation that caused the collapse of this civilization? 5. It was John Lloyd Stephens who published *Incidents of Travel in Central America, Chiapa, and Yucatan* in 1841. 6. It was the English artist Frederick Catherwood who drew amazing pictures of the ruins covered by jungle growth. 7. It was the Mayans who (that) created the Sun Stone, an elaborate calendar. 8. It was the Mayans who (that) invented the concept of zero. 9. It was Mayan geometric architecture that amazed archeologists. 10. It was the famous conductor Leopold Stokowski who spent four days trying to understand the acoustics of the Great Ball Court at Chichen Itza.

5 Page 126.

Read the instructions. Have students edit the paragraph and compare their results in pairs. Encourage them to read their paragraphs aloud.

Sample Answers (may vary):
The Yucatan is a peninsula that juts into the western Caribbean Sea. The Yucatan is the site of many impressive Mayan ruins, many of which are amazing. However, it is Chichen Itza, which was the most important city in the peninsula from the 10th to 12th century, that is perhaps the most amazing.

Chichen Itza is filled with structures that are enormous and awe inspiring. For example, at Chichen Itza is an impressive ball court whose acoustics are phenomenal. In fact, the acoustics of the Ball Court still baffle scientists and musicians who have spent long hours analyzing its construction. Dominating the ruins is the famous 98-foot-tall El Castillo pyramid, which is the most impressive monument in Chichen Itza. El Castillo is a masterpiece of Toltec-Maya architectural design and genius.

Using What You've Learned

6 **Page 126.**
Read the instructions and the example. Have students check meanings of the words in the dictionary, if they need to, but ultimately write each definition in one sentence using an adjective clause. To add a game element, give them (or have them find) a few more words related to reading passages in this chapter. Then have teams or pairs write the definitions (without the words) in quiz form and give them to another team or pair to solve. The first group to guess all the words correctly wins.

Part 3 Adjective Clauses: Replacement of Objects

Setting the Context

Have students discuss the prereading questions about the Inca Empire in groups or as a class. Then have them read the passage individually.

Discussing Ideas

Have students discuss the passage and the questions in small groups. Encourage them to paraphrase the ideas in their own words. If time permits, you could also have students do a little extra research on the Web or in the library to find some additional information about the Nazca Lines to share with the class. You could also bring in some additional pictures of the Nazca Lines, if possible, to spark conversation.

A. Clauses with *Whom, Which,* or *That* (1)

Students are often confused about when to use *whom*, as well as about clauses used to replace objects in general, so take time to present the information in this section. Read the explanation above the chart. Have students read the examples in the chart out loud. You might have them label the parts of speech in the first sentence of each set so they see how the adjective clauses in the second sentence of each set replace the word in the object position. Point out the degrees of formality in descending order in the examples. Also point out that the relative pronoun can be omitted altogether in sentences with restrictive adjective clauses that replace objects; however, this is informal.

1 **Page 128.**
Read the instructions and the example. Students can do this activity individually or in pairs.

Answers: 1. Why did the Indians make designs and figures that (which) they could not appreciate from the ground? (relative pronoun can be omitted) 2. Some argue that the Nazca figures were created by extraterrestrials, whom (which) the Indians might have treated as gods. (Note that the choice of relative pronoun here could be debatable, depending on whether we choose to think of extraterrestrials as people or not) 3. A more conventional theory holds that the Nazca figures were dedicated to the mountain gods whom (who, that) the Indians worshipped. (relative pronoun can be omitted) 4. Newer evidence suggests some of the designs acted as solar calendars that (which) the Indians used to determine when to plant new crops. (relative pronoun can be omitted) 5. In fact, some of the lines which (that) the Indians drew point directly to the places where the sun sets on winter and summer solstice days. (relative pronoun can be omitted)

B. Clauses with *Whom, Which,* or *That* (2)

Read the explanation above the chart. Have students read the examples in the chart out loud. You might have them label the parts of speech in the first sentence of each set so they see how the adjective clauses in the second sentence of each set replace the object of a preposition. Point out the degrees of formality in descending order in the examples. You might also point out that it is best to avoid ending a clause or sentence with a preposition for formal writing in English.

2 Page 129.

Read the instructions and the examples. Have students work individually or in pairs, and compare answers in groups or as a class. You might suggest to students that they read through all the sentences first and circle the prepositions. Encourage them to list the different variations in descending order of formality.

Answers: 1. The Nazca figures about which so much has been written are at least 3,000 years old. / The Nazca figures that so much has been written about are at least 3,000 years old. / The Nazca figures which so much has been written about are at least 3,000 years old. / The Nazca figures so much has been written about are at least 3,000 years old. 2. The plateau on which the figures are located is about 20 miles wide. / The plateau that the figures are located on is about 20 miles wide. / The plateau which the figures are located on is about 20 miles wide. / The plateau the figures are located is about 20 miles wide. 3. The gods for whom the Indians probably drew the lines were thought to reside in distant mountains. / The gods that the Indians probably drew the lines for were thought to reside in distant mountains. / The gods which the Indians probably drew the lines for were thought to reside in distant mountains. / The gods the Indians probably drew the lines for were thought to reside in distant mountains. 4. A German named Maria Reiche, to whom the world owes a great debt, is responsible for preventing the destruction of the figures. / A German named Maria Reiche, whom the world owes a great debt to, is responsible for preventing the destruction of the figures. / A German named Maria Reiche, who the world owes a great debt to, is responsible for preventing the destruction of the figures. / A German named Maria Reiche, that the world owes a great debt to, is responsible for preventing the destruction of the figures.

C. Clauses with *Whose*

Read the explanation above the chart. Have students read the example in the chart. Point out how these clauses with *whose* differ from those presented earlier because these clauses replace objects of verbs and prepositions. They do not replace subjects. Give some incorrect examples for contrast to show how whose cannot be omitted. For example: *Little is known about these Indians, drawings scientists have studied for decades.*

3 Page 130.

Read the instructions and the example. Have students combine the sentences individually and compare their answers in pairs.

Answers: 1. Some lines , whose function scientists still argue about, extend for miles and are almost perfectly straight. 2. The geometrical designs, whose lines the Nazca Indians drew with astounding accuracy, range from rectangles and triangles to spirals.
3. How could a society from 1000 B.C. construct figures and lines whose precision would be difficult to duplicate today?
4. Maria Reiche, whose life we are about to examine, has spent 40 years studying the lines.

4 Page 130.

Read the instructions. Have students read the passage individually, perhaps while you read it aloud. Have students edit the paragraph and compare their results in pairs. Encourage them to read their edited paragraphs aloud.

Sample Answers (may vary):

Maria Reiche slowly made her way to the terrace on which a group of tourists had gathered to hear her speak. Though trembling from Parkinson's disease and nearly blind, this 84-year-old ex-mathematics teacher had a commanding presence. Using one of her five languages, Maria Reiche spoke to the audience for over an hour of the abiding passion to which she has devoted four decades.

If Maria is a celebrity today, it has not always been so for this ex-school teacher from Germany whom local people now call "Santa Maroa." In fact, the admiration in which she is now held is relatively new. When she began to study and protect the lines of Nazca over 40 years ago, few outsiders knew of her work, and most of the people of the region thought she was mad.

At the end of the talk, Maria's listeners were invited to buy copies of her book *Mystery on the Desert*. She uses the book's proceeds to pay the salaries of the guards, whom Maria employs to protect the ancient lines.

Using What You've Learned

5 Page 131.
Read the instructions. Have students work individually or in pairs to research an ancient city on the Web or in the library. Have them write their information in a paragraph or a short report. Have students exchange completed reports to edit for content and grammar, focusing the use of adjective clauses.

Optional Activity: Have students write up their discussion notes for Activity 6 into a short argumentative essay. Have students exchange essays in pairs to proofread for errors and to give feedback on the overall organization and ideas. Allow time for revisions.

Part 4 Other Adjective Clause Constructions

Setting the Context

Have students discuss the prereading question in groups or as a class. Then have them read the passage individually.

Discussing Ideas

Have students discuss the passage and the questions in groups. Have groups share their theories with the class. If time permits, have them do a little extra research on Easter Island and find some information to share with the class.

A. Clauses with *When* and *Where*

Read the explanation above the charts. Have students read the examples in the chart. Emphasize the fact that the relative pronoun *when* cannot be omitted with a nonrestrictive clause (as in the example in the second row). Elicit or give additional sets of simple sentences modeled after those in the example, and have students tell you how to combine them into complex sentences.

1 Page 133.
Read the instructions and the example. Have students complete the exercise in individually or in pairs. Encourage students to read through all the sentences first and circle time and place words like *then* and *there*; this will help them to identify more quickly which relative pronoun to use. Check answers as a class, and encourage them to state other possible ways to combine the sentences, and in which sentences the relative pronoun can be omitted.

Answers:

1. The statues were built during the sixteenth and seventeenth centuries, when a mysterious society ruled the island.
2. By 1722, when the Dutch visited the island, the society that made the statues had vanished.

3. On this island, where the Dutch had gone in search of supplies, there were only 4,000 inhabitants. OR: On this island, to which the Dutch had gone in search of supplies, there were only 4,000 inhabitants. OR: On this island, which the Dutch had gone to in search of supplies, there were only 4,000 inhabitants.
4. The Dutch left a few days later, recording that the island was a place where tremendous stone figures stood facing the ocean. OR: The Dutch left a few days later, recording that the island was a place in which tremendous stone figures stood facing the ocean. OR: The Dutch left a few days later, recording that the island was a place which/that tremendous stone figures stood facing the ocean on. (also, relative pronoun can be omitted)
5. Fifty years later, when Captain James Cook visited Easter Island, all the statues were lying face down.
6. Recently, archaeologists have gone to Easter Island, where they have used modern machinery to stand some of the statues upright.

B. Nonrestrictive Adjective Clauses and Expressions of Quantity

Read the explanation above the chart. Have students read the examples of simple and complex sentences in the chart out loud. For a more hands-on approach, you could have them cover up the right-hand (complex sentences) column while they read the simple sentences and have them try to convert the simple sentences to complex on their own before checking the right-hand column.

2 Page 134.

Read the instructions and the example. Have students do the exercise individually or in pairs and correct answers with other pairs.

Answers: 1. These huge stones, several of which weigh 20 tons or more, certainly could not have been carried. 2. It seems unlikely that they were dragged over the land, much of which is extremely rough. 3. Some archeologists think that the islanders used huge wooden platforms, the remains of which were never found. 4. The wood for these platforms would have had to come from large forests, none of which existed on the island.
5. A number of authors, most of whom archeologists totally disregard, suggest that extraterrestrials moved the statues.
6. According to the islanders, the finished statues were transported by the island's kings, all of whom had magical powers.

C. Adjective Clauses and Subject/Verb Agreement

Read the explanation above the chart. Remind students that this group of adjective clauses replace the subject of a sentence (the last few sections have focused on adjective clauses that replace objects). Have students read the examples and notes in the chart out loud. Give them some incorrect examples of subject-verb agreement for contrast: *The islanders who was kidnapped later died. / It was the only one of the islands that were formed by volcanoes. / It is one of the islands that was formed by volcanoes.* The distinction between the last two examples in the chart may be the most difficult for students to master (*the only one vs. one of the*); you may wish to elicit additional examples following these models, perhaps on a topic more immediately familiar to the students.

3 Page 135.

Read the instructions and the example. Have students complete the exercise individually or in pairs. Check answers as a class.

Answers: 1. believes 2. has 3. have 4. suggest 5. has

Optional Activity: Have students rewrite the sentences in Activity 3 to use the verb forms that they did not choose. (In other words, have them rewrite a sentence so that the singular verb form could be used instead of the plural used in the original, and vice versa). They will need to change the subject of each sentence.

4 Page 136.
Read the instructions. Encourage students to read the entire passage once first for overall comprehension. You could also suggest that they underline the nouns in the main clauses that serve as referents for the relative clauses. Have students complete the exercise individually and compare answers in pairs.

Answers: 1. have 2. needs 3. were 4. contain 5. were 6. were 7. were 8. have 9. was 10. was 11. was 12. was 13. was 14. were 15. were 16. was 17. have 18. remain 19. have

5 Page 137.
Review of Adjective Clauses. Read the instructions and the example. Have students complete the sentences with their own information and then add commas. Have them compare answers with a partner and check each other's punctuation and subject-verb agreement.

Optional Activity: Have students write a ten-sentence paragraph about a trip that they took somewhere, modeling the sentences after those in Activity 5 and incorporating adjective clauses.

Using What You've Learned

6 Page 137.
Read the instructions and the example. Have students work in pairs to write a long sentence with a string of adjective clauses. You could add a game element by awarding a prize to the pair who writes the most humorous sentence, and/or the most serious.

Optional Activity: As an alternative, students could do Activity 6 as a chain writing activity, passing one paper around a circle (with ten people, or going around twice with groups of five) and having everyone add an adjective clause until the sentence is complete.

7 Page 137.
Read the instructions and the examples. Have groups write quizzes about the content presented in this unit, and/or the structures taught. Tell them that they should be able to answer the questions themselves; they should create an answer key on a separate piece of paper, which another group can use to check their answers.

Focus on Testing

Set a time limit for students to complete this test individually. Go over the answers as a class.

Answers:
Part 1: 1. b 2. c 3. c 4. b
Part 2: 1. b 2. a 3. b 4. a

Part 5 Review of Chapters 1–4

1 Page 139.
This activity reviews verb tenses covered in Chapter One. Read the instructions. Have students complete the exercise individually and compare answers with a partner. Encourage them to read the entire passage through once first for overall comprehension (and perhaps also to identify and circle time expressions that will be useful for helping them choose the best verb tense). When they share their answers, encourage them to state other verb forms that are possible in some sentences.

Answers: 1. is 2. consists 3. have interested 4. built 5. did 6. take 7. was 8. have speculated 9. is 10. was 11. was 12. are still arguing (or: still argue) 13. began 14. started 15. ended 16. had probably worked (or: had probably been working) 17. have studied (or: have been studying) 18. is still 19. are 20. will never know 21. now believe 22. served

2 Page 140.
This activity reviews articles, which were covered in Chapter Two. Read the instructions. Have students complete the exercise individually and compare answers with a partner. Encourage them to read the entire passage through once first for overall comprehension (and perhaps also to identify and circle time count and noncount nouns that will be useful for helping them choose the best article).

Answers: 1. X 2. X 3. the 4. X 5. the 6. the 7. a 8. X 9. a 10. the 11. X 12. The 13. the 14. The 15. a 16. the 17. X

3 Page 141.
This activity reviews connecting words that were covered in Chapter 3. Read the instructions and the examples. Students can work individually to complete the sentences in their own words and then compare answers with a partner. You might encourage them to read through all the sentences first and identify the function of each type of connecting word: is it to show cause/effect? Contrast? Additional information? Identifying the function first will help them to choose the best way to complete the sentence. Answers will vary.

Punctuation: 1. ; therefore, 2. , yet 3. ; in fact, 4. , for 5. , so 6. ; in addition, 7. , nor did 8. ; nevertheless, 9. ; however, 10. , and 11. ; otherwise, 12. ; as a matter of fact,

Optional Activity: Have students use the sentence beginnings in Activity 3 as models and write similar sentences about themselves, using the same sets of transition words.

4 Page 141.
Read the instructions and the example. This activity reviews adjective clauses presented in this chapter. Read the instructions and the example. Students can work individually to combine the sentences and then compare answers with a partner. Remind them that in some cases more than one answer may be possible; discuss the various options.

Answers: 1. Machu Picchu, which is a famous archaeological site in Peru, is now very popular with tourists. 2. It's a place whose history is fascinating. 3. It's located above a river valley in the Andes Mountains, where the Inca Indians fled from the Spanish conquerors. (OR: It's located above a river valley in the Andes Mountains, which/that the Inca Indians fled to from the Spanish conquerors). 4. Tourist trains, all of which are rather expensive, take most foreigners to Machu Picchu. 5. It is also possible to walk to Machu Picchu on a trail which (that) the Incas built hundreds of years ago. (also possible to omit the relative pronoun) 6. I arrived on the train one morning when it was raining. 7. I climbed the adjacent mountain called Huayna Picchu, whose beauty many photographers have captured. 8. The view that (which) climbers have of the ruins is spectacular. (also possible to omit the relative pronoun). 9. Our guide, with whom we hiked for several hours, had a bachelor's degree in antiquities. (OR: Our guide, whom/who we hiked with for several hours, had a bachelor's degree in antiquities.) 10. Next to the archeological site there is a hotel which (that) we found very comfortable. (also possible to omit the relative pronoun).

Video Activities: Abduction by Aliens

Before You Watch
Have students discuss the questions in small groups.

Answer to 2: b

Watch [on video]
Have students read the questions before having them watch the video. Play the video. Give students time to answer the questions. Play the video again, if necessary. Go over the answers as a class.

Answers: 1. a 2. They have big pear-shaped heads, huge eyes, small bodies—an average of 3½ feet tall. 3. a 4. b 5. b

Watch Again [on video]

Have students read the questions. Play the video and have students answer the questions. Put them in pairs to check their answers. Replay the video, if necessary.

Answers: 1. four 2. her sister 3. 1983 4. three 5. He is a Psychology Professor at Harvard Medical School; he wrote the forward to a book about UFO abductions 6. He believes that people's alien abduction experiences are real, and that these people are traumatized and need counseling.

After You Watch

Read the instructions. Have students combine the sentences individually and compare answers in groups.

Answers: 1. Ruth Foley, who is about 45 years old, was first abducted when she was four. 2. Her sister saw a beam of light that (which) took Ruth to the spaceship. 3. Ruth doesn't remember the spaceship where they took her. (OR: Ruth doesn't remember the spaceship to which they took her. OR: Ruth doesn't remember the spaceship which they took her to. 4. Many people have reported abductions whose purpose is not known.

Focus on Testing

Set a time limit for students to complete this test individually, keeping in mind that this testing section is slightly longer than the ones in previous chapters because it is a review. You may wish to lengthen the time accordingly. Go over the answers as a class.

Answers:

Part 1: 1. a 2. b 3. d 4. b 5. a 6. a 7. c 8. c

Part 2: 1. d 2. c 3. b 4. b 5. a 6. d 7. c 8. c

Transitions

Goals

- Clauses and related structures of time: future time
- Clauses and related structures of time: present and unspecified time
- Clauses and related structures of cause and result
- Clauses and related structures of time: past time

Introduction

You can use this introductory passage as not only a way to introduce the theme of the chapter but also as a diagnostic. Have the students discuss it at length and then write a paragraph summarizing and analyzing the passage, or a brief reaction. Look specifically for the presence and/or correct use of the clauses to be covered in this chapter. Alternatively, you could collect this writing sample and return it at the end of the chapter for students to revise incorporating the structures that they covered in the chapter.

Before having students read the passage, have a brief pre-reading discussion as a class or in small groups. Then have students read the passage individually.

Discussing Ideas

Have students discuss the passage and the questions in small groups. Have groups report their examples and future predictions of changes to the class.

Part 1 Clauses and Related Structures of Time: Future Time

Setting the Context

Have students discuss the prereading question in pairs or groups. Then have students read the passage individually.

Discussing Ideas

Have students discuss the passage and the questions in small groups or pairs. Encourage them to take notes on their discussion by writing them in categories (childhood, adolescence, young adulthood, middle- aged adulthood, old age) and share their ideas of changes at each stage with the class.

A. Transitions of Sequence

Students have already practiced recognizing and using some different kinds of transitions in Chapter 3. To review the concept of transitions, elicit from students what transitions do in a sentence and what some examples are. Read the explanation above the chart. Have students read the examples in the chart out loud. Point out the use of future tense in the examples. Go over the notes that give additional examples of sequence transitions. For a quick practice, and to get them to use some of the other transitions listed in the "notes" column of the chart, have students describe what they will do later that day, or in this class, using the transitions.

1 Page 148.

Read the instructions and the example. Students can do this activity orally or in writing, individually or as a class. They can refer back to the transition words listed in the chart on page 147. Their choice of sequence transitions will vary. Answers will vary. The correct order of events is given at the bottom of Student Book page 148. Check answers as a class and be sure that the future tense is used correctly in each sentence.

2 Page 148.
Read the instructions. Students can work individually or in pairs to select one or two processes and write the steps of the process using sequence transitions. Note that they should continue to use the future tense. Answers will vary.

Optional Activity: Have students write a brief "How to" paragraph describing a process that can be carried out in class—for example, tying one's shoe or making a paper airplane. Have them incorporate sequence words into the instructions. Do not let them draw pictures or use numbers. Then have students exchange process paragraphs in pairs and try to do each others' tasks, following the instructions exactly. Then discuss which instructions were successful, and what made peoples' instructions easy or difficult to follow.

B. Time Clauses with the Present, Present Perfect, and Future Tenses

Read the information above the chart. Have students read the examples and the notes in the chart. Point out the fact that the emphasis is usually on the main clause, since the time words indicate a dependent clause. (Students should be familiar with this concept as it was presented in Chapter 3, but you may wish to review it briefly here by having students underline the main clauses in each of the examples and state the focus of each sentence).

C. Time Clauses with the Simple Present and Future Perfect (Continuous) Tenses

Have students read the example and notes in the chart. Briefly review the difference between a clause and a phrase. (A clause includes a subject and a verb; a phrase is merely a group of words, such as a prepositional phrase, that does not include both a subject and verb). You can have students label the parts of speech in the example sentences in the chart to see the difference more clearly. In the first column of the chart, point out that with the phrase *By the time that*, the word *that* is optional. Review the formation of the future perfect tense which is used in the main clause: *will* + *have* + past participle. For a quick practice with this structure, write some future times and events on the board (for example: *when this class is over, by lunchtime, by tomorrow*) and have students make statements about their plans in complete sentences with the future perfect tense.

D. Placement and Punctuation of Adverb Clauses and Phrases

Read the explanation above the chart. Have students read the examples in the chart and note the change in comma use when the adverb clause begins or ends the sentence. Point out in the last section of the chart (under "other time expressions") the range of choices for an adverb of frequency (you can also substitute different adverbs of frequency for review, such as *seldom, rarely, never*). Give an incorrect example to show the error of separating a subject and a verb with an adverb of frequency: *We feed almost always the baby before he takes his nap.*

3 Page 150.
Read the instructions. Students can complete the exercise individually or in pairs. Encourage students to read the passage once first for overall comprehension and context. Check answers as a class and have students state all possibilities in cases where more than one verb tense is possible.

Answers: 1. will 2. will follow 3. have given 4. will look 5. will 6. go through 7. will start 8. is still 9. will develop 10. is 11. will actively begin 12. will do 13. will not 14. has reached 15. will take 16. will start 17. turns 18. will have entered 19. will have developed 20. will be preparing 21. involves 22. goes 23. will develop

Optional Activity: Since the passage in Activity 3 is a lecture, you could do Activity 3 as a cloze activity. Read the passage aloud, with the correct answers, and have students listen and fill in the blanks. You may need to read the passage more than once.

4 **Page 151.**
Read the instructions and the examples. Point out that the actual cues for the exercise are listed before the notes on Student Book page 152. Have students work individually or in pairs and compare answers. Answers will vary.

Sample Answers: 1. By the time the baby is two months old, it should begin to lift its head. 2. Before the baby is four months old, it should be able to focus its eyes and coordinate stares. 3. When the baby is 20 weeks old, it will be able to open its hand to grasp an object. 4. Until the baby is 24 weeks old, it cannot grasp objects with its palm, fingers, and thumb all together. 5. Before the baby is eight months old, it will sit alone without support for a short time. 6. By the time the baby is eight months old, it can stand with minimum help. 7. After the baby is ten months old, it will walk without help. 8. When the baby is 12 months old, it should be able to stop putting objects in its mouth.

5 **Page 152.**
Read the explanation and the example. Have students work individually to draw on their own knowledge and write sentences about child development. Then have them exchange sentences with a partner and check for correct use of transition words and verb tenses in adverb clauses.

Using What You've Learned

6 **Page 152.**
Read the instructions and the examples. Have students role-play fortune-telling in pairs. As they do, go around the room and listen for any problems or common errors to go over later as a class.

7 **Page 153.**
Read the instructions. Have students discuss serious issues of the future in pairs. As they do, go around the room and listen for any problems or common errors to go over later as a class.

Optional Activity: Have students write a short personal essay about their personal and professional goals for the future based on the information they gave in Activity 7.

Part 2 Clauses and Related Structures of Time: Present and Unspecified Time

Setting the Context

Have students discuss the prereading questions in groups or as a class. Then have students read the passage individually.

Discussing Ideas

Have students discuss the passage in pairs or small groups. Have them summarize the passage in their own words and add their own commentary about it.

A. Time Clauses with the Simple Present, Present Continuous, and Present Perfect Tenses

Read the explanation above the chart. Have students read the examples in the chart out loud. Go over the notes as a class and elicit additional examples of sentences using the various time words before you move on to the next section of the chart. If students seem confused about verb tenses in each clause, have them underline and label the verb tenses in the example sentences.

1 **Page 155.**
Read the instructions. Students can complete this exercise individually or in pairs. Encourage them to read the entire passage once first for general context. Check answers as a class. Point out that in some cases there may be more than one possibility.

Sample Answers: 1. work 2. have 3. cooperate 4. are (or: can be) 5. began 6. has steadily evolved 7. is 8. can function 9. must develop 10. have 11. (can) communicate 12. (can) use 13. need 14. has ever developed

2 Page 155.

Read the instructions. Have students work individually and compare answers in pairs or groups. Have them discuss the differences in emphasis and meaning in their answers; they may need to refer back to the chart on page 154 to do so.

Answers:

1. Before people can build settled communities, they must have a way of producing a steady supply of food. / After people have a way of producing a steady supply of food, they can build settled communities. Meaning: The meaning is basically the same, but the first sentence gives more emphasis to what must happen first, and the second sentence gives more emphasis to what can happen after.
2. After people build villages, large marketplaces develop. / Large marketplaces develop when people build villages. Meaning: The meaning is different in these two sentences. In the first sentence, there is a definite sequence: first people build villages, and after that large marketplaces develop. In the second sentence, these events seem to happen at or around the same time.
3. As commerce expands, cities develop. / As soon as commerce expands, cities develop. Meaning: The meaning is different in these two sentences. In the first sentence, the two actions happen at about the same time. In the second sentence, the two actions happen close in time, but there is a sequence: commerce expands and then cities develop.
4. Until the population reaches 500 to 1,000, the social structure of a village remains generally constant. / Up to the time that the population reaches 500 to 1,000, the social structure of a village remains generally constant. Meaning: The meaning is the same in both sentences.
5. When towns grow in size, their character changes drastically. / Once towns grow in size, their character changes drastically. Meaning: The meaning is similar (both sentences describe a sequence), but there is a difference in emphasis. In the first sentence, the two actions happen one immediately after the other. In the second sentence, it is not clear how quickly the second action follows the first.

3 Page 156.

Read the instructions and the examples. You may need to give or elicit a definition of the word *continuum* in the first line of the instructions. See if they can use the context of the activity to define this word after you have looked at the examples, or if they can guess the meaning from other words that it looks like (such as *continuation, continuity*). (The definition of *continuum* is something that continues without interruption). Have students work in pairs to study the charts and write eight sentences using the information. Have students compare answers in groups.

Sample Answers: When people live in a small village, they exhibit uniform group behavior. Once the population increases, more individualistic lifestyles emerge. As soon as individualistic lifestyles emerge, specific guidelines for behavior become relaxed.

Optional Activity: Have students write a short paragraph, or a few sentences, as they did in Activity 3 but about another kind of continuum—perhaps of language learning or adjusting to life in another country. (In other words, something they can describe based on their own knowledge or experience).

4 Page 157.

Read the instructions and the example. Have students work individually or in pairs and compare answers in groups. Note that in Activity 7 students will have the opportunity to expand on this activity.

Answers: Answers will vary, as students will be using their own information and ideas and a wide range of time expressions. Check answers for correct use of verb tenses in clauses and correct punctuation.

Using What You've Learned

5 **Page 157.**
Read the instructions. Help students prepare for this essay-writing assignment by allowing some time for brainstorming ideas to use in the essay. First have them list some possible things that can happen with urban migration. Then have them circle ones that they would like to include in their essay. After that, have them brainstorm specific examples they could use to support each point. Next, have them state their opinion in one statement. After they have written the essay, have them exchange drafts in pairs to check for overall comprehension as well as correct use of transitions and adverb clauses.

6 **Page 157.**
Read the instructions. Have students work in pairs or groups to return to their notes or answers for Activity 4 and expand them by creating a chart and listing subsequent breakthroughs and innovations. They may need time to do a little research on the Web or in the library. Have them narrow their focus onto one area of interest to everyone in the group. Encourage listeners to ask questions. To add a creative element to this activity, you could present it as groups being a "panel of experts" on each topic.

7 **Page 157.**
Have students first look at the Rube Goldberg invention on page 158 without reading the words on the left of it. Have them try to explain what is going on in their own words before comparing their description with the text on the cartoon. Then read the instructions and the example. Encourage students to draw the invention and write the sequence of steps.

Part 3 Clauses and Related Structures of Cause and Result

Setting the Context

Have students discuss the prereading questions about charisma in groups or as a class. Resist giving them the definition of the word right away (it means a special quality that some individuals have who show an ability to lead and win over large numbers of people). See if they can define the word from the context, if not before they read the passage then after. Have them read the passage individually.

Discussing Ideas

Have students discuss the passage and the questions in small groups. Encourage them to list ideas of charismatic leaders and share them with the class. If time permits, you could have students bring in pictures of charismatic leaders of their choice and briefly talk about these individuals to the class.

A. Adverb Clauses and Related Structures of Cause and Result

Read the explanation above the chart. Have students read the examples and notes out loud. Have them substitute each possible phrase in each example so that they can practice using all of them. Review the punctuation rules in the third column; students covered this material in Chapter 3. You could write some incorrect sentences on the board to have students correct as a form of review.

1 **Page 160.**
Read the instructions. Do this activity all together as a class.

Answers:

1. *because of* (line 3) is followed by a noun phrase (human nature). Because (line 5) is followed by a clause: *people are usually more willing to fight or die for a leader than an idea.*

2. Substitutions for *because of*: as a result of, due to, owing to. Substitutions for *because*: Due to the fact that, Since.

2 Page 160.

Read the instructions and the examples. Review the terms *complex and compound sentences* by eliciting definitions from the students or telling them: a compound sentence is two independent clauses joined by a coordinating conjunction. A complex sentence is an independent clause joined with a dependent clause. You might encourage them to first read each sentence and decide if it is compound or complex, as the task is to convert compound to complex and vice versa. In the example, the original sentence is complex, and the revision is compound. Have students work individually or in pairs to form new sentences, and compare answers in groups or as a class. Encourage them to use a variety of transitions in their revisions.

Sample Answers: 1. Many South Americans had resented Spanish rule for years; as a consequence, they were prepared to revolt. 2. Due to the fact that South America had a mixture of races and interest groups, it was difficult to unite all the people. 3. The various colonial groups disagreed with each other; hence, one leader was needed to unite all of these groups. 4. Simon Bolivar was able to appeal to a wide variety of people; therefore, he ultimately became the political and military leader of the South Americans. "5. Since Bolivar could see beyond immediate problems and conflicts, he was able to develop long-term military and political goals.
6. Because Bolivar directed the war for independence throughout much of South America, he is known today as "the Liberator."
7. Due to the fact that Bolivar believed in a united South America, he struggled to unite the region into one nation—"Gran Colombia."
8. Individual groups and regions had their own interests in mind; thus, most leaders resisted the idea of one nation in South America. 9. Most areas are separated into distinct regions by major geographic boundaries such as the Amazon and the Andes Mountains; consequently, even without political or cultural differences, South America would be difficult to unite. 10. Perhaps because many geographical, political, and cultural differences exist among regions in South America, one united country has never been achieved.

3 Page 161.

Read the instructions and the example. Have students complete the sentences individually and compare their answers in pairs. When they check answers, encourage them to state whether the transition words for each sentence introduce phrases or clauses.

Answers (choice of transition words may vary): 1. As a result of... 2. Due to the fact that... 3. Owing to... 4. Since... 5. Due to... 6. Because... 7. Because of... 8. Due to...

4 Page 162.

Read the instructions and the example. Have students rewrite the sentences individually and compare their results in pairs or groups. You may wish to point out that the text before the italicized text in for each item is merely to provide some context. They are only to combine and rewrite the sentences in italics.

Answers (may vary):

1. Kemal dreamed of modernizing Turkey; therefore, he toured every part of his country to learn the conditions and needs of the people. Focus: Equal focus on both clauses / Because Kemal dreamed of modernizing Turkey, he toured every part of his country to learn the conditions and needs of the people. Focus: Kemal's tour of Turkey to learn about its peoples' needs. / Because of his dream of modernizing Turkey, Kemal toured every part of his country to learn the conditions and needs of the people. Focus: Kemal's tour of Turkey to learn about its peoples' needs.
2. Martin Luther King, Jr. was successful in uniting people in nonviolent protest; thus, he attracted worldwide attention and was

awarded the 1964 Nobel Prize. Focus: Equal focus on both clauses. / Since Martin Luther King, Jr. was successful in uniting people in nonviolent protest, he attracted worldwide attention and was awarded the 1964 Nobel Prize. Focus: MLK Jr's international fame and Nobel Prize. / As a result of Martin Luther King, Jr.'s success in uniting people in nonviolent protest, he attracted worldwide attention and was awarded the 1964 Nobel Prize. Focus: MLK Jr's international fame and Nobel Prize.

3. Because Mother Teresa worked tirelessly for the hungry, the homeless, and the sick, she was awarded the Nobel Peace Prize in 1979. Focus: Mother Teresa's Nobel Prize. / Owing to Mother Teresa's tireless work for the hungry, the homeless, and the sick, she was awarded the Nobel Peace Prize in 1979. Focus: Mother Teresa's Nobel Prize. / Mother Teresa worked tirelessly for the hungry, the homeless, and the sick; thus, she was awarded the Nobel Peace Prize in 1979. Focus: Equal focus on both clauses.

5 Page 162.
Read the instructions. Have students work individually or in pairs to combine the sentences in various ways. Have them discuss the differences in focus. Answers will vary.

Using What You've Learned

6 Page 163.
Read the instructions. If students discussed various charismatic leaders at the beginning of Part 3, they could refer back to their notes or recall that discussion to get ideas for their composition. Allow time for students to research the leader they will write about, if necessary, and to organize their ideas into outline form before writing. Have students exchange completed compositions in pairs and give feedback on content and structures.

7 Page 163.
Read the instructions and talk about the rules and purposes of formal debating. You might ask students in what contexts people hold debates (for example: elections). Once a topic has been decided, allow students plenty of time to prepare in their groups by listing supporting reasons for their position and anticipating the other group's points. You might also require everyone in the group to be responsible for a certain section of the debate (for example, opening remarks) to ensure equal participation.

Part 4 Clauses and Related Structures of Time: Past Time

Setting the Context

Have students discuss the prereading question in groups or as a class. Then have them read the passage individually.

Discussing Ideas

Have students discuss the passage and the questions in groups. If time permits, have them do a little extra research on other revolutions and share the information with the class.

A. Time Clauses and Phrases with the Simple Past and Past Perfect Tenses

Read the explanation above the charts. Have students read the examples in the chart out loud. Go over the notes for each example. Have students underline the verb tenses in each example sentence. You can also have them write "1" and "2" by the first and second event in each sentence, to show that the first event does not always come first in the sentence; the verb tenses and the time expressions are the keys to understanding what happened first and second.

Optional Activity: Have students work in pairs or groups to draw timelines or some means of visually representing the differences in meaning for each of the example sentences.

B. Time Clauses and Phrases with the Simple Past and Past Continuous Tenses

Read the information above the chart. Have students read the examples in the chart out loud. Go over the notes for each example together. Have students label the subject and verb in the examples of clauses, to stress the difference between clauses and phrases (there is no verb to label in the last example). Elicit additional examples of events that happened simultaneously, perhaps on a topic that is more familiar to or immediate for your students. As a prompt, you could write events in sets of two and have students combine them with the appropriate time expressions.

1 Page 166.

Read the instructions and the example. Have students complete the exercise in individually or in pairs. Encourage students to read through all the sentences first and circle time expressions.

Answers: 1. were settling, were facing 2. were, was, was not 3. died 4. was, had signed 5. had produced 6. had arrived, grew 7. lived 8. had increased 9. continued, started 10. began, were

2 Page 167.

Read the instructions and the example. Have students do the exercise individually or as a class, with yourself or one student reading the second paragraph aloud.

Answers: There are two complex sentences in paragraph 2. 1. While the American Revolution was taking place, the forces behind the French Revolution were building. (lines 15–16) The two events were happening at the same time. 2. When it [the American revolution] ended some six years later, over 40,000 people had been executed, and a new social order was in place. (lines 2–22) First, over 40,000 people were executed and a new social order was instituted. After that, the revolution ended.

3 Page 167.

Read the instructions and the example. Have students complete the exercise individually or in pairs. Encourage them to read all the sentences first and decide on the order of events. They can write a "1" by the first event and a "2" by the second. Then they should combine the sentences, keeping in mind that the past perfect will be used before the first event. Check answers as a class.

Answers: 1. Until the British started taxing the colonies, most of the colonists had felt loyal to Britain. 2. After the British Parliament had started to collect the new import taxes, the American merchants began to rebel. (The simple past can also be used) 3. By the time the British started to collect the new import taxes, the colonists had begun to organize a rebellion. 4. Boston had already been a center of rebellion for years by the time the first armed conflict occurred there in March of 1770. 5. Soon after the fighting around Boston had stopped, the British Parliament passed the Tea Act of 1773, another new set of import taxes. (The simple past can also be used) 6. After British soldiers had started enforcing the Tea Act, Boston merchants disguised as Indians attacked a British ship. (The simple past can also be used) 7. When these merchants had secretly boarded the British ship they dumped over 300 chests of British tea into the ocean. (The simple past can also be used) 8. After the British had learned of the dumping of their tea, British soldiers closed Boston Harbor to all trade. (The simple past can also be used) 9. Only a few people had been killed or injured in the rebellion before the British closed the harbor. (The simple past can also be used) 10. Until the first real battles were fought at Lexington and Concord on April 19, 1775, the rebellion had continued to grow.

4 Page 168.

Read the instructions and the example. Have students complete the exercise individually and compare answers in pairs.

Sample Answers (the order of the clauses and the choice of *while* or *as* may vary): 1.

While Louis XVI was ruling France, he did little to help the poor. 2. While France was suffering an economic crisis, Louis XVI nearly bankrupted the country by sending large sums of money to the American revolutionaries. 3. As French incomes were falling dramatically, prices seemed to rise daily. 4. As shortages of bread were occurring regularly, the price of bread skyrocketed. 5. While the wealth of the upper class was increasing, the life of peasants was become steadily worse. 6. While thousands of Parisians were searching for work, unemployed peasants looking for jobs were flooding Paris. 7. As his people lost their jobs and their homes, Louis XVI was relaxing in his palace at Versailles, 30 miles from Paris. 8. While Louis XVI was staying in Versailles, he had virtually no contact with the French people.

5 Page 169.

Read the instructions and the example. Have students change the selected clauses to phrases and check answers as a class.

Answers: Sentence 1: During Louis XVI's rule, he did little to help the poor. Sentence 2: During France's economic crisis, Louis XVI nearly bankrupted the country by sending large sums of money to the American revolutionaries. Sentence 4: During the bread shortages that were occurring regularly, the price of bread skyrocketed. Sentence 8: During Louis XVI's stay in Versailles, he had virtually no contact with the French people.

6 Page 169.

Read the instructions and the example. Have students work in pairs to change the headlines into complete and grammatically correct sentences. Point out that they may need to combine information in some of the headlines in order to use *when* effectively.

Optional Activity: Bring in some headlines from a current newspaper and have students select some to rewrite grammatically, using *when* and possibly additional time words, as they did in Activity 6.

7 Page 169.

Read the instructions. Note that this activity asks students to combine sequence connecting words with cause/effect connecting words. Have students complete the passage individually and compare answers in groups. Note that in some cases more than one word will be possible, but students should try not to repeat connecting words. Encourage them to read the passage once before starting, for overall content. (They might also underline the verb tenses as they read; this will help them to choose the best time words later). Have them read the passage aloud when they have finished to see if the connecting words sound natural.

Answers (may vary): 2. While 3. Because 4. Since 5. When 6. due to the fact that 7. As soon as 8. Because 9. As soon as 10. By the time 11. Because of

8 Page 170.

Read the instructions and the example. Have students write the paragraph individually and then trade paragraphs with a partner to check for overall comprehension and use of time words and clauses. Answers will vary.

9 Page 171.

Read the instructions and the example. Have students write their answers individually and then trade answers with a partner to check for overall comprehension and use of time words and clauses. Answers will vary.

Using What You've Learned

10 Page 171.

Read the instructions. Help students prepare for this presentation by allowing some time for them to brainstorm possible holidays to talk about and then choosing the one that seem most interesting or least known to the rest of the class. Encourage students to bring in visual aids to enhance their presentations. Also help them to organize their ideas first; they might talk about background information first and then tell how it is celebrated today.

Optional Activity: Expand Activity 9 by having students use their presentation notes to write a short report about the holiday.

Video Activities: College Graduation

Before You Watch

Have students discuss the questions in small groups.

Watch [on video]

Have students read the questions before having them watch the video. Play the video. Give students time to answer the questions. Play the video again, if necessary. Go over the answers as a class.

Answers: 1. b 2. a 3. c

Watch Again [on video]

Have students read the questions. Play the video and have students answer the questions. Put them in pairs to check their answers. Replay the video, if necessary.

Answers: 1. b 2. d 3. a 4. c 5. e

After You Watch

Read the instructions. Have students complete the sentences individually and compare answers in groups. Encourage them to state all the possibilities for completing each sentence (all the connecting words that could be used for each sentence).

Answers: 1. Because of / As a result of / Due to 2. Because / Since 3. because / since 4. Because of / Due to / As a result of 5. because of / due to / as a result of

Focus on Testing

Set a time limit for students to complete this test individually. Go over the answers as a class.

Answers:
Part 1: 1. c 2. d 3. d 4. a
Part 2: 1. c 2. d 3. a 4. a

The Mind

Goals

- Clauses and related structures of contrast: concession
- Clauses and related structures of contrast: opposition
- Clauses and phrases of purpose
- Clauses and related structures of comparison
- Clauses of result

Introduction

As with Chapter 5, this chapter presents more types of clauses, phrases, and related structures in detail. You can use this introductory passage as not only a way to introduce the theme of the chapter but also as a diagnostic. Have the students discuss it at length and then write a paragraph summarizing and analyzing the passage, or a brief reaction. Look specifically for the presence and/or correct use of the clauses to be covered in this chapter. Alternatively, you could collect this writing sample and return it at the end of the chapter for students to revise incorporating the structures that they covered in the chapter.

Before having students read the passage, have a brief pre-reading discussion about the mind as a class or in small groups. Then have students read the passage individually.

Discussing Ideas

Have students discuss the passage and the questions in small groups. Have groups report their theories and information to the class.

Part 1 Clauses and Related Structures of Contrast: Concession

Setting the Context

Have students discuss the prereading questions in pairs, groups, or as a class. Then have students read the passage individually.

Discussing Ideas

Have students discuss the passage and the questions in groups or pairs. If time permits, have them do a little research in the library or on the Web to find out more about how the central nervous system works and share their information with the class.

A. Adverb Clauses and Related Structures of Contrast: Concession

Students have already practiced recognizing and using some different kinds of transitions in Chapter 3 and Chapter 5, so the concepts of clauses versus phrases, as well as transitions, should be familiar by now. Read the explanation above the chart. Have students read the examples in the chart out loud. Point out the punctuation change when clauses begin or end the sentence. Have students rewrite the example clauses with the clauses in reverse order and the addition or subtraction of a comma, as appropriate. In the third section of the chart, point out the punctuation used with transitions that separate two independent clauses; remind them that the semicolon could also be replaced with a period to make two separate sentences. Also point out that with these last examples, the order of the clauses cannot be reversed; it would be grammatically correct, but the sentence would not make sense. Finally, with despite and in spite of, point out some common errors: *She was able to sleep despite of the noise. / She was able to sleep inspite the noise. / She was able to sleep despite that the noise continued.*

Chapter 6

1 Page 178.

Read the instructions. Do this exercise together as a class.

Answers: 1. connecting words: even though (lines 1–2), in spite of (lines 2–3), although (line 4), however (line 8). 2. All of these connecting words express ideas or information that is different from our expectations. 3. even though: connects clauses; in spite of: connects phrases; although: connects clauses; however: connects phrases that, combined, make one clause. 4. No punctuation is used with these connecting words except for commas before and after *however*, a word which is interrupting an independent clause.

2 Page 178.

Read the instructions. Students can work individually or in pairs to rewrite the sentences. By now they should be familiar with the terms compound sentence and complex sentence, but review them if necessary. (A compound sentence is two independent clauses joined by a coordinating conjunction. A complex sentence is an independent clause joined with a dependent clause). Encourage students to read their revised sentences aloud when they check answers to check for repetitive words that should be changed.

Answers: 1. A large and a small box may be exactly the same weight; however, the large box will feel heavier. 2. Although a person wearing blue- tinted glasses sees a blue world at first, the blue effect soon disappears, and the world looks normal again. 3. The sound of the phone does not change; still, the phone appears to ring much louder when we are expecting a call. 4. Five people may witness the same accident; nevertheless, each person will remember the accident differently. 5. The air seems damper on a cloudy day than on a sunny day, in spite of the fact that the humidity level may be exactly the same. 6. Time seems to pass quickly on some days, even though it goes slowly on others.

Optional Activity: Have students look over their rewritten sentences in Activity 2 and write down or state additional transitions and time expressions that could be used in each sentence. (For example: In sentence number 1, *however could be substituted with nevertheless, still, even so, and all the same)* .

3 Page 179.

Read the instructions. Students can complete the exercise individually or in pairs. You might encourage students to read the sentences first and identify the clauses versus phrases; this will facilitate their selection of time expressions. When students compare their answers, have them write or state all the possible time words that could be used for each sentence.

Answers:

1. Sentence One: Despite (In spite of) Sentence Two: Despite the fact that (in spite of the fact that)
2. Sentence One: Despite the fact that (In spite of the fact that) Sentence Two: Despite (In spite of)
3. Sentence One: Despite the fact that (In spite of the fact that) Sentence Two: Despite (In spite of)
4. Sentence One: despite the fact that (in spite of the fact that) Sentence Two: despite (in spite of)

4 Page 180.

Read the instructions and the example. Have students work individually or in pairs and compare answers. Choice of transition words may vary somewhat; be sure that they are using the correct expressions and punctuation for phrases versus clauses.

Sample Answers: 1. However, 2. Nevertheless, 3. Still, / , however, 4. Even though / Although many treatments had been tried, none had been successful (note comma after the first clause) / Even so, / All the same

5 Page 181.

Read the instructions and the example. Have students work individually to combine the sentences and compare answers in pairs.

Encourage them to read their rephrased sentences aloud to check for unnecessary repetition. Choice of connecting words will vary somewhat.

Sample Answers: 1. The adult brain uses up to 25 percent of the blood's oxygen supply, even though it does not perform physical work. 2. Despite the fact that the brain comprises only 2 percent of the body's weight, it receives 20 percent of all the blood pumped from the heart. 3. All parts of the brain receive blood; however, areas that control intellectual activity have the most blood vessels. 4. Blood pressure often changes in other parts of the body; nevertheless, it stays relatively constant in the brain. 5. Great amounts of energy are consumed in the production of thought; even so, the exact process is still not understood. 6. A loss of blood in a body part only causes numbness, though a 15-second interruption in the blood flow to the brain results in unconsciousness.

Optional Activity: Have students rewrite the sentences they wrote in Activity 5 one more way. If their original sentence was a compound, they should make it complex, and vice versa, using different connecting words.

6 **Page 181.**
Read the instructions and the example. Have students complete the sentences individually, with their own words and ideas, and compare their answers in pairs or groups. As an alternative to having students suggest different connectors for each of their sentences, you could have partners suggest different connectors for each others' sentences. Answers will vary.

Using What You've Learned

7 **Page 181.**
Read the instructions. Students should not need to do any additional research for this activity. They can use information from the reading passages and exercises (especially Activity 5) in this section, but make sure that they are using their own words as much as possible. Have students exchange finished paragraphs and check for sentence variety and correct use of adverb clauses.

8 **Page 181.**
Have one student read the information about vision and optical illusions out loud. (It might be one student from each group, or one student for the whole class). Have groups discuss their impressions of the four pictures. Encourage the use of clauses to show concession in their discussion. (For example: *Even though at first I thought it was a picture of a rabbit, I now think it is a duck*). Go around and listen for their use of clauses and connecting words. Go over any common mistakes or problems as a class.

9 **Page 182.**
Read the instructions and the questions. Have groups discuss the questions. Go around and listen for their use of clauses and connecting words. Go over any common mistakes or problems as a class.

Optional Activity: Have students find a psychological or personality test on the Web (there are many; students can do a keyword search under "psychological tests.") Or have students design a psychological test of their own. Have them test their classmates, and/or people outside the class, and present their findings to the class in an oral or written report, using as many clauses of concession as they can. They might write such clauses more easily if they think about results that they would expect to find (before they conduct the test) and compare them later with what they really found.

10 **Page 182.**
Read the instructions and the example. Help students prepare for their paragraph-writing task by allowing some time to brainstorm ideas. They could make a chart listing the five senses at the top and then list or freewrite ideas under each category heading. Then they can select the most important information to include in the paragraph and write the paragraph. Have students exchange finished paragraphs to check for overall

comprehension and use of clauses. Finally, have students gather in groups and share their paragraphs by speaking from them rather than reading them word for word.

Part 2 Clauses and Related Structures of Contrast: Opposition

Setting the Context

Have students discuss the prereading questions in groups or as a class. Then have students read the passage individually.

Discussing Ideas

Have students discuss the passage in pairs or small groups. Have them summarize the theory expressed in the passage. Then have them come up with other theories about how the brain functions, or about the right brain versus the left brain.

A. Adverb Clauses and Related Structures of Contrast: Opposition

Read the explanation above the chart. Have students read the examples in the chart out loud. Go over the notes as a class and elicit additional examples of sentences using the various time words before you move on to the next section of the chart. You may wish to discuss the difference between *opposition* and *contrast* to explain why this group of words is used for a slightly different purpose than those in Part 1. Also point out that *in contrast* and *on the other hand* can relate contrasting ideas (quite different ideas) that need not be direct opposites.

1 Page 184.

Read the instructions. Do this exercise together as a class.

Answers:

1. *whereas* (line 2); connects clauses / *While* (line 4); connects clauses / *on the other hand* (line 8); connects phrases (interrupts one clause) / *where* (line 10); connects clauses
2. Punctuation—*whereas* is preceded by a comma, following the main clause. *While* introduces a dependent clause that is followed by a comma before the main clause. *On the other hand* has a comma before and after because it interrupts an independent clause. *Where* is preceded by a comma (because it follows an introductory transition word) and it introduces a dependent clause that is followed by a comma before the main clause.
3. <u>The second sentence</u> = The right hemisphere mainly controls the left side of the body, whereas the left hemisphere directs the body's right side. Focus: the right hemisphere controls the left side of the body. Rephrased: Whereas the right hemisphere mainly controls the left side of the body, the left hemisphere directs the body's right side. New Focus: the left hemisphere directs the body's right side. <u>The last sentence</u> = Thus, where the left hemisphere is more analytical and sequential, the right is more holistic and relational. Focus: The right side is more holistic and relational. Rephrased: Thus, the left hemisphere is more analytical and sequential, where the right is more holistic and relational. New Focus: the left hemisphere is more analytical and sequential

2 Page 185.

Read the instructions. Have students work individually and compare rephrased sentences in pairs. Have them discuss the differences in focus.

Answers:

1. Focus of original sentence: both an adult's brain and a child's brain

   Rephrased: While an adult brain is more specialized, a child's brain has large areas that are uncommitted.

   New Focus: a child's brain

Rephrased: An adult brain is more specialized, whereas a child's brain has large areas that are uncommitted.

New Focus: an adult brain

2. Focus of original sentence: adults have a hard time learning new things

   Rephrased: Children can learn many things easily, while adults often have a much harder time.

   New Focus: children learn easily

   Rephrased: Children can learn many things easily; in contrast, adults often have a much harder time.

   New Focus: how both adults and children learn

3. Focus of original sentence: on both adults and children and how they learn languages differently

   Rephrased: Whereas few adults can learn to use a new language without mistakes or accent, children frequently become completely fluent in new languages.

   New Focus: children can become fluent in new languages

   Rephrased: Few adults can learn to use a new language without mistakes or accent, whereas children frequently become completely fluent in new languages.

   New Focus: adults have difficulty learning new languages

4. Focus of original sentence: most adults are either right-handed or left-handed.

   Rephrased: Most children do not favor either hand until they are about five years old, whereas most adults are either right-handed or left-handed.

   New Focus: children do not tend to favor one hand over the other

   Rephrased: Most children do not favor either hand until they are about five years old; in contrast, most adults are either right-handed or left-handed.

   New Focus: on both children and adults and how they do or do not favor the right or left hand

5. Focus of original sentence: on both research that has been done on the brain and what has actually been mapped

   Rephrased: While considerable research is being done on the geography of the brain, only a few areas have actually been mapped.

   New Focus: only a few areas of the brain have been mapped

   Rephrased: Considerable research is being done on the geography of the brain, while only a few areas have actually been mapped.

   New Focus: considerable research is being done on the geography of the brain

3 Page 185.

Read the instructions and the examples. Encourage students to read the passage once for context and overall comprehension. You might also suggest that they first identify clauses and phrases that will follow the connecting words to be added. Have them work individually and compare their answers in pairs.

Answers (will vary in choice of connecting words): 1. However, 2. , in contrast, 3. Whereas computers are complex, (note comma needed after first clause) 4. , on the other hand, 5. , in contrast, 6. whereas

Optional Activity: Have students write a short paragraph, or a few sentences, modeled after those in Activity 3 but on a topic immediately familiar to them—perhaps something related to an activity they do or a special interest that they have.

4 Page 186.

Read the instructions and the example. Have students work individually or in pairs to rephrase the sentences. Check answers as a class.

Answers: 1. Unlike a brain, which is capable of emotions and dreams, a computer only processes information. / Instead of being capable of emotions and dreams like a brain, a computer only processes information. 2. Unlike a computer, which may weigh hundreds of pounds, a brain weighs only about three pounds. / Instead of weighing hundreds of pounds like a computer, a brain weighs only about three pounds. 3. Unlike a computer, which can cover a desk, a brain fits neatly into the top of the skull. / Instead of covering a desk like a computer, a brain fits neatly into the top of the skull. 4. Unlike a brain, which is aware of its own existence, a computer has no such sense of being. / Instead of being aware of its own existence like a brain, a computer has no sense of being.

Optional Activity: Have students write sentences like those in Activity 4 comparing two things and noting the differences. The subject could be something more immediately familiar to the students or reflective of their personal interests or knowledge.

5 Page 187.

Read the instructions. Remind or elicit from students what the difference between *on the contrary* and *on the other hand* is. Note that either phrase works grammatically in all of the sentences in this activity, but the meaning is different. *On the other hand* expresses different ideas that are not necessarily opposite. *On the contrary* expresses indicates that the opposite of some idea is true; it reinforces the negative idea in the preceding sentence. Have students complete the sentences individually or in pairs. Go over the answers as a class.

Answers: 1. On the contrary, 2. On the other hand, 3. On the other hand, 4. On the contrary, 5. On the other hand, 6. On the contrary,

6 Page 187.

Read the instructions and the example. Have students complete the sentences individually, with their own ideas, and compare them in pairs or groups, checking to be sure that the meaning is clear with each choice of phrase.

Sample Answers: 1. On the contrary, both words are used to refer to basically the same thing. 2. On the other hand, adults often struggle to learn foreign languages. 3. On the contrary, they find it quite difficult and frustrating. 4. On the other hand, his younger brother has had a fairly easy time learning Spanish. 5. In contrast, scientists and mathematicians seldom have trouble with it. 6. On the contrary, it is done primarily by using the left side. 7. In contrast, art and creative writing are done primarily by using the right side. 8. On the contrary, we are enjoying it!

7 Page 187.

Read the instructions and the example. Have students work individually to complete each sentence with their own word and ideas. Have them compare answers in groups and check each others' sentences for correct meaning and structure.

8 Page 188.

Read the instructions. Have students work individually to combine the two paragraphs into one. Explain that the general statement suggested in the instructions is a *topic sentence*, which expresses the main idea to be developed in the paragraph. Since the paragraph will discuss both the left and right brain, both of these elements need to be mentioned in the topic sentence. Encourage them to read their final version out loud to help check for repetitiveness and correct use of clauses, phrases, and punctuation. You could also have students exchange finished paragraphs and check them for these elements. Answers will vary.

9 Page 188.

Read the instructions and the example. Have students work individually or in pairs to find and correct the errors. Note that there may be more than one way to correct some errors. One sentence is correct.

Answers (may vary; corrected errors are underlined where possible):

1. Whereas the right brain processes information sequentially, the left brain handles information simultaneously. (omit *on the other hand*).

2. Keesia studied left- brain functions last semester; in contrast, Mike focused on the right. (add semicolon before transition phrase and comma after)
3. Unlike the left brain, which is responsible for language, the right brain specializes in recognition of faces.
4. Where I love studying the brain, Shirley thinks it is boring. (need a word in contrast to *fascinating*)
5. Though I have spent nine months in China, I still cannot communicate in Chinese. (add comma after the first clause, which is a dependent clause)
6. Even though Chinese is very difficult, it is possible to learn it. (Omit *however*)
7. correct
8. Although migraine headaches are associated with women, millions of men have the same problem. (comma should appear after the first clause, not after the connecting word).
9. Despite the fact that Mary has taken four aspirin, she still has a terrible headache.
10. In spite of the fact that Mary has seen several doctors, none has been able to help her.

Using What You've Learned

10 Page 189.

Read the instructions. Have students write their paragraphs individually. Encourage them to include specific examples to support their assertion that they are mostly right-brained or left-brained. These examples might be short anecdotes, or brief facts such as "I have always been very good at music but terrible at math." Then have them share the ideas in groups. As they do, go around and listen for their use of contrast words. Go over any problems or common errors as a class.

11 Page 189.

Read the instructions. Have students study the two pictures in pairs or groups and describe the differences. As they do, go around and listen for their use of contrast words. Go over any problems or common errors as a class.

Part 3 Clauses and Related Structures of Cause and Result

Setting the Context

Have students discuss the prereading questions and discuss what they know about Alzheimer's Disease. Have them read the passage individually.

Discussing Ideas

Have students discuss the passage and the question in small groups. If time permits, you could have students find more information on Alzheimer's Disease or on Dr. Alois Alzheimer, to share with the class.

A. Adverb Clauses and Phrases of Purpose

Read the explanation above the chart. Have students read the examples in the chart out loud. Go over the notes for each example together. Point out the fact that modal auxiliaries are typically used in the dependent clause with ***in order that*** or ***so that***. With the second example sentence, show how the two phrases linked by the phrase ***in order to*** can appear in reverse order, unlike the clauses linked by ***in order that / so that***. Write some incorrect sentences on the board to show common errors with these expressions: ***In order they can understand more about learning, scientists are studying the brain. / So that they can understand more about learning, scientists are studying the brain.*** Have students refer to the chart if necessary and state what is wrong with these sentences; then have them correct the errors. Also point out the note at the bottom of the chart and emphasize the difference between purpose and result. Elicit additional examples of sentences that show purpose versus result.

1 **Page 191.**
Read the instructions and the example. Do this activity all together as a class.

Answers (note that *so that and in order that* can be used interchangeable in these answers because all of these sentences deal with clauses): 1. Tests are being developed so that we can diagnose AD easily. 2. Researchers are working on a vaccine in order that they can eliminate the disease. 3. Mice were used in experiments so that researchers could see how effective the vaccine was. 4. Information on the research is posted on Websites in order that people can know the latest developments. 5. The disease was named Alzheimer's so that everyone would be able to recognize who discovered it. 6. I hope the vaccine is successful in order that Alzheimer's disease will disappear.

2 **Page 191.**
Read the instructions and the example. In this exercise, students will be converting clauses to phrases and changing the time expression accordingly. Have students work individually to rephrase the sentences and compare answers in pairs.

Answers: 1. In the 1970s, Western scientists traveled to India in order to study the powers that yogis were rumored to have. 2. The scientists used electronic instruments in order to test yogis' ability to control involuntary body functions such as heartbeat and reaction to pain. 3. In one experiment, a yogi pushed a rusty needle completely through his arm in order to demonstrate his ability to block all pain. 4. He used meditation in order to ignore this pain. 5. Yogis undergo years of training in order to control their bodily functions through meditation. 6. Now some patients in the West are using biofeedback in order to control their involuntary nervous systems like yogis. 7. The patients use machines in order to see and hear a problem and then consciously solve it. 8. Other people practice transcendental meditation in order to control their nervous system without the help of machines.

3 **Page 193.**
Read the instructions and the example. Have students complete the sentences individually and compare their answers in pairs. Answers will vary.

Optional Activity: Have students write their own questions, similar to those in Activity 3, and then have them ask and answer their questions in pairs, using *so that*, *in order that*, or *in order* in their responses.

Using What You've Learned

4 **Page 193.**
Read the instructions. Have students take turns reading the descriptions of the scientists out loud. Have students discuss them in small groups and add any other information they may know about them. Then have students individually choose a scientist to research. Have them write questions about things they would like to know about this person and possible places to look for information. When students are doing their research, remind them to write down information about the sources they consult: the title of the book, article, or web site; the author; the place and date of publication; the page numbers. When they write their reports, they should indicate where the information they use came from. Have students exchange drafts of their reports in pairs and give feedback on content, organization, and correct grammar, paying particular attention to clauses and connecting words.

Part 4 Clauses and Related Structures of Comparison

Setting the Context

Have students discuss the prereading question in groups or as a class. Then have them read the passage individually.

Discussing Ideas

Have students discuss the passage and the questions in groups. Have them paraphrase the main idea of the first sentence; you might encourage them to close the book in order to force them to use their own words.

A. Comparative and Superlative Forms of Adjectives and Adverbs

Have students look at the drawing of a human brain and a bird brain on Student Book pg. 194. Have them state or write sentences comparing the two brains. You can do this as a diagnostic activity to find out how much students already know or remember about comparative structures. Students at this level will have learned these structures at some point in the past, but may have difficulty remembering certain forms or rules, especially when speaking. Then read the explanation above the charts. Have students read the examples in the chart out loud. Elicit example sentences using these various adjectives and adverbs in their comparative and superlative forms. You could have them rewrite or state comparisons about the two brains on pg. 194.

Optional Activity: Have them discuss similarities and differences among themselves, perhaps in small groups. As they discuss, go around and listen for errors or common problems that you can review as a class after the activity.

B. Clauses and Phrases Showing Comparison

Write two simple sentences on the board, perhaps about students in the class. For example: *Martine studies for one hour a night. Juan studies for three hours a night.* Then have students try to put them together in a compound sentence using a comparative adjective. See if they can use a comparative form with these clauses on their own. If not, give them a possible answer: *Martine studies hard, but Juan studies harder*. Show them other possibilities for expressing this idea: *Martine studies hard, but Juan studies harder than Martine studies./ Martine studies hard, but Juan studies harder than Martine does.* Ask students to explain the differences in structure among the three sentences. Then read the explanation above the chart. Elicit additional examples by having students state comparative sentences about themselves and their classmates. Then have students read the examples in the chart out loud. Go over the notes together. Elicit additional examples for each type of connecting word. Under "Transitions," in the last section, point out that these transitions are punctuated the same way as transitions in the last two chapter; the only difference is their purpose. Therefore, the transition similarly can be punctuated in the same way as likewise, and vice versa. Either word can come between two independent clauses with a semicolon and a comma, or can begin a new sentence.

1 Page 197.

Read the instructions and the example. Have students complete the exercise in individually or in pairs, or orally, going around the room as a class.

Answers: 1. taller, the tallest 2. stockier, the stockiest 3. more quickly, the most quickly 4. less interesting, the least interesting 5. more slowly, the most slowly 6. worse, the worst 7. good, the best 8. less tired, the least tired

Optional Activity: To add a game element to Activity 1, have teams compete to give the correct comparative and superlative forms of adjectives and adverbs as you call them out (you could read them off the chart in random order in order to add more words and make the activity more challenging). Two people (one representative from each team) could compete at a time by having to say or write on the board the comparative and superlative forms of the word you give before the other person. Or, if that sounds too pressured, have representatives from each team take turns answering your question and earning points for their team. You could score up to two points per answer, giving one point for a correct comparative and one point for a correct superlative.

2 Page 198.

Read the instructions and the examples. Have students complete the exercise individually and compare their answers in groups, checking for correct comparative and superlative forms in each others' sentences. Answers will vary.

3 Page 198.
Read the instructions. Have students complete the exercise individually and compare answers in pairs. Encourage them to read the passage once first for context.

Answers: 1. least developed 2. more developed 3. higher 4. more primitive 5. smaller 6. smoother 7. higher 8. more advanced (or: the most advanced) 9. larger 10. greater

4 Page 198.
Read the instructions and the example. Have students work individually or in pairs. Check answers as a class, paying particular attention to punctuation.

Answers: 1. Gorillas walk on their hind legs; likewise, people stand upright on two legs. 2. Gorillas don't live to the same age as people. 3. Elephants can live past 60; similarly, dolphins survive six decades or more. 4. Both Anne and Harry are fascinated by various types of snakes. 5. At the zoo, Anne devotes most of her time to watching snakes; likewise, Harry can spend hours at the snake exhibit. 6. A worm isn't as developed as a crab.

Optional Activity: To expand Activity 4, have students rephrase the sentences so that they fit with the connecting words that were incorrect.

5 Page 199.
Read the instructions. Have students work individually to complete the sentences. Then have them try to answer the questions in pairs. Encourage them to continue using connecting words in their answers.

Answers: 1. fast, faster, the fastest 2. far, farther, the farthest 3. well, better, the best 4. tall, taller, the tallest

6 Page 199.
Read the instructions. Have students work individually, in pairs, or in groups to write their sentence sets. Have them agree on three topics and list adjectives and adverbs to use first; then have them write their sentence sets modeled after those in Activity 5. Answers will vary.

7 Page 199.
Have students work individually or in pairs to find and correct the errors. Have them compare answers in groups. Encourage them to state the reason behind the error. In some cases, there may be more than one way to correct the error.

Answers (corrections are underlined where possible): 1. Humans are not <u>as strong as</u> most other animals the same size. 2. We cannot run as <u>quickly</u> as dogs or deer can. 3. We seem to be <u>clumsier</u> than most creatures. 4. Horses are herbivores; likewise, cows eat only vegetarian. 5. Many animals are less clever than chimpanzees. 6. Orangutans eat a mixed diet of seeds, nuts, fruit, and a little meet. Similarly, tigers are <u>herbivores</u>. 7. To some people, the coat of a leopard looks the same <u>as</u> the coat of a tiger. 8. Both sheep and deer <u>provide</u> meat to predators, including humans.

Using What You've Learned

8 Page 200.
Read the instructions. Remind students that they need to be able to answer their own questions, so they should write an answer key on a separate sheet of paper. This can be used to "grade" their classmates' finished quizzes.

Part 5 Clauses of Result

Setting the Context

Have students discuss the prereading questions about memory in pairs, groups, or as a class. Have them look at the title of the passage and make predictions about points that the author might make. Then have them read the passage individually.

Discussing Ideas

Have students discuss the passage and the questions in small groups. You might also ask them to discuss what things they often tend to forget or remember, and to describe any strategies or "tricks" they might have for remembering things. (For example: people who often forget people's names might try to use the person's name in conversation as much as possible when they first meet).

A. Adverb Clauses of Result

Read the information above the chart. Have students read the examples in the chart out loud. Go over the notes together for each example. You may need to briefly review quantity words used with count and noncount nouns (this was covered in Chapter 2); Activity 1 lets students review this in more detail. If students seem comfortable with *much* and *many*, you could omit Activity 1.

1 Page 202.

This activity reviews much and many with count/noncount nouns, and could be omitted or done very quickly as an oral exercise if students seem comfortable with these structures.

Answers: 1. many perceptions, much input, many colors, much noise, many shapes 2. much more information, many more details, many people 3. much more information, much more easily, many things 4. Many scientists, much more complicated, many electrical and chemical processes 5. much research, many of these experiments, many of the day's activities

2 Page 203.

Read the instructions and the example. Have students complete the sentences individually, adding their own ideas at the end. Then have them compare answers in groups, checking against the chart for correct use of comparative structures and comparing their endings.

Sample Answers (the following underlined comparative structures must be used; endings to the sentences will vary): 1. The weather was <u>so</u> beautiful that we decided to go to the beach. / It was <u>such</u> beautiful weather that we decided to go to the beach. 2. They sang <u>so</u> wonderfully that we were moved to tears. / They have <u>such</u> wonderful voices that we are always moved to tears. 3. It was <u>such</u> a loud noise that I thought a gun had been fired. / The noise was <u>so</u> loud that I thought a gun had been fired. 4. The article was <u>so</u> interesting that I read it twice. / It was <u>such</u> an interesting article that I read it twice. 5. She got <u>such</u> a bad sunburn that she could hardly move. / She got <u>so</u> badly sunburned that she could hardly moved. 6. The race was <u>so</u> exciting that we couldn't take our eyes off it. / It was <u>such</u> an exciting race that we couldn't take our eyes off it.

3 Page 203.

Read the instructions and the example. Have students complete the sentences in their own words and write the paragraph out on a separate piece of paper. Have them exchange finished paragraphs in pairs and check for correct use of comparative structures.

Answers (sentence endings will vary, but comparative structures should be as follows): 1. so many 2. such a 3. so (adjective) that 4. so (adjective) that 5. so much 6. such 7. so (adjective) that 8. so many 9. such 10. so many 11. so 12. such a

4 Page 204.

Read the instructions. Have students work in pairs or groups to combine sentences using a variety of connecting words. Point out that this activity asks them to recall a variety of types of connecting words and structures. Have pairs or groups combine into larger groups to compare and discuss their choices.

Sample Answers: 1. Psychoanalysis is a type of therapy developed by Sigmund Freud that involves remembering and analyzing dreams. 2. Freudian analysts use dreams in order to unlock the secrets of their patients' minds. 3. According to psychoanalysts, our dreams represent ideas or emotions that we are trying to suppress. 4. When we suppress these ideas and emotions that create conflicts, we cannot resolve the conflicts. 5. Many current brain researchers who believe dreams have a different purpose disagree with psychoanalysis. 6. According to them, the brain collects too much information, all of which it cannot store. 7. The brain may use dreaming so that it can forget incorrect or useless information. 8. Attempting to remember dreams may not be helpful; moreover, it may interfere with the brain's housecleaning. 9. Brain researchers and psychoanalysts, both of whom are attempting to unlock secrets that are held in our minds, do not agree. 10. Both groups continue to search for answers whose mysteries we may one day understand.

5 Page 205.

Have students work individually or in pairs to find and correct the errors. Have them compare answers in groups. Encourage them to state the reason behind the error. In all cases, there will be more than one way to correct the error.

Sample Answers (answers will vary; corrections are underlined):

1. Despite the fact that he had been unknown in the French capital, Mesmer soon became a celebrity. OR: Although he had been unknown in the French capital, Mesmer soon became a celebrity.
2. Thousands flocked to his salon in order to be cured of every illness imaginable. OR: Thousands flocked to his salon in order so that they could be cured of every illness imaginable.
3. In fact, so many patients came for help that Mesmer had to turn large numbers of them away. OR: In fact, patients had so much demand for his help that Mesmer had to turn large numbers of them away.
4. Mesmer's treatment gained so much popularity that crowds gathered outside his salon demanding treatment. OR: Mesmer's treatment gained so many people believing in its popularity that crowds gathered outside his salon demanding treatment.
5. At one point, the crowds became so uncontrollable that he devised a special treatment. OR: At one point, there was such an uncontrollable crowd that he devised a special treatment.
6. Mesmer "magnetized" a tree and had these people hang from ropes in order to cure them. OR: Mesmer "magnetized" a tree and had these people hang from ropes so that he could cure them.
7. Although Dr. Mesmer developed a large group of supporters, others were more skeptical of the doctor and his treatments. OR: Dr. Mesmer developed a large group of supporters; however, others were more skeptical of the doctor and his treatments.
8. In particular, government officials in Paris were so unimpressed by animal magnetism that in spite of Mesmer's local followers, a French Royal Commission declared it dangerous. OR: In particular, government officials in Paris were unimpressed by animal magnetism; therefore, in spite of Mesmer's local followers, a French Royal Commission declared it dangerous.
9. This was such an important judgment that Mesmer was forced to leave Paris in disgrace. OR: This judgment was so important that Mesmer was forced to leave Paris in disgrace.
10. Mesmer was discredited; nevertheless, hypnotism eventually became a respected treatment. OR: In spite of the fact that Mesmer was discredited, hypnotism eventually became a respected treatment.

Using What You've Learned

6 **Page 206.**
Read the instructions and the examples. Have students discuss the adjectives on the list first. They should guess at meanings of unfamiliar words and then check them in a dictionary. Then set a two-minute time limit and have the pairs discuss a topic of their choice (school, the weather, food, etc.) using as many words as possible. They could check them off as they use them, but it is probably best to strive for speed and fluency. If you like, you can repeat the activity a couple of times and have them try to use the adjectives for an entirely different topic of conversation.

Video Activities: Social Phobia

Before You Watch

Have students discuss the questions in small groups.

Answer to 1: A phobia is (b) a fear
2. Answers will vary.

Watch [on video]

Have students read the questions before having them watch the video. Play the video. Give students time to answer the questions. Play the video again, if necessary. Go over the answers as a class.

Answers: 1. social phobia 2. a 3. b

Watch Again [on video]

Have students read the questions. Play the video and have students answer the questions. Put them in pairs to check their answers. Replay the video, if necessary.

Answers: 1. b 2. c 3. c 4. b 5. c 6. b 7. c 8. a

After You Watch

Read the instructions. Have students rephrase the sentences individually and compare originals with the rewritten versions in groups. Encourage them to discuss other possibilities for rephrasing the sentences.

Answers: 1. Despite the fact that she struggled for many years, Katherine Whizmore only recently overcame her phobia. 2. People with phobias usually understand that their fears are groundless; nevertheless, it is very difficult for them to defeat them. 3. In spite of the fact that millions of Americans suffer from social phobia, many doctors do not understand this disease. 4. Hundreds of millions of dollars are spent every year on research into physical illnesses; in contrast, relatively little is spent on mental illnesses.

Focus on Testing

Set a time limit for students to complete this test individually. Go over the answers as a class.

Answers:
Part 1: 1. c 2. b 3. a 4. b
Part 2: 1. b 2. c 3. c 4. c

Chapter 7

Working

Goals

- Clauses with *that;* reported speech
- Clauses with embedded questions
- Statements and requests of urgency
- Clauses as subjects of sentences
- Reduction of noun clauses to infinitive phrases

Introduction

Tell students that the U.S. Census is a governmental institution, and that it gathers information about people living in the United States. Ask students what kinds of information they think that the U.S. Census gathers. Provide these prompts on the board: *who, what, where, how much, how many*, and *when*. Record their ideas in the form of noun clauses, e.g., *how many immigrants come to the U.S., how much money Americans spend*, and so on. Tell students that these phrases are noun clauses. As students read "The U.S. Workforce," ask them to underline all the noun clauses that they see in the article.

Answers: who is or isn't working, what kinds of jobs people hold, where they find the jobs, how much money they make, how they spend their earnings, how often they change their jobs, how many people are injured on the job, when men and women retire, what recent census information has shown, that Americans are better educated, what the statistics do not show

Discussing Ideas

Invite students to share their responses to the questions. You can extend the conversation by searching the Internet for the latest U.S. Census report. Abbreviated versions of the report are often available in almanacs as well.

Part 1 Clauses with *That;* Reported Speech

Setting the Context

Engage students in a brainstorm of jobs in three categories: Declining, Steady, and Increasing. List their ideas on the board in three columns. Then tell students that the article "The Changing U.S. Job Market" will give them statistics about job trends.

Discussing Ideas

Ask students if their predictions were confirmed by the reading. Have them determine whether the jobs they listed in the brainstorm belong to a service- producing or goods- producing market. Then have students respond to the questions in the Student Book.

A. Introduction to Noun Clauses

1 Page 212.

Sample Answers: 1. The chart shows that the number of bank tellers will decrease slightly. 2. The chart indicates that the number of computer engineers will increase tremendously. 3. The chart tells us that there are more computer systems analysts than database administrators. 4. The chart illustrates that the number of word processors will decrease slightly more than the number of bookkeepers. 5. The chart indicates that there are almost as many home care aids as medical assistants. 6. The chart says that the number of farmers will drop dramatically.

D. Changes in Modal Auxiliaries with Reported Speech

2 Page 213.
Answers: 1. The study showed that this trend would continue indefinitely. 2. The study indicated that computer-related jobs were becoming more and more popular. 3. The study noted that the number of teaching jobs had begun to increase. 4. The study proved that many bank tellers had lost their jobs. 5. The study demonstrated that many clerical workers might be replaced by new office machines. 6. The study found that some fields of medicine were already overstaffed. 7. The study showed that the job market in other areas of medicine, such as nursing and physical therapy, would probably grow. 8. The study reported that a higher percentage of older people are going to work. 9. The study illustrated that a good education had become more important in finding a well-paying job. 10. The study indicated that most areas of computer work would continue to offer opportunities.

F. Changing Commands to Reported Speech

3 Page 214.
Sample Answers: 1. My boss told me to be at my desk by 9:00. 2. My boss told me that I shouldn't take more 15 minutes for my breaks. 3. My boss told me that I should leave for lunch at the scheduled time. 4. My boss told me that shouldn't make personal phone calls while I was working. 5. My boss said that I should call as early as possible if I was sick. 6. My boss said that I should schedule my vacations as far in advance as possible.

4 Page 215.
Sample Answers: 1. Our teacher says that we can look at our notes during the test. 2. Teachers say that we must not chew gum in class. 3. Most teachers say that their students must be on time. 4. The teacher told her class that they must pay attention. 5. Teachers tell their students to get under their desks during an emergency drill. 6. A teacher told a Haitian student that she could not speak French in class.

5 Page 215.
Answers:

1. Molly told me that she was a computer programmer around San Francisco but had grown up in India. She said that she had helped design several new Websites. She added that there was a lot of pressure in this type of work, and that shipping and playing golf seemed to relieve some of the tension.
2. Stan says that he has been moving furniture for five years. He told me that had made a local delivery yesterday. He said that he would be working on a job about 20 miles from here tonight. Next week, he might be halfway across the country. He said he didn't think he could ever sit at a desk all day.
3. Ty told me that he started delivering papers when he was seven. According to him, the work was hard and he didn't make very much money. Now he works in a coal mine, and his wife works, too. He said that they still don't make enough money, though. Ty believes that the more things stay the same, the more they stay the same.
4. Mariel told me that she is a tennis instructor, and that she loves her job. She says that she can really help people better when they listen to her. She also said that she might do something else in a few years. She is thinking about joining an organization and doing some volunteer work.

Using What You've Learned

6 Page 216.
Have students form pairs of students of and ask each other the list of questions in the Student

Book. Students should take notes during the interview. Afterward, invite students to report on their partners' responses.

7 Page 216.
This activity directs students to conduct an interview with somebody they know about his or her job. Students should draw up a list of questions beforehand, and take good notes during the interview. Afterward, ask students to paraphrase and use reported speech to convey what their interview subjects had to say about their jobs.

Part 2 Clauses with Embedded Questions

Setting the Context

Read the Prereading Questions aloud with students. Then, brainstorm a list of questions that an employer might ask during a job interview, and write these on the board. Invite students to take turns role-playing a job interview using these questions.

Finally, look at the illustrations with the class and ask students why they think the woman appears to be so stressed in the second picture. She is recuperating from the job interview and has a headache. The dialogue on the following page is intended to go with this illustration. Ask two students to read it aloud for the class.

Discussing Ideas

Guide students to the conclusion that Sentence B is more polite because it is less direct. In general, the more direct a statement or question is, the more likely it is that it will sound rude. Sentences that are formed in such short, direct ways are best used with close friends and family members. When a guest arrives at your place of work, for example, you might ask "Would you like a cup of coffee?" whereas you might simply say to a friend visiting you at home "Want coffee?" Have students help you brainstorm a list of familiar requests, offers, and statements. Students can then help you transform each sentence into a more formal version.

A. Clauses with Embedded Questions

1 Page 216.
Answers: 1. On an application, you might be asked where you went to school. 2. On an application, you might be asked where you live. 3. On an application, you might be asked what kind of work experience you have. 4. On an application, you might be asked why you want to work in that particular place. 5. During an interview, you might be asked about your strengths and weaknesses. 6. During an interview, you might be asked why the employer should hire you. 7. During an interview, you might be asked how you would describe yourself. 8. During an interview, you might be asked how much money you hope to earn.

B. Clauses with *If* and *Whether*

2 Page 218.
Answers: 1. I may be asked if I have my college transcripts. 2. I might be asked if I have any letters of recommendation. 3. I might be asked whether my family is supporting me. They might want to know if I have a scholarship and need financial aid. 4. They might ask me I have taken the TOEFL test. The may want to know whether certain sections were more difficult than others. 5. I might be asked if I have taken the admissions test. They may want to know whether or not I have received the scores. 6. I might be asked if I am planning to live with my parents. They may want to know if I have ever lived on my own.

3 Page 218.
Sample Answers:
1. The interviewer asked about my typing speed and whether I could use a fax machine. She wanted to know about any software I was familiar with and whether or not I was comfortable on the Internet.

2. They asked me if I had a license for driving trucks. They wanted to know if I had ever hauled a load over ten tons. They also asked about my driving record and my last job.
3. The interviewer asked who had worked for, which design software programs I had used, and whether I had had any experience with digital imaging. He also asked if he could see my portfolio.
4. The interviewer wanted to know how many people I had supervised. He asked about the kinds of restaurants I had worked in and how many meals the restaurant served per day. He also wanted to know what hours the restaurant was open.

4 Page 219.
Sample Answers:

1. A. Did she say what she wanted?
   B. No, she didn't say.
2. A. Did she say whether she would call back?
   B. Yes, she said she would call back.
3. A. Did she say when she would call back?
   B. No, she didn't.
4. A. Did she say how long she would be in town?
   B. Yes, she said she'd be in town until Wednesday.
5. A. Did she say where she'd call from?
   B. Yes, she said she would call from the hotel.
6. A. Did she say whether it was important?
   B. Yes, she said it was very important.
7. A. Did she say how she got my number?
   B. No, she didn't.
8. A. Did she say whether she would be free tomorrow?
   B. She said she'd be busy all day.

5 Page 220.
Sample Answers: 1. Did she tell you why she was angry? 2. Do you know whether she's going to fire me? 3. I need to know when she is coming back. 4. Did she mention where she was going?

6 Page 220.
Sample Answers: 1. I'm concerned about whether there will be any good jobs available. 2. I'm interested in how much computer programmers make. 3. I don't really care about whether I make a lot of money or not. 4. I'm not worried about where I live. 5. I've been thinking about when I have to start paying back my loan. 6. So far, I haven't paid attention to whether or not this school has a good placement rate. 7. Sometimes I'm nervous about how what I'll do after graduation. 8. Right now I'm tired of what other people think.

Using What You've Learned

7 Page 220.
Form pairs of students. Have students create a list of questions for one of the jobs listed in the Student Book.Then have students switch partners and take turns asking each other questions for the designated job. Encourage students to be imaginative-their answers can be as outlandish as they care to make them.

Part 3 Statements and Requests of Urgency

Setting the Context

Look at the two photos with students and compare the two different lifestyles that they depict. Start two word webs on the board, one labeled "wealthy" and the other labeled "poor." Ask students to brainstorm words for each web and record their ideas under the appropriate heading.

Then read "Equality for All?" on page 222 of the Student Book.

Discussing Ideas

Use the questions in the Student Book to engage students in a discussion of the ideas contained in the article. Summarize students' ideas on the board. You can extend the discussion by challenging some of these ideas and asking students to defend their proposals with supporting reasons and examples.

A. Statements of Urgency with *That*

1 Page 223.

Sample Answers: 1. It is vital that the gap between the rich and poor be closed. 2. It is mandatory that sex or race not be used to judge workers. 3. It imperative that employees not discriminate against women or minorities. 4. It is desirable that every qualified person have equal opportunity for employment. 5. It is crucial that every person in the country have access to a quality education. 6. It is advisable that the company hire people from all parts of the population. 7. It is important that there be more minorities in management positions. 8. It is essential that there be more economic development in poorer areas.

B. Urgent Requests with *That*

2 Page 224.

Sample Answers: 1. My boss asks that I not make personal calls. 2. My boss insists that I keep my breaks to 15 minutes. 3. My boss requests that I not leave before five o'clock. 4. My boss recommends that I plan my vacations in advance. 5. My boss prefers that I work fast as possible without making mistakes. 6. My boss suggests that we be friendly but efficient. 7. My boss demands that I stay off the Internet. 8. My boss suggests that I come to him if I have any problems.

3 Page 224.

Answers: 1. The union asked that Macrohard provide health insurance to all employees. 2. The union asked that the company provide child care. 3. The workers demanded that they be given equal pay for equal work. 4. The union requested that the company publicize all job openings. 5. The workers demanded that they be given equal consideration for promotions. 6. The union insisted that the company forbid all forms of sexual harassment. 7. The workers asked that the company allow job sharing. 8. The union advised that Macrohard allow flexible schedules. 9. The union insisted that the company give one-month vacations.

4 Page 225.

Sample Answers: 1. I will ask that Truck Drivers' Local 441 provide free back massages. 2. I will demand that the Farm Workers' Local 70 stop using all chemical pesticides. 3. In my opinion, it's necessary that Textile Workers' Local 55 provide better health insurance. 4. In fact, it's vital that Restaurant Workers' Local 12 establish of policy for the sharing of tips. 5. Because of numerous lawsuits, it's vital that Brain Surgeons' Local 617 provide malpractice insurance. 6. In conclusion, I request that Secret Agents' Local 007 throw a yearly masquerade party.

5 Page 225.

Sample Answers:

Mrs. Jones told me I was late and she reminded me that I was late the day before. She said she hoped I wouldn't continue with this behavior. I assured her I was sorry and told her that the bus had broken down. When she asked what had happened the day before, I told her that I had forgotten to tell her about my doctor's appointment. The appointment was for 7:45, but the doctor was late, so I wasn't able to see him until 8:15. Mrs. Jones said that was understandable, but that I should tell her about these things. She also requested that I come on time. She reminded me how essential it is that we run on schedule. I apologized once again and said that I hoped she would forgive me. She said it was alright but not to let it happen again. Then she asked about the report that I had promised her. She also asked when I would be finished with the Weir account and whether I had all the information that I needed.

Using What You've Learned

6 Page 225.
Ask students to create a dialogue between an employer and an employee. They can choose from the situations suggested in the Student Book or create an original situation. In either case, they should write the dialogue together and then practice it. Afterward, invite partners to share their dialogues with the class.

Part 4 Clauses as Subjects of Sentences

Setting the Context

Some students may not understand the visual pun being made with the two photos, as they rely on English metaphors that compare corporate quarters to various animal habitats. Ask: How is this office like a rabbit's den? Point out that both environments are made up of narrow tunnels and cubicles (or burrows). Then read the Prereading Questions and ask students to share their responses.

Discussing Ideas

Record student responses in the form of two lists: Boring Jobs, and Interesting Jobs. Ask students to compare the two lists. What generalities can be made about each list?

B. Anticipatory *It* Clauses with *That*

1 Page 227.
Answers: 1. It's obvious that Harry is unhappy in his job. 2. It's surprising that he hasn't already quit. 3. It amazes me that he has stayed at this job so long. 4. It is almost certain that he will quit soon. 5. It is essential that he find a better- paying job. 6. It worries us that he might not make enough to support his family.

2 Page 228.
Sample Answers: 1. It's fairly certain that I'll get a job in the Bay Area. 2. It's hopeful that the economy will be in good shape. 3. It's doubtful that I'll get a job as soon as I graduate.

3 Page 229.
Answers: 1. Where Harry might be is a mystery to me. 2. Why he isn't at work isn't important. 3. Whether he is sick again or not is none of our business. 4. Why he has so many days off doesn't really concern us. 5. How he gets any work done doesn't really matter. 6. Whether the boss has decided to fire him is his business. 7. How much he makes is his business. 8. Whether he has a company car is confidential.

4 Page 229.
Sample Answers: 1. What I like to do most is to spend time outdoors. 2. Why I like to do it is for religious reasons. 3. What I like to do least is clean house. 4. How I work best is under pressure. 5. Where I work best is in an office, because there are too many distractions at home. 6. When I work best is in the morning, because I am too tired in the afternoon. 7. What I like to wear to work are dress pants and shirt but no tie. 8. When I take breaks isn't something I think about.

5 Page 229.
Sample Answers: 1. How much money I make concerns me because I have two children to support. 2. Whether or child care is provided worries me because I have children. 3. How many hours a day I work matters to me because I go to school. 4. How much responsibility I have is important to me because I want a good challenge. 5. What kind of

benefits are included doesn't concern me because my parents take care of me. 6. What kind of work doesn't worry me so long as I work. 7. How many sick days I get doesn't matter to me because I'm never sick. 8. How much job security there is isn't important to me because I plan on changing careers anyway.

6 Page 230.
Answers: 1. The workers asked why the company was going to lay off 50 workers. 2. The management told them that the company was losing money. 3. The workers asked the management if the company had considered alternatives. 4. According to management, it was necessary to lay workers off. 5. The workers told management that they would like to discuss the situation. 6. The workers suggested that everyone take pay cuts. 7. What that would do is to save all the jobs. 8. Working together, the workers and management decided how the would solve the problem.

Using What You've Learned

7 Page 230.
Ask pairs of students to take turns role-playing one of the situations shown in the Student Book. They should try to use as many of the expressions shown as possible. After they have role-played for about five minutes, ask them to write down their dialogues, adding or changing any lines as they wish. When they are finished, partners can read their dialogues aloud for the class.

8 Page 230.
Have students follow the same steps as in Activity 7. Encourage students to create humorous dialogues. The activity may be even more fun if they create dialogues for real public figures that they know.

Part 5 Reduction of Noun Clauses to Infinitive Phrases

Setting the Context

Start a chart on the board with the headings "Causes of Stress," "Effects of Stress," and "Ways to Relieve Stress." Engage students in a brainstorm and record their ideas in the appropriate column. Discuss the Prereading Questions, and then have students read "Job Stress" silently.

Discussing Ideas

Ask a volunteer to summarize the reading in his or her own words. Afterward, ask the questions in this section to relate the reading to students' own personal experience.

A. Reduction of *That* Clauses in the Subjunctive Mood

1 Page 231.
Answers: 1. It is good to have a pleasant place to relax. 2. It is advisable to get regular exercise time on the job. 3. It is crucial to work in a healthy environment. 4. It is essential to have proper lighting. 5. It is vital to breathe clean air. 6. It is imperative to feel safe. 7. It is necessary to provide training on new equipment. 8. It is important to have regular safety reviews.

2 Page 233.
Answers: 1. Workers have asked management to allow them to participate in major decisions. 2. Negotiators have advised management to give workers more responsibility. 3. Workers have urged companies to reward employees for suggesting improvements. 4. Workers have asked management to allow them to do more of their work at home. 5. Workers have urged management to meet regularly with employees. 6. Negotiators have advised management to treat employees with respect. 7. Workers have

asked management to consider dramatic changes. 8. Management has asked workers to be patient.

3 **Page 233.**
Sample Answers:

1. a. In my opinion, it's important to focus only on work while working.
   b. It's also necessary to take breaks and tend to personal matters.
   c. In fact, it's essential to do this so that you can concentrate on work.
   d. It's best to take a break about once every two hours.
2. a. I would ask that the company provide updated safety equipment.
   b. In fact, I have asked for a new pair of gloves and face shield.
   c. The government should require private companies to protect workers in dangerous occupations.
   d. I strongly urge other workers to sign this petition.

B. Reduction of Indirect Commands, Requests, and Embedded Questions

4 **Page 235.**
Answers: 1. I would like to know how long to wait before applying for another job. 2. I would like to know what kind of job to look for. 3. I would like to know how much money to expect. 4. I would like to know where to look. 5. I would like to know what to write on my resume. 6. I would like to know what to do with so much free time. 7. I would like to know how to avoid becoming depressed. 8. I would like to know how to qualify for unemployment benefits.

5 **Page 235.**
Answers: 1. I don't know whether to go back to school. 2. I don't know whether to wait for a good job. 3. I don't know whether to take a low-paying job. 4. I don't know whether to ask my family for help. 5. I don't know whether to give up my apartment. 6. I don't know whether to move in with my parents. 7. I don't know whether to get a roommate. 8. I don't know whether to go to an employment agency.

6 **Page 236.**
Answers: 1. I would tell my friend to read the want ads. 2. I would urge my friend to ask everyone she knows about possible jobs. 3. I would advise my friend not to wait for people to call him. 4. I would tell my friend to visit all the major businesses in the area. 5. I would try to persuade my friend to talk to the counselors at school. 6. I would advise him to put an ad in the paper under "Situations Wanted." 7. I would encourage her not to give up. 8. I would urge him to try every possible method.

7 **Page 236.**
Sample Answers: 1. I would tell them to look in the yellow pages of the phone book. 2. I would advise them to follow up with personal visits. 3. I would encourage them to keep a positive attitude.

Using What You've Learned

8 **Page 236.**
Form two teams of students. Appoint one team "management" and the other team "personnel." You might also appoint one or two students to play the role of mediator, or you can play this role yourself. Have students read the instructions on page 236 to conduct a labor dispute role-play. Each team should first draw up a list of demands and suggestions that they propose will help to cut company expenses by 25 percent. The team should list these points on chart paper. As the instructions indicate, teams should decide before the role-play which points, if any, are non-negotiable. The mediators can facilitate the negotiation by indicating whose turn it is to speak and summarizing each team's major points. As students talk, listen for opportunities to use

expressions with infinitives and noun clauses. The list on page 237 will help to give you ideas. Restate any such utterances, encouraging the speaker to repeat after you.

Video Activities: Telecommuting

Before You Watch

Sample Answers:

Advantages to Workers

Advantages to Employers

Savings on lunch prepared at home

Able to care for children while working

Less money spent on utilities

Better morale among staff

Disadvantages to Workers

Disadvantages to Employers

More money spent on utilities

Isolated from staff

Not as able to monitor employee

Staff communication is more difficult

Watch [on video]

Answers:

1. Saved money on clothes and dry cleaning; flexibility in hours so that children can be dropped off and picked up at day care; no time wasted in traffic
2. Less pollution; less money spent on utilities; workers tend to be more productive

Watch Again [on video]

Answers:

1. a. estimated number of telecommuters b. average commuter miles per year c. dollars a year saved by a company for each telecommuter d. cost of commuting that is saved by workers
2. b
3. c
4. a
5. c

After You Watch

1. One worker said that telecommuting had changed his life.
2. The reporter asked how companies benefited from allowing employees to work at home.
3. The narrator said that telecommuting had become so popular that AOL was adding 40,000 modems a month.
4. One employer said that if he gave his employees a quota of x and the produced 2x, he didn't care if they were watching "Oprah" and eating bonbons.

Focus on Testing

Answers:

Part 1: 1. c 2. c 3. d 4. d

Part 2: 1. b 2. b 3. a 4. a

Breakthroughs

Goals

- The simple tenses
- The perfect tenses
- The continuous tenses
- The modal auxiliaries
- The passive tense
- Express personal experiences and opinions

Introduction

Point to a light bulb in the class and ask students *Who invented the light bulb?* Recast the answer in the passive: *The light bulb was invented by Thomas Edison*, and write this sentence on the board. Tell students that they will review the passive tense in this chapter. Underline *was* and *invented* in the sample sentence, and tell students that the passive is formed with a form of the verb *to be* and the past participle of the main verb. Then ask students to read "The Gifts of History" silently. Afterward, direct students' attention to these passive constructions in the article: *is associated, could not even have been recognized, has so much been done, have been made, are based, were discovered, should not be viewed, has been accumulated.* Tell students they will review the tenses of these constructions throughout the chapter.

Discussing Ideas

Explain that the expression *the fruit of our technological inheritance* means "the benefits accrued from past inventions and advances in technology." These advances have led to improvements in our quality of life and have made new innovations possible. Ask students to think of innovations on past inventions. The telephone had to be invented before the message machine, for example, and the television set had to be invented before the VCR. Ask students to speculate on future innovations on current technology.

Part 1 The Simple Tenses

Setting the Context

With students, brainstorm a list of machines, appliances, and other forms of technology that we use in our daily lives. You might help students generate ideas by asking them to think about machines that they use from the moment they get up until the time they go to bed at night. Then ask a volunteer to read "No Escape!" aloud for the class.

Discussing Ideas

Invite students to share their responses to the questions at the end of the reading. Encourage use of passive constructions by modeling sentences such as *Laundry could not be done without machines*, and so on.

A. Introduction to the Passive Voice

1 Page 244.

Answers:

1. passive Since 1876, many advances have been made in the field of communications.

   active Since 1876, we have made many advances in the field of communications.

2. active Several companies began to produce personal computers in the 1970s

   passive Personal computers began to be produced by several companies in the 1970s

3. active Today computers make some sales calls.

   passive Today some sales calls are made by computers.

4. passive By the early 1990s, the Internet was being used to communicate all over the world.

   active By the early 1990s, people were using the Internet to communicate all over the world.

5. active By last year, technicians should have connected most colleges in the United States to the Internet.

   passive By last year, most colleges in the United States should have been connected to the Internet.

6. active Now, hundreds of thousand of students are doing research electronically.

   passive Now, research is being done electronically by hundreds of thousands of students.

7. passive How will our lives be changed by this technology in the future?

   active How will this technology change our lives in the future?

B. The Simple Tenses

2 Page 245.

Answers:

No Escape!

How important is technology? Take a moment and look around. It hardly matters what time it is or where you are. Almost everything that you own, use, or even touch in the course of a normal day was created through technology.

In the morning, your toast is made and the coffee is brewed by electronic machines. You are transported to school or work by bus, train, car, or bike. During the day, you receive messages that are transmitted via phone, fax, or the Internet. Back home, dinner is prepared in a microwave, and programs are delivered to your television via antenna, cable, or satellite dish. And these are only a few examples.

You may like technology or hate it, but one thing is certain. In today's world, technology is almost impossible to escape.

3 Page 245.

Answers:

1. New technological advances usually arrive in major cities first.
2. Satellites transmit overseas telephone calls.

   Telephone calls are transmitted overseas by satellites.
3. Computers design cars.

   Cars are designed by computers.
4. Athletes use computers to monitor their workouts.

   Athletes' workouts are monitored by computers.
5. Laser scanners read food prices in supermarkets.

   Food prices in supermarkets are read by laser scanners.
6. Scientists compete to be the first to develop new products.

   New products are developed by competing scientists.
7. Hundreds of new products flood the market each year.

   The market is flooded each year by hundreds of new products.
8. Some technologies spread very quickly.

C. *By* + Agent

4 Page 246.

Answers:

1. Television was originally created ~~by people~~ purely for entertainment.
2. Today, television is used ~~by people~~ for all types of purposes.
3. Television was made possible ~~by researchers~~ through a variety of technological breakthroughs.
4. In 1884, a scanner disk was developed by a German, Paul Nipkow.
5. Using this disk, an image was broken down into thousands of dots ~~by Nipkow~~.
6. Later, a device was created by V.K. Zworykin that was used ~~by him~~ to scan and duplicate images using electron beams.
7. The cathode-ray picture tube was perfected and the first TV sets were produced by Allen B. DuMont in 1939.

8. On February 1, 1940, the first official program was broadcast in the United States by the National Broadcasting Company (NBC).
9. Soon, a variety of programs was being broadcast ~~by the companies~~ around the United States.
10. These early programs were transmitted ~~by the companies~~ in black and white.
11. Later, color transmissions were achieved ~~by researchers~~.
12. Today, very clear color transmissions are sent ~~by companies~~ across the globe in a matter of seconds.

5 Page 246.
Answers:

1. The first modern elevator was exhibited by Elisha Otis at the New York World's Fair in 1853.
2. The steel-making process was improved from the 1850s to the 1880s.
3. Tall building were made possible by the cheap production of steel.
4. Using steel construction and elevators, structures were soon built with more than five or six stories.
5. The first electric lamps were produced simultaneously in the 1870s by Thomas Edison of the United States and Joseph Swan of Great Britain.
6. Air conditioning was invented by Willis Carrier in 1911.
7. Entire new parts of the United States and the world were opened up for habitation.
8. Hundreds of new houses were built in hot places like Houston, Texas, and Phoenix, Arizona.

D. Common Expressions in the Passive Voice

6 Page 247.
Answers: 1. are still accustomed 2. is made 3. will be equipped 4. will be connected 5. will be used 6. used 7. will be located 8. will not be covered

7 Page 248.
Sample Answers: 1. I get frustrated when I'm stuck in traffic. 2. I always get sick when I smoke. 3. When I'm late for class, I get embarrassed. 4. Before difficult exams, I get nervous. 5. If I don't sleep well, I get a headache. 6. I get bored when my assignments are too easy. 7. I get really excited when I learn new things. 8. I get confused when I listen to two people talking at the same time.

F. Anticipatory *It*

8 Page 248.
Sample Answers: 1. It was believed that telephones would be too expensive for most people to have. 2. It was predicted that television would eliminate the movie industry. 3. It was said that faxes were only useful in large businesses. 4. It was feared that computers were too complicated for ordinary people to use. 5. It was believed the employees had to work in the office every day. 6. It was feared that it was too dangerous to have automatic tellers. 7. It was felt that most people didn't want to have a lot of electronic gadgets in their homes. 8. It was thought that videotape was only useful for advertising firms.

9 Page 248.
Answers: 1. took 2. were sometimes given 3. were organized 4. are overwhelmed 5. offer/are offering 6. are equipped 7. will be linked

10 Page 249.
Sample Rewrite:

Refineries

A variety of techniques are used to refine oil, but the most common one is separation. The separation process has several steps. First, the oil is heated in a large furnace, and from there it is sent into a fractionating tower. This tower is a steel cylinder about 130 feet (40 meters) high. When the hot oil enters the tower, it turns into vapor. This vapor rises naturally. As it rises, its temperature begins to fall, and the components of the oil separate according to their weight. At this time, the heavy oil is taken from the bottom of the tower. During the process, lubricating oil, kerosene, and gasoline are also removed from higher points. Uncondensed gas rises to the top of the tower, where it is released through a pipe, where it is recycled for further separation.

Using What You've Learned

11 Page 250.

To do this activity, students should think of an activity which lends itself to passive constructions. Hobbies and occupations that are involved in the production of a good or service are good candidates. Activities such as reading, writing, and traveling will be difficult to write about in the passive. When students are finished writing, invite them to read their papers aloud for the class. As each student reads, ask his or her classmates to listen for verbs in the passive and to note them. Students can share their notes with the speaker after the presentation to make sure that all the passive constructions were accounted for by the class.

Part 2 The Perfect Tenses

Setting the Context

Restate students' respond to the Prereading Questions using the present perfect tense, saying for example, Scientist have developed operating techniques with lasers, or We have discovered how to store fresh blood. Then read "Miracles in Medicine" aloud.

Discussing Ideas

Sample Answers: 1. The rate of Malaria has been decreased. 2. Small pox has nearly been eliminated. 3. Chemical therapies have been developed for cancer. 4. Drugs have been discovered that help to minimize the effects of AIDS.

A. The Perfect Tenses

1 Page 252.
Answers:

Subject	Passive Verb	Agent
remedies	had been developed	
cinchona bark	was used	
digitalis	was used	
medicine	has been completely transformed	large number of discoveries
smallpox	has been virtually eliminated	

2 Page 252.
Answers:

1. passive; subject: idea; verb: had been regarded; no agent
2. active; subject: doctors; verb: had believed; object: diseases
3. passive; subject: patients; verb: had been viewed; no agent
4. passive: subject: bloodletting; verb: had been seen; no agent
5. passive; subject: tooth extractions and surgeries; verb: had been performed; no agent
6. active; subject: Joseph Lister; verb: developed; object: antiseptics
7. active; subject: antibiotics; verb: have become; no object
8. passive; subject: many diseases; verb: have been eradicated; no agent
9. active; subject: postsurgical infections; verb: have declined; no object

10. active; subject: pure drinking water and pasteurized milk; verb: have helped to eliminate; object: cholera, typhoid, typhus
11. passive; subject: research; verb: has been devoted; no agent
12. passive; subject: breakthroughs; verb: will have been made; no agent

3 Page 253.
Answers:
1. Before antibiotics, sulfa drugs had been prescribed for infections.
2. Before antibiotics, brandy, cold water, and castor oil had been used to treat pneumonia.
3. Before antibiotics, bloodletting had been recommended for almost any disease.
4. Before antibiotics, whisky had been given for exhaustion.
5. Before antibiotics, opium had been used for many ailments.
6. Before antibiotics, small doses of mercury had been prescribed to treat syphilis.

4 Page 253.
Answers:
1. All of these remedies have been tested "clinically" in China over centuries.
2. The gingko tree has been used in Chinese medicine for almost 4,000 years.
3. Asthma, bronchitis, and tuberculosis have been treated with gingko seeds and fruit for hundreds of years.
4. Gingko leaves have prescribed in Europe for strokes and blocked arteries.
5. Dried sea horse has been used to treat swollen thyroid glands for thousands of years.
6. Ulcers have been treated with licorice root.
7. Licorice root has been found to have steroid-like characteristics.
8. Dried mandarin orange rind has been burned to keep mosquitoes away for over a thousand years.
9. Orange rind has been used as a cure for digestive ailments for many centuries.
10. Sweet wormwood has been successfully prescribed for malaria for over 1,500 years.

5 Page 254.
Answers:
1. A. Has the patient's temperature been taken?
   B. Taken.
2. A. Has his blood pressure been checked?
   B. Checked.
3. A. Has the patient's pulse been taken?
   B. Taken.
4. A. Has the patient been treated for shock?
   B. Treated.
5. A. Have the blood samples been drawn?
   B. Drawn.
6. A. Have the X rays been ordered?
   B. Ordered.
7. A. Have his wounds been bandaged?
   B. Bandaged.
8. A. Has the patient been given plasma?
   B. Given.

6 Page 254.
Answers: 1. will have been completely transformed 2. will have been learned 3. will have been developed 4. will have been created 5. will have been performed 6. will have been developed 7. will have been perfected 8. will have certainly been made

7 Page 255.
Answers: 1. is 2. are sold 3. are derived 4. are developed 5. buy 6. is altered 7. have already been extracted 8. have been

pressed 9. scooped 10. have 11. have been derived / are derived

8 Page 255.

Answers: 1. was used 2. had 3. noticed 4. grew 5. were damp 6. remained 7. reasoned 8. was protected 9. is 10. irritates 11. was often prescribed 12. not always taken 13. felt 14. was 15. came 16. worked 17. discovered 18. is perhaps 19. is used 20. has been easing 21. suffer

Using What You've Learned

9 Page 257.

Form groups of students and have groups share what they know about the remedies shown in the Student Book. Ask groups to appoint a scribe to take notes during their discussion. Afterward, have groups summarize their discussion for the class. You might add, if it is not brought up by students, that castor oil, celery juice, garlic, and ginseng are traditionally used as tonics. That is, they are used to improve overall health and a sense of well-being. They are also reputed to improve one's immune system. Of these, ginseng is the closest to an established "drug," as it has been a part of Chinese pharmacology since ancient times. The mold that grows on bread is also ingested by some people to cure common bacterial infections. This is a home remedy that is based partly on scientific fact, as penicillin is derived from blue bread mold. Copper bracelets are used to qualm nausea and dizziness, although their efficacy has not been clinically established.

10 Page 257.

Instruct students to choose one of the topics listed in the Student Book and to prepare a short report for the class on it. They can use encyclopedias, medical journals, and do key word searches on the Internet to gather information. Tell students they need not prepare a formal essay. Instead, they should organize their notes into a logical order and focus on the oral presentation.

Part 3 The Continuous Tense

Setting the Context

Direct students' attention to the photos and use these as a starting point for talking about changes in farming methods over the last two or three centuries. Ask students to name tasks that have been replaced by machines. Model the use of the present continuous with sentences such as *Today farmers are using tractors to plow fields. A hundred years ago, farmers were using hand tools.*

Discussing Ideas

Invite students to respond to the questions in the context of their home cultures. Ask them to tell about crops that are important in their countries of origin, and how these crops are raised.

A. The Continuous Tenses

1 Page 258.

were first being discovered (past continuous); were being cultivated and harvested (past continuous passive); were actually being imported and exported (past continuous); methods were being introduced (past continuous); surplus of food products is being produced (present continuous); none of the passive sentences have agents

2 Page 258.

Answers: 1. were being produced 2. was being grown / were being raised 3. was being harvested / was being cultivated 4. were being used / was still being done 5. were being used 6. were being attached 7. was still being done 8. were being used

3 Page 259.

Answers: 1. New techniques are being developed to allow for direct planting of rice. 2. Soybeans are being used to make variety of new high-protein food products. 3. Shorter wheat stalks are being developed to withstand damage from storms. 4. Strawberries are being bred to resist damage from frost. 5. Beans are being engineered to create their own fertilizer. 6. Gene banks are being established in many countries to preserve important seed material. 7. Freeze-drying is being perfected to allow for rapid, economical preservation of many vegetables. 8. Potatoes are being bred to grow in a much wider variety of climates.

4 **Page 260.**
Answers: 1. were needed 2. took 3. would not cooperate 4. was considered 5. tried 6. had been successfully colonized 7. did / had 8. fail / failed 9. grouped 10. fought 11. ate 12. failed 13. persisted 14. was 15. had been found 16. was 17. as 18. are currently being used 19. are continuing 20. has begun 21. determines 22. will be used

Using What You've Learned

5 **Page 261.**
Review the following principles of public speaking with students before they give their speeches:

1) Write the beginning of your speech word for word on index cards.
2) Take notes for additional information on other index cards and arrange the cards in order. It is not necessary to write complete sentences on these cards, the body of your speech. In fact, it is advisable not to do this, as it will interfere with your ability to speak naturally.
3) Write the ending word for word on the final index cards.
4) Stand tall during the speech and make eye contact with the audience.
5) Speak loudly and clearly.
6) Allow time at the end for questions.

Part 4 The Modal Auxiliaries

Setting the Context

Engage students in a discussion about the future of our energy resources, using the questions provided in the Student Book. Tell students that the article "Low on Energy" will discuss the future of fossil fuels — a finite and non-renewable source of energy.

Discussing Ideas

Use the questions in the Student Book to brainstorm a list of alternatives to fossil fuels. Add the terms *methane gas, geothermal energy, hydroelectricity, nuclear energy, wind farms*, and *solar energy* if they are not mentioned by students. The meanings of most of these terms will be taught later in the chapter.

A. The Modal Auxiliaries

1 **Page 263.**
Answers: 1. Solar power should have been developed sooner. 2. Methane could be used now instead of other fuels. 3. New biodegradable plastics ought to be developed. 4. (It is not possible to put this sentence into the passive.) 5. People must be educated about energy. 6. Alternative energy sources should have been researched a long time ago.

2 **Page 263.**
Answers: 1. will have become / can be accomplished 2. will be needed / can be replaced by 3. should be used / can be produced / must come 4. cannot be abandoned / should be used 5. should be avoided / cannot be found 6. can find 7. can be recovered / will be required 8. can find 9. can be produced / can be controlled / can be collected 10. can be put / might replace

3 Page 264.
Sample Rewrite:

Energy Planning

Since the 1880s, when oil first became an important resource, we have known that the supply could not last forever. Today, it is obvious that these supplies should not be used freely. In fact, many people believe that they should be regulated by governments.

A general energy plan should have been created decades ago. Just when the government could have enacted such a plan is debatable. However, surely after World War II, the direction of our industrial development was clear, and something should have been done.

Today, with the size and complexity of our industrial system, it would be extremely difficult to begin a strict energy plan. However, if a plan had been developed in the 1940s, it probably could have been enforced. In this way, our resources might have been managed in a more efficient way.

4 Page 264.
Sample Answers: 1. Three times as much power can be delivered by the legs as by the arms. 2. By the late 1890s, tools such as saws and grinding wheels were being powered by bicycle-like machines. 3. (no errors) 4. However, it has been recently "rediscovered." 5. Today, "people-powered" tools are being made by several different manufacturers. 6. These tools are being used by some craftspeople and farmers. 7. (no errors) 8. For example, grain can be ground, water can be pumped, and land can be cleared, plowed, and cultivated by "people-powered" tools.

5 Page 265.
Answers: 1. is produced 2. can be put 3. has been used 4. are heated 5. can also be generated 6.are powered 7. has been developed 8. has been reduced 9. has brought 10. has been cut 11. have followed 12. are blessed 13. can be exploited 14. can be provided 15. has taken 16. are used 17. to produce

6 Page 266.
Answers: 1. is regularly renewed 2. does not pollute 3. are being exploited 4. are provided 5. are not found 6. are found 7. exist 8. are not being exploited

7 Page 267.
Answers: 1. was funded 2. was believed 3. could become 4. had almost disappeared 5. have not been abandoned 6. are still pursuing 7. is being used 8. is produced 9. is produced 10. have persisted 11. have to be made 12. have to be built 13. have to be designed 14. are being planned 15. is expected

Using What You've Learned

8 Page 268.
Form small groups of students. Have groups follow the steps outlined in the Student Book to create a list of "best practices" in their chosen field. Afterward, invite a speaker from each group to read their list aloud to the class. Recast these points in the passive with modals for students as necessary.

9 Page 268.
Form small groups of students and have groups follow the same procedure as in the preceding activity.

Focus on Testing

Answers:

Part 1: 1. d 2. a 3. c 4. a

Part 2: 1. c 2. a 3. b 4. c

Part 5 Review of Chapters 5 to 8

1 **Page 270.**
Answers: 1. was born 2. first revealed 3. was projected 4. was located 5. was seated 6. could be viewed 7. was used 8. was 9. was used 10. had invented 11. was not 12. showed 13. was entering 14. were leaving 15. was shown 16. reported 17. believed 18. would have 19. refused 20. finally obtained 21. produced 22. were developing 23. was working 24. had created 25. made 26. was 27. included 28. have exploded 29. have delighted 30. frightened 31. bored 32. astounded 33. have reached 34. has evolved 35. have been developed

2 **Page 271.**
Answers: 1. that 2. when 3. who 4. where 5. who 6. which 7. which 8. that / which 9. so 10. since 11. that 12. that 13. when 14. that 15. Since 16. than 17. whether 18. how 19. which 20. that 21. which 22. who

3 **Page 273.**
Sample Rewrite:

Improvisational Technology

Tina told Steve not to worry. She suggested they get out of the car and start walking. She was sure help wasn't too far away. As Tina said this, she dismantled the rearview mirror from the car.

Gail asked what she was doing.

Tina said she was taking the mirror so that they would have it with them. She explained that they might need it to signal someone for help.

Gail agreed that it was a good idea, and then she began to take a hubcap off the car.

Frank asked what she was doing. He was the last one to get out of the car.

Gail told him that she was taking the hubcap. She explained that they could use it to shade themselves from the sun if it got really hot.

Frank said that was smart, and then he looked around him. He said he was going to take the radiator. He told Gail and Tina that that way they would have water to drink if they got thirsty.

Gail and Tina both agreed that was a good idea.

Then, when they were ready to begin walking, Gail, Tina, and Frank noticed that Steve had taken off one of the car doors and was trying to carry it.

Gail, Tina, and Frank asked Steve what he was doing with the door at the top of their voices.

As he dragged the door over to where they stood, Steve explained that if it got hot, they could roll down the window.

4 **Page 273.**
Answers:
The Berlin Wall, which had stood as a physical and psychological barrier between East and West for almost 30 years, was torn down in the fall of 1989. In September 1989, the first noncommunist government since World War II was elected in Poland. The Polish people elected a new type of leader who had been a communist. It was also in 1989 that Hungary, Czechoslovakia, East Germany, and the former Soviet Union all opened their borders to the West. Many of the changes which occurred in 1989 had been put in motion decades earlier. One can see the influence of the events of the 1870s, 1920s, and the 1940s on the events of 1989. Many of the countries which gained freedom in the 1980s had been parts of larger empires years earlier. The new borders that were created in recent years may change again someday soon.

Chapter 8

Video Activities: Advances in Medicine

Before You Watch

Use the questions to engage students in a discussion about degenerative diseases of the central nervous system, such as MS and ALS. Talk to students about the effects of these diseases and available treatments. Tell students that they will learn more about ALS from the video.

Watch [on video]

Answers: 1. c 2. c 3. b

Watch Again [on video]

Answers: 1. 2 years 2. BDNF 3. pump, implanted, abdomen, catheter, inserted, vertebrae, release, spinal fluid 4. diagnosis 5. optimistic 6. a. mindboggling b. neurologist c. prolonged d. hypothesis

After You Watch

Answers: 1. were not given 2. is not performed 3. will be helped 4. implanted / inserted 5. suffer *or* are suffering

Focus on Testing

Answers:

Part 1: 1. b 2. d 3. b 4. c 5. b 6. c 7. a 8. d

Part 2: 1. c 2. a 3. c 4. c 5. b 6. c 7. a 8. a

Art and Entertainment

Goals

- Gerunds
- Infinitives
- Verbs followed by either infinitives or gerunds
- Infinitives and gerunds as subjects and complements; parallelism

Introduction

Tell students that they will be studying the gerund and infinitive throughout this chapter. Remind students that a gerund is a verb form that ends in ing and is used as a noun. Review these basic spelling rules for the formation of gerunds:

- In verbs that end in *-e*, the *-e* is dropped before adding *-ing*.
- In verbs that end in a short vowel plus the consonants *-b, -d, -g, -l, -m, -n, -p, -s, -t*, or *-z*, the consonant is often doubled before adding *-ing*.
- In verbs that end in a double consonant, the double consonant is kept.

Write the following list of verbs on the board and have students dictate the spelling of the gerund form to you.

buzz	read
create	rid
keep	rob
kill	sing
listen	stop
make	swim
mop	win
play	

When you are finished, invite a volunteer to read the article "What Is Art?" aloud for the class.

Discussing Ideas

With the class, brainstorm as many different kinds of art as you can think of and list these on the board. Invite students to describe specific works in each category that they know about. Ask them to try to define why they think these works qualify (or do not qualify) as "art."

Part 1 Gerunds

Setting the Context

If possible, play a sample of a classic jazz recording for the class. Some of the jazz artists mentioned in this chapter include Miles Davis, Dizzy Gillespie, Louis Armstrong, and Wynton Marsalis. The video for this chapter features women artists in the field of jazz. Taking time to listen to some of these artists will help to create context for this material. Afterward, invite students to respond to the Prereading Questions.

Discussing Ideas

In the context of this activity, you might provide the following definition of *improvise* for students: "to compose or play a musical piece without preparation; to make up a melody as one plays." Encourage students to compare jazz to other forms of music by having them respond to the questions in the Student Book. Invite students to share about music from their countries of origin.

C. *To* + Gerund

1 **Page 282.**
Sample Answers: 1. in learning 2. at appreciating 3. on buying 4. of listening to 5. of going 6. to going 7. about going to see a play

2 Page 283.
Sample Answers: 1. I'm not interested in learning how to play a wind instrument. 2. Some people object to paying high prices for a show. 3. I look forward to hearing some good music tonight. 4. I'm used to hearing loud music from my neighbors. 5. Let's plan on meeting around eight o'clock. 6. It takes talent to be successful at playing more than one kind of instrument.

3 Page 283.
Answers: 1. At first in New York, he made money by working several odd jobs. 2. He learned more about a new movement in jazz called "bebop" by playing with jazz greats Dizzy Gillespie and Charlie Parker. 3. Eventually, he gave himself more musical freedom by starting his own band. 4. In the following years, he created his own special sound by blending many types of jazz. 5. While playing, he often kept his concentration by turning his back to the audience. 6. In the 1950s, he tried to escape his loneliness by using illegal drugs. 7. He improved his health by giving up drugs in the 1960s. 8. Throughout most of his career, Miles gave his music a wider audience by traveling around the world.

D. Gerunds as Objects of Verbs

4 Page 284.
Answers: 1. It was certainly worth seeing. 2. I wouldn't mind seeing that group again. 3. I admit no liking all the music. 4. We certainly appreciated you giving us the tickets. 5. We are considering going to another concert. 6. It will involve making plans well in advance. 7. I'd recommend you buying tickets soon. 8. I suggest calling the box office today.

5 Page 284.
Sample Answers: 1. I'd appreciate taking some time off. 2. Would you consider returning a favor? 3. Let's discuss returning earlier than we planned. 4. I can't imagine seeing her in person. 5. The trip involves planning months in advance. 6. I don't mind driving into the city. 7. I recommend seeing that movie. 8. Let's spend some time visiting the sights. 9. He suggested going to the museum. 10. I can't help wondering what happened backstage.

6 Page 284.
Form pairs of students. Partners can use the questions in the Student Book to have a short discussion about their musical preferences. Afterward, invite students to tell the class a few things that they learned about their partners.

7 Page 284.
Form pairs of students once again. One student can take the role of a ticket agent while the other student takes the role of customer. Have students sit back to back and role play a telephone conversation in which the customer has called the agent about the availability of tickets for an upcoming show.

E. Subjects of Gerunds

8 Page 285.
Answers: 1. his improvising / his "bending" 2. Representing / understanding / Complementing / Training / playing / dedicating / performing / appearing 3. Billie Holiday's singing / Joe Williams's singing / Ella Fitzgerald's singing

F. Direct Objects of Gerunds

9 Page 286.
Answers: 1. the mixing of different races, cultures, and music 2. the blending of work songs, spirituals, blues, folk, and traditional music 3. the interweaving of black and white music 4. the playing of musical notes 5. the expressing of one's individuality 6. the releasing of tension

Using What You've Learned

10 Page 287.
Form small groups of students. Have group members share their ideas on music by responding to the questions in the Student Book. Ask one member of the group to write down a few quotes from the discussion to share with the class.

11 Page 287.
Ask students to write a short paragraph about a sport, musical instrument, or other art form that they have some personal knowledge about. Students should include as many instances of gerunds within the paragraph as they can. Collect students' work and check it for correct grammar and usage. Circle errors so that students can identify and correct the errors themselves. Check the corrections later and ask for further revisions if necessary.

Part 2 Infinitives

Setting the Context

Invite students to share about traditional forms of art from their native countries and the tools that are used to create those works. Students may want to draw simple illustrations on the board to support their descriptions.

Discussing Ideas

The questions ask students to think of examples of art that has been taken or destroyed by outsiders. The Philistines are a well-known example of this. They were a non-Semitic people who lived in Palestine from the 12th century B.C. The Philistines were hostile to the Israelites and destroyed much of their art in their frequent raids. To this day, a "Philistine" is therefore known as a person who is indifferent or hostile to artistic and cultural values. In more recent times, the Nazis were reputed to have plundered many works of art throughout Eastern Europe in the years preceding World War II. The fate of some paintings and sculptures from this period is still unknown. In addition, the means by which major museums and art institutions acquire important works of art from foreign countries is often called into question. You can add these and other examples to students' own ideas.

B. Infinitives As Objects of Verbs

1 Page 289.
Answers: 1. Everyone agreed to meet at the museum. 2. There appeared to be hundreds of people at the museum. 3. We happened to choose a busy day. 4. We had hoped to go when it wasn't crowded. 5. We waited for the crowds to leave. 6. We decided not to stay. 7. We agreed to come back later. 8. We never plan to go there on a holiday again.

2 Page 289.
Sample Story:
I used to walk my daughter home from school every day. I had agreed to wait for her on the corner by the school, but one day I decided not to go. Actually, she asked me to stay home. She wanted to find her own way. I hoped she would return to her senses, but she was firm about it. Most of all, I was worried about her safety. She had learned not to ask strangers for directions, and I told her not to let people offer her help. She has a cell phone, so she can call me anytime. On the first day she was supposed to walk by herself, she was preparing to leave the school. She called me and said she was going to be late. She didn't seem to want to tell me why. One hour later, she arrived with several friends. I realized that my little girl was much older than I had thought. Since then I've managed to understand her need to be more independent.

C. Verbs That May Be Followed by (Pro)nouns and Infinitives

3 Page 290.
Answers: 1. He chose not to stay. 2. The extra money helped pay for the trip. 3. The extra money enabled me to stay longer.

4. They told us to stay. 5. We were told to stay.

4 Page 290.

Form pairs of students. Have students use the prompts in the Student Book to ask each other questions about a trip to South America that they would take if they could. Postcards, travel magazines, art albums, and other images from South America may help, if you have these available. Students can also refer to the map on page 291 of the Student Book for ideas.

E. Adverbs, Adjectives, and Nouns Followed by Infinitives

5 Page 292.

Sample Answers: 1. I wonder if it was difficult to carve such small details into stone. 2. How did the artists get enough gold for these works of art? 3. How were they able to cut stone? 4. These pieces seem too intact to have withstood the test of time. 5. The artists must have worked hard to achieve such intricacy of detail. 6. In wonder who was the first person to discover these works? 7. I wonder if it was easy to move around while wearing such elaborate jewelry. 8. It would be nice to have a replica of the jaguar. 9. I would like to know where I can see pre-Colombian works on display.

6 Page 292.

Answers: 1. to master / working 2. to heat 3. to stretch / hammer / breaking 4. to break 5. melting / pouring 6. to use / to be / working 7. to do 8. working

7 Page 293.

Answers: 1. pound 2. to use 3. reflecting 4. to dig 5. to make 6. to make 7. to date 8. trading 9. trading 10. to pound 11. beat 12. breaking 13. to use 14. to add 15. to strengthen

8 Page 294.

Answers: 1. to bring 2. to become 3. discovering 4. to accept 5. to employ 6. Coating 7. conducting 8. to make 9. to form

9 Page 294.

Answers: 1. I would enjoy learning how to make jewelry. 2. She asked me to go with her to South America. 3. Everyone agreed to meet me at the steps in front of the concert hall. 4. Marguerite refused to help me with the painting. 5. Miles Davis's playing is beautiful. 6. Playing jazz is a difficult art form. 7. I can't help going at least once a week. 8. The students are very excited about visiting the Louvre Museum. 9. Marina isn't used to practicing the piano yet. 10. I like to relax by painting with oil.

Using What You've Learned

10 Page 295.

You might post some or all of the following sentences on the board as model sentences for partners to use in their discussion.

It's fun to paint.

It's boring to go to a museum.

It's enjoyable to hear music outdoors.

It's interesting to read about the making of a film.

It's relaxing to listen to music at the end of the day.

I'm accustomed to practicing piano at least two hours a day.

I'm interested in learning how to play the saxophone.

I avoid going to foreign films.

My friend encouraged me to learn how to dance salsa.

I enjoy almost any kind of sport.

My trainer expects me to be able to lift 100 pounds in three months.

I plan on visiting the Art Institute of Chicago this summer.

11 Page 295.

Tell students that they can write the description in the first person if they wish. In other words, they can write as if the tool or appliance is speaking for itself. You might share the following description with students to help them get started:

People use me to make all kinds of drinks and sauces. To use me, you have to follow certain steps. First you have to put the necessary ingredients inside of me. Next, put a lid on top to avoid making a mess. Then push my button to mix all the ingredients. Can you guess what I am? (a blender)

12 Page 295.

This activity asks students to describe an art form that is indigenous to their country of origin. Although students may be familiar with the use and function of a certain art form, they won't necessarily be informed as to how it is created. Encourage students to visit the library and check out materials that outline the steps in this process. They can summarize these steps in one or two paragraphs and then describe the use and function of this art form. Remind students to include as many infinitives and gerunds as possible. Invite students to take turns reading their papers aloud to the class, and allow time for classmates to ask questions after each presentation.

Part 3 Verbs Followed by Either Infinitives or Gerunds

Setting the Context

You can preview the paintings *Impression, Sunrise* (page 296), *The Bar at the Folies Bergere* (page 300), and *Burning of the Houses of Parliament* (page 301) to familiarize students with impressionist art, and to help them respond to the Prereading Questions.

Discussing Ideas

Modern painting is not as popular among the general public as it once was, and many people are unaware of the diversity of approaches in the art world today. There are a number of journals and magazines available that showcase contemporary art. You may be able to find a copy of such a publication in the art department of your school. If so, you might want to show students a few examples of innovative art to help them respond to the questions. There may also be works of art displayed on campus that can provide the stimulus for this discussion.

A. Verbs Followed by Either Infinitives or Gerunds

1 Page 298.

Answers:

1. to take (The infinitive must be used to indicate two separate actions.)
2. to go (The infinitive must be used as *love* is in the conditional.)
3. to spend / spending
4. to visit / visiting
5. to visit (The infinitive is used after *remember* when giving advice.)
6. to spend / spending
7. to spend (The infinitive is used after *mean* to show intent.)
8. changing (The gerund is used after *mean* to show what an action involves.)
9. you telling (The gerund is used after *remember* to show that the action happened at an earlier time.)
10. to go / going
11. talking (The gerund is used after *stop* as a command.)
12. packing (The gerund is used after *stop* as a command.)

2 **Page 299.**
Answers: 1. That museum does not permit you to take pictures. 2. At least, they do not permit using a flash. 3. You are forbidden to use a flash. 4. My friend teaches people how to take pictures without a flash. 5. She could teach you how to take good pictures without your flash. 6. Flash cameras can cause the colors to fade. 7. The museum encourages people to buy prints there instead. 8. The prints are very good. I advise you to buy several.

3 **Page 299.**
Answers: 1. to adopt 2. they could find 3. painting 4. to define 5. to consider 6. analyzing 7. to see 8. reproducing 9. to be 10. to know 11. to reproduce

4 **Page 300.**
Answers: 1. to gain 2. to not understand 3. to shake 4. to begin 5. following 6. His handling 7. thinking 8. to ask 9. to imitate 10. to create 11. to come 12. imitating 13. taking 14. redefining 15. to define 16. exploring

Using What You've Learned

5 **Page 301.**
Form small groups of students and ask groups to discuss the paintings shown on pages 301 and 302 of the Student Book. These paintings were all created by innovative artists working during the last half of the nineteenth century. You can expand the activity to include works by twentieth-century artists as well, such as Jackson Pollock, Andy Warhol, and Robert Rauschenberg. You may be able to find reproductions of paintings by these and other artists in the art department or library of your school. If so, display them in the class to provide stimulus for the group discussions. Encourage students to speculate as to the intent of the various artists, and to share their reactions to the paintings.

Part 4 Infinitives and Gerunds as Subjects and Complements; Parallelism

Setting the Context

Using the questions in the Student Book, invite students to share what they know about different forms of African art, including dance, music, and sculpture.

Discussing Ideas

If possible, play a sample of traditional African drumming for students. This will help to provide some context for the discussion. Invite students to talk about the influence of African rhythms on different forms of contemporary popular music.

A. Infinitives and Gerunds As Subjects and Complements

1 **Page 304.**
Sample Answers: 1. It would be a shame to lose the expertise of past generations. 2. It's difficult for folk artists to support themselves in today's world. 3. It's much more interesting to have an original work of art than a reproduction. 4. It's better to embrace technology than to ignore it. 5. It would also be fascinating to see how folk artists in other countries approach technology. 6. It's hard to reach a large audience without mass production. 7. It's necessary to change with the times. 8. It's impossible to avoid mechanization these days.

1. Losing the expertise of past generations would be a shame. 2. Supporting oneself as a folk artist is difficult in today's world.
3. Having an original work of art is much more interesting than having a reproduction.
4. Embracing technology is better than ignoring it. 5. Seeing how folk artists around the world approach technology would also be fascinating. 6. Reaching a large audience is hard without mass production. 7. Changing

with the times is necessary. 8. Avoiding mechanization is impossible these days.

B. Parallelism

2 Page 305.

Answers: 1. Dancing / to unite 2. marking / giving 3. to commemorate / to celebrate 4. to honor / for people to enjoy 5. dancing / moving 6. drumming / creating / following / responding 7. to produce / to make 8. for Westerners to duplicate / to follow

3 Page 306.

Answers: 1. to create (creating) 2. Attracting / keeping 3. Expressing 4. to combine 5. Wearing 6. Collecting 7. carving / producing 8. to find

4 Page 307.

Answers:

1. Long before Europeans came ~~for~~ to explore tropical Africa, the powerful nation of Benin had been flourishing in what is now southern Nigeria.
2. (no errors)
3. In spite of not ~~to have~~ having a written language, the Beninese left beautiful bronze plaques and figures as records of their civilization.
4. (no errors)
5. These plaques recorded numerous scenes of life in Benin, and many showed two important aspects of the culture: hunting and ~~to trade~~ trading.
6. Only the strongest Beninese men could become hunters and then only after to complete completing rigorous training.
7. Young hunters had to learn how to track animals, ~~moving~~ to move quickly and quietly, and ~~surviving~~ to survive in the forest for days without food.
8. When European explorers arrived, they couldn't help ~~to be~~ being amazed at the amount of commerce in Bening.
9. Benin was the commercial center of western Africa, and Beninese merchants were clever enough ~~outhinking~~ to outthink the Europeans, who had expected ~~dealing~~ to deal with simple natives.
10. Beninese merchants had an elaborate money system, and they dealt in the buying and ~~to sell~~ selling of ironwork, weapons, farm tools, wood carvings, and food.

Using What You've Learned

5 Page 307.

Form small groups of students. Have group members take turns telling a story from their cultural heritage, following the suggestions in the Student Book. Tell students to listen carefully to each group member's story. Afterward, invite a volunteer from each group to retell a group member's story—not his or her own story—for the class.

Video Activities: Women in Jazz

Before You Watch

Answers: 1. a 2. Students' answers will vary. Tell students that the video they are about to watch is about female artists in the field of jazz music.

Watch [on video]

Answers: 1. c 2. b 3. a 4. a, c, d

Watch Again [on video

1. a. Ida Cox (Woman)
   b. Neta May McKinney (Woman)
   c. Maxine Sullivan (Woman)
   d. Lester Young
   e. Cab Calloway
   f. Duke Ellington

g. Count Basie
h. Helen Humes (Woman)

2. b
3. a
4. b

After You Watch

Answers: 1. listening 2. becoming 3. to preserve 4. playing 5. to play

Focus on Testing

Answers:

Part 1: 1. c 2. c 3. b 4. a

Part 2: 1. b 2. b 3. b 4. b

Conflict and Reconciliation

Goals

- ***Hope* versus *wish***
- **Imaginary conditions: present and unspecified time**
- **Perfect modal auxiliaries**
- **Imaginary conditions: past and present time**
- **Factual conditions: present, future, and unspecified time**

Introduction

Tell students that this chapter will present information about different problems in the world today-political upheavals, natural disasters, and especially the critical state of our environment. It will also present possible solutions and ways to express hopes for a better future. Ask students to read the introductory article silently to themselves.

Discussing Ideas

Invite students to share their responses to the discussion questions. Rephrase students' responses using conditional tenses, e.g., *If we tried to limit our consumption, there wouldn't be such a terrible problem with waste.* Write a few of these sentences on the board, and tell students they will be learning how to create sentences about imaginary conditions.

Part 1 *Hope* versus *Wish*

Setting the Context

Write two headings on the board: *Problems* and *Solutions.* With students, brainstorm a list of problems in today's world and some possible solutions. Tell students that the article "Taking Responsibility" is about two different approaches to the world's problems. Then invite a volunteer to read the article aloud for the class.

Discussing Ideas

Ask students to think of ways that they can or do contribute to solutions to the world's problems. It doesn't necessarily have to be in the form of political activism. Some people are very conscientious about recycling. Others choose to patronize businesses that support their personal values. Engage students in a discussion about the ways in which ordinary citizens can contribute to a better world in their daily lives.

A. *Hope* Versus *Wish*

1 Page 313.

Answers: [Note: The "tenses" do not refer to the inflection of the verb, but the time frame in which it is hoped or wished that the action occur.]

1. are concerned: present
2. recognize: present
3. were: present
4. had begun: past
5. had: present
6. had faced: past
7. had cared: past
8. were: present
9. were working: present
10. could: present
11. will have: future
12. will face: future

B. Subjunctive Forms with *Wish*

2 Page 314.

Answers:

1. These people often wish that the situation were (present) different and that our problems had never developed (past).

2. They may hope that solutions <u>are</u> (present) possible or that the problems <u>will disappear</u> (future).

3 Page 315.
Answers: 1. realized 2. had begun 3. are 4. begin 5. understand 6. knew 7. had never learned 8. understood 9. realized 10. will change 11. would join 12. could see 13. will start

4 Page 316.
Answers: 1. is still being done 2. has already been ruined 3. are being affected / are affected 4. are injured / are being 5. are dying 6. are assassinated / are being assassinated 7. wish 8. had ever happened 9. wish 10. had had 11. wish 12. had never started 13. were not dying 14. were not now being drafted 15. would stop 16. could come 17. do 18. hope 19. only hope / am only hoping 20. would hope 21. could be 22. help 23. would hope 24. could help 25. could share 26. would 27. could once again

5 Page 319.
This activity provides an excellent opportunity for students to educate each other about important issues being faced in their home countries. Have students follow the steps outlined in the Student Book and ask them to study the example provided. Afterward, invite students to take turns reading their essays aloud for the class.

Using What You've Learned

6 Page 320.
The activity asks students to write two statements expressing a wish and a hope about the issues raised so far in the chapter. To publish students' work, you or an assistant can gather students' papers and input them all together into a single document. Put quotation marks around each statement and cite the author. Make copies of the document and distribute it to students so that they can read their classmates' ideas.

7 Page 320.
This activity encourages students to draft a petition to the United Nations. If students wish to actually send their petition, they can address it to: United Nations, New York, NY, 10017, to the attention of the appropriate agency or program. To find out more about the U.N. system, students can visit its website at: http://www.unsystem.org. They can also visit the website for the U.N. Headquarters at: http://www.un.org

8 Page 320.
Following are the names of environmental agencies which students may wish to investigate:

- Bureau of Land Management
- Environmental Protection Agency
- National Biological Service
- National Park Service
- U.S. Geological Survey
- United States Fish and Wildlife Service

Part 2 Imaginary Conditions: Present and Unspecified Time

Setting the Context

Use the Prereading Questions to prepare students for the article, then ask a volunteer to read the article aloud for the class.

Discussing Ideas

You might offer the following definition of *shortcomings* to students: "a failing or weak point in achieving a certain goal." Then ask students to think of shortcomings of modern societies to care and respect for all its members, including the environment.

A. *Otherwise*: Present Time

1 **Page 321.**

Sample Answers:

1. Otherwise, Sabelia might have more qualified teachers.
2. Otherwise, Sabelia might have a more developed economy.
3. Otherwise, Sabelia would have more money available for industrial development.
4. Otherwise, there might be more skilled workers in other areas.
5. Otherwise, there might be less hunger.
6. Otherwise, there might be less disease.

B. Imaginary Conditions: Present and Unspecified Time

2 **Page 322.**

Sample Answers: 1. If the industries were more concerned about pollution, we wouldn't be in the middle of an environmental crisis. 2. If Technologica had its own source of energy, we wouldn't be subject to price increases. 3. If the government managed the economy better, we could plan how to save and spend more wisely. 4. If the wealth of the country were distributed more equally, there wouldn't be any poverty. 5. If Technologica produced more of its own food, we wouldn't be so dependent on foreign countries. 6. If we had more natural resources, we could exploit them and make more money.

3 **Page 323.**

For this activity, you might encourage students to take a controversial position, or a position that is contrary to students' actual way of thinking. This is a good exercise in developing logical arguments, and may help students to focus on form.

Sample Answer: 1.. In my model society, there would be only one ethnic group. If there were only one ethnic group, there would be no differences. And if there were no differences, there'd be no war, only peace.

4 **Page 323.**

Form small groups of students and have them enter several ideas in each column of each table. They can then write sentences in the conditional tense using their notes. The following is an example of one completed activity.

Sample Answers:
see chart below

	Advantages	**Disadvantages**
capitalist	economy develops very quickly, some people very rich	a large class of poor people, inflation, unemployment
socialist	sense of ownership among workers, guaranteed medical care	limited range of products, lack of choice

If we had a capitalist economy, the economy would develop quickly and some people would become very rich. However, a large class of poor people might form, and inflation and unemployment would be constant problems. If we had a socialist system, there might be a feeling among workers that they owned the means of production, but there would be a limited range of products. There would also be a lack of choice in other areas of life, such as healthcare, although essential services would be guaranteed for all.

5 Page 325.

Sample Answer:

In my model society, there would be a capitalist economy. A capitalist economy has several advantages over a socialist economy. It would develop much more quickly than a socialist economy, and there would be plenty of opportunities for material advancement for those who were motivated and willing to work hard. It's true that some people would be much wealthier than others, but increased productivity would result in an improved infrastructure for the whole society.

C. Imaginary Conditions with *Should* or *Were* + Infinitive

6 Page 325.

Answers:

1. Should you steal a car, you would go to prison for five years.

   Were you to steal a car, you would go to prison for five years.
2. Should you participate in a riot, you would pay a fine of $1,000.

   Were you to participate in a riot, you would pay a fine of $1,000.
3. Should you try to overthrow the government, you might be imprisoned for life.

   Were you to try to overthrow the government, you might be imprisoned for life.
4. Should you throw a tomato at the supreme leader, you would be in big trouble.

   Were you throw a tomato at the supreme leader, you would be in big trouble.
5. Should you spy for a hostile country, you would be guilty of treason.

   Were you to spy for a hostile country, you would be guilty of treason.
6. Should you buy goods on the black market, you would be in great danger.

   Were you to buy goods on the black market, you would be in great danger.

7 Page 325.

Answers: 1. is still 2. were constructed 3. would surround 4. were 5. would have 6. could walk 7. could get 8. would help 9. would also know 10. be 11. would cut 12. began 13. designed 14. flock 15. were 16. did

Using What You've Learned

8 Page 327.

Many people have a superstition that a wish will not come true if the speaker announces it to other people. To preserve the anonymity of "wishers," have students write five wishes on a piece of paper without writing their names. Collect the papers and correct grammatical errors. Then place the papers on a table where students can collect their work, and perhaps sneak a peek at the wishes of their classmates.

9 Page 327.

Students can find out the penalty for various misdemeanors and felonies by obtaining a copy of their local ordinances. This is usually available at the local library or students may try to call the local sheriff, who can direct them to the appropriate agency or resource. Students can then use this information to write conditional sentences about different crimes and their punishments.

10 Page 327.

Ask a volunteer to come forward and help you perform a role-play for the class. With the volunteer, read the mini-dialogue in the Student Book aloud. Here are some other problems that can be used to extend the dialogue:

- unemployment
- corruption
- lack of adequate health care
- unskilled workers
- undereducated population

Then, ask students to form pairs and continue the role-play, with one student taking the role of leader and the other taking the role of adviser.

After a few minutes, ask students to stop and switch roles.

11 Page 327.

Form groups and have groups follow the steps outlined in the Student Book to design a model society for a newly formed island in the Pacific. Invite a representative from each group to present the principles of its model society to the class. After each presentation, ask students from other groups to recapitulate the main points of the presentation. After all groups have made their presentations, ask students to name those principles which were common to all or most of the model societies described.

Part 3 Perfect Modal Auxiliaries

Setting the Context

Following is a list of the world's ten largest urban areas, in order of population. Ask students to share what they know about the living conditions in these cities:

- Tokyo, Japan
- Mumbai (Bombay), India
- São Paulo, Brazil
- Shanghai, China
- New York, U.S.
- Mexico City, Mexico
- Beijing, China
- Jakarta, Indonesia
- Lagos, Nigeria
- Los Angeles, U.S.

Discussing Ideas

Ask students to rate the quality of life in the city or town in which they live. What are some of the problems facing the community? How can they be improved?

A. Perfect Modal Auxiliaries

1 Page 329.

Answers:

1. Modal auxiliaries and verbs in the second and third paragraphs: could have avoided; might have managed; could have provided; should have limited...and developed, might have, could have, should have done. These do not refer to real events, but things the author thinks should have happened.
2. The main verbs after the modal auxiliaries are in the form of past participle.

2 Page 329.

Answers: 1. We should have left. 2. They couldn't have helped us. 3. It must have been right. 4. He may have had a problem. 5. I should have gone. 6. It might not have worked. 7. She may have called. 8. I wouldn't have tried that. 9. He would have rather stayed home. 10. We might have gone there. 11. It couldn't have been true. 12. We would have liked to discuss it. 13. She could have done it. 14. We should have told him. 15. They might have stopped him.

3 Page 330.

Sample Answers: 1. They would have done something to clean the air, but there are more important problems right now. 2. They would have moved to Rio, but they don't speak Portuguese. 3. I would have gone with them, but I wasn't finished with my studies. 4. I would have gone to a doctor, but I'm too busy. 5. I would have paid it, but my boss hasn't paid my salary yet. 6. I would have handed it in, but my printer ran out of ink.

4 Page 330.

Answers: 1. He would rather have been at home. 2. He would rather have driven in the comfort of his car. 3. He would rather have gone in the subway, but it was too far away. 4. He would rather have eaten something a little healthier. 5. He would rather have had a fishburger. 6. He would rather have slept in a hotel.

5 **Page 331.**
Sample Answers:
1. Dreckville should have planned its growth more carefully. It could have established a city center and controlled subsequent growth. The city should have sponsored a more comprehensive transportation system.
2. The bus service and subway system could have been integrated in a better way. Bus routes should have been drawn so that they service subway stops. If the service were more frequent and more efficient, perhaps the fares could be reduced.
3. Dreckville should have regulated industry more closely. It could have avoided the problem with pollution if it had done this.
4. Dreckville should have anticipated this problem. They could have installed fresh oxygen lines in the public schools for smog-alert days.

6 **Page 331.**
Sample Answers:
1. The bus could have had a flat tire. The driver could have abandoned the bus.
2. She could have walked. Or she might have taken a taxi, if she had enough money.
3. They might have died from all the pollution. Although its' unusual for so many to die at the same time, they could have died from natural causes.
4. He could have scolded her for being late and then told her to get to work.
5. A robber could have broken into the house. He could have trashed the place while looking for valuables.
6. She might have called police. She might have cleaned the house up. In either case, she might have cried.

Part 4 Imaginary Conditions: Past and Present Time

Setting the Context

With students, brainstorm a list of technological discoveries and inventions of the last century. Talk about the dangers and benefits of each discovery. Your list might include some of the following:

- anesthetics
- computers
- engines and fuel
- lasers
- nuclear energy
- penicillin
- vaccines
- X-rays

Discussing Ideas

Revisit the list you generated in Setting the Context. Ask students to make statements about how our lives might be worse or better without these inventions.

A. *Otherwise*: Past Time

1 **Page 333.**
Answers: 1. Tribes no longer had to follow herds of animals; otherwise, they wouldn't have been able to settle in permanent villages. 2. People had more than enough food; otherwise, they would have spent all their time on survival needs. 3. People had more free time; otherwise, they wouldn't have had any time for creative pursuits. 4. Some areas were naturally suited for agriculture; otherwise, tribes wouldn't have had to fight over territory. 5. War became a common occurrence; otherwise, people wouldn't have had any reason to develop new and more sophisticated weapons. 6. Humans learned how to use metal; otherwise, they wouldn't have been able to manufacture spears, knives, and guns.

B. Imaginary Conditions: Past Time

2 Page 334.
Answers:
1. If the Chinese hadn't invented gunpowder, they wouldn't have invented fireworks.
2. If ancient Egyptians hadn't needed a sharp, durable tool for harvesting wheat, they wouldn't have made the first metal sword.
3. If ancient East Africans hadn't developed an iron industry, they wouldn't have made new and effective spears and knives to defeat invaders and become successful invaders.
4. If Europeans hadn't traveled to China in the 13th century, they wouldn't have started to import spices, found new ways to preserve meat, learn about gunpowder, and developed firearms.

3 Page 335.
Answers:
1. hadn't been / wouldn't have been able to
2. not studied / would have taken
3. would not have moved / had not had
4. wouldn't have flown / had not developed
5. wouldn't have developed / hadn't succeeded
6. not broken out / would have taken

4 Page 336.
Sample Answers:
1. They could create tools, and the tools increased their productivity. If people hadn't learned how to use metal, they wouldn't have been able to make tools which enabled them to hunt, cook, and farm.
2. The boats allowed them to visit other cultures. If they hadn't developed ocean-going boats, there would have never been contact between peoples of different cultures.
3. Columbus' discovery led to the colonization of native peoples in the Americas. If Columbus hadn't discovered the "New World," native peoples might have been able to further develop their own civilizations.
4. The engine made it possible for machines to do labor-intensive work for people. If Watt hadn't invented the engine, we would still be farming by hand.
5. Mendel's work eventually led to current research known as the genome project. If Mendel hadn't made his discoveries, we would know much less about ourselves.
6. Penicillin has made it possible for us to combat many forms of bacteria. If Fleming hadn't discovered penicillin, people would be much more vulnerable to disease today.
7. Radium is used in medical radiography. If Curie hadn't isolated radium, there would be no X-rays today.
8. Einstein's theories led to the development of the atom bomb. If Einstein hadn't developed these theories, we would have never developed the capacity for mass destruction that is now available.

C. Imaginary Conditions: Past and Present Time

5 Page 336.
Sample Answers: 1. If humans hadn't developed systems for writing, there would be no way to know anything about our past. 2. Had the gun been banned 50 years ago, there might be far less violence in our society today. 3. If aircraft had never been developed, spacecraft wouldn't have been developed either. 4. If penicillin hadn't been discovered, millions of children might have died from simple infections. 5. If satellites had never been launched, we wouldn't be able to predict hurricanes. 6. If a nuclear war had started five years ago, we might all be living in caves.

6 Page 336.
Sample Answers:

1. If there had been no nuclear testing in Nevada in the 1950s, there wouldn't be deadly radiation throughout the area today. Thousands of sheep wouldn't have died, and there wouldn't be so many people suffering from cancer.
2. If the farmer hadn't fertilized his field so early, the pellets would have sunk into the ground and dissolved. The birds wouldn't have mistaken the pellets for food, and they would have lived.
3. If copper mining had not been allowed so close to the river, there wouldn't have been so much contamination. The rice crops wouldn't have been destroyed. Farmers wouldn't have lost their crops.
4. If so many hardwood trees hadn't been harvested, the ecosystem wouldn't have been upset. The rats wouldn't have been forced to eat coconuts. The Maldives wouldn't have lost its main export.

7 Page 337.
Answers: 1. had never happened 2. had not decided 3. would have been 4. would have been damaged 5. had not controlled 6. would have continued 7. would have moved 8. had continued 9. would have been able to provide 10. would have been 11. wouldn't have been

Using What You've Learned

8 Page 338.
Here is a short list of topics students can choose from to do this writing activity:

- the atomic bomb
- biologically engineered food
- capitalism
- colonization
- the Internet
- public education
- vaccines

9 Page 338.
Have students write a short essay about how their lives might have been taken another course under different conditions. The prompts in the Student Book will help them to generate ideas for the writing activity. When they are finished, have students get together in small groups and read their papers aloud to each other.

Focus on Testing

Answers:
Part 1: 1. b 2. b 3. d 4. a
Part 2: 1. d 2. c 3. b 4. a

Part 5 Factual Conditions: Present, Future, and Unspecified Time

Setting the Context

Most students will be able to appreciate that Native Americans lived in greater harmony with the natural environment than we do today. They did not waste as we do. After killing a buffalo, for example, virtually every part of the animal was used. The meat and internal organs were eaten or smoked and stored. The hide was used for clothing and shelter, and even the animal's sinews and tendons were used for sewing. Many Native American rituals were practiced to give thanks to the earth and to establish a sense of balance. Ask students to share about other Native American customs and lifeways they know about in preparation for the article.

Discussing Ideas

Chief Seattle is of course describing the newly arrived white settlers in North America. Ask students to summarize the values that Chief Seattle wanted to impart in their own words.

1 **Page 341.**
Answers: 1. are combined 2. produce 3. stay 4. travels 5. returns 6. causes 7. has 8. is

A. Factual Conditions: Present or Unspecified Time

2 **Page 342.**
Answers: 1. When sulfur dioxide mixes with clouds, drops of acid rain form. 2. When acid rain falls to the ground, soil becomes acidic. 3. When forests become acidic, young trees die. 4. When the acid contents of rivers rise, fish stop reproducing. 5. If drinking water becomes more acidic, water pipes will dissolve.

B. Factual Conditions: Future Time

3 **Page 342.**
Sample Answers: 1. If farmers use pesticides, their harvests will increase dramatically. 2. If farmers use pesticides, their losses during storage are lower. 3. If farmers use pesticides, their crops are easier to export. 4. If farmers don't use pesticides, pests will not be as resistant to the chemicals. 5. If farmers don't use pesticides, natural enemies of the pests will be allowed to survive. 6. If farmers don't use pesticides, the chemicals won't accumulate in nature and reach lethal amounts.

4 **Page 343.**
Answers: 1. Unless farmers use pesticides, their harvests will decrease dramatically. 2. Unless farmers use pesticides, their losses during storage will increase. 3. Unless farmers use pesticides, their crops won't be as easy to export. 4. Unless farmers don't use pesticides, pests will be more resistant to the chemicals. 5. Unless farmers don't use pesticides, natural enemies of the pests won't be allowed to survive. 6. Unless farmers don't use pesticides, the chemicals will accumulate in nature and reach lethal amounts.

5 **Page 343.**
Answers: 1. Whenever we use pesticides, we also affect birds and animals that feed on the pest. 2. Whenever aphids eat crops that have been sprayed, the poison enters the aphids' systems. 3. If a ladybug eats poisoned aphids, the poison accumulates in the ladybug. 4. When a sparrow eats the ladybug, the sparrow absorbs the poison. 5. Whenever a bird such as a hawk eats the sparrow, the bird also eats the accumulated poison from thousands of insects. 6. If a hawk consumes large amounts of the poison, the hawk is not able to reproduce.

6 **Page 343.**
Answers:

1. a. The temperature would be equal to the surface of the sun.
   b. Nobody living within 20 miles of the explosion would survive.
   c. Every person living in the area would be vaporized instantly.
2. a. I would slowly die of radiation poisoning.
   b. I would probably get very sick.
   c. I would have to leave to get safe food and water.
3. a. Food and water supplies would still be contaminated, so I would not be safe.
   b. There would be disruptions in government and other essential services.
   c. Future generations might be born with birth defects.
4. a. I would contact my family and make arrangements with them.
   b. I would stock up on bottled water and canned food.

Using What You've Learned

7 **Page 344.**
Form small groups of students, and have groups discuss one or more of the issues listed in the Student Book. Group members should take notes

during the discussion, and use these notes as the basis for a composition. Later, groups can reconvene and read their compositions aloud for each other. Then collect students' work and check them for grammatical errors. Circle the errors without correcting them, and return them to students for revisions. Check their final drafts and make any necessary corrections.

Video Activities: A Strike

Before You Watch

Sample Answers:

1. Workers often go on strike to improve working conditions and to seek an increase in salary.
2. With few exceptions, government workers are not allowed to go on strike, because this would result in an interruption in necessary services. This is especially true of federal employees. Strikes sometimes do occur at the level of city and county governments.

Watch [on video]

Answers: 1. b 2. b 3. b

Watch Again [on video]

Answers:

1. a. librarians b. nurses c. building maintenance workers f. typists g. cashiers
2. nurses
3. a, b
4. a
5. b
6. c

After You Watch

Answers: 1. would rule in their favor 2. they would probably give the workers a raise 3. If they had adequate salaries 4. they will go back to work 5. If the strikers lose their case,

Focus on Testing

Answers:

Part 1: 1. d 2. b 3. a 4. d

Part 2: 1. c 2. d 3. a 4. d

Medicine and Science

Goals

- Adjective clause to phrase reduction
- Verbs followed by participial constructions; the verbs *lay/lie, raise/rise*
- Adverb clause to phrase reduction
- Causative and structurally related verbs

Introduction

Write the following sentence on the board: *Aging is one of the few things that is assured in this changeable world.* Ask students to rephrase the sentence in their own words to check comprehension. Then ask students to compare it to the first sentence in the article "Aging." How are the two sentences different? In the article, the adjectival clause *that is assured* has been reduced to the participle *assured.* Tell students that the reduction of clauses into phrases will be the focus of this chapter.

Discussing Ideas

Invite students to share their responses to the discussion questions. Create a word web with the word *old age.* Keep this word web hand throughout the chapter, as you may wish to return to it as a starting point for other discussions on aging.

Part 1 Adjective Clause to Phrase Reduction

Setting the Context

Here are some procedures and techniques you might mention in your discussion:

- angioplasty
- CAT scans
- heart transplant
- laser surgery
- MRIs
- organ transplant

B. Reduction of Adjective Clauses with Verbs in the Active Voice

1 Page 352.

Answers:

1. Still, after age 60, people begin to suffer from a number of complications <u>that eventually lead to disability and death</u>.

   Still, after age 60, people begin to suffer from a number of complications eventually leading to disability and death.
2. Most people <u>who are still living at the age of 70</u> die within ten years.

   Most people still living at the age of 70 die within ten years.
3. The number of Americans <u>who live past 90</u> represents less than .5 percent of the population.

   The number of Americans living past 90 represents less than .5 percent of the population.
4. Only around 13,000 people <u>who reside in the United States</u> are currently over 100.

   Only around 13,000 people residing in the United States are currently over 100.

5. There are only a few verified cases of Americans who survived past 110.

   There are only a few verified cases of Americans surviving past 110.

C. Reduction of Adjective Clauses with Simple-Tense Verbs in the Passive Voice

2 Page 352.

Answers:

1. Sequoias and redwoods, which are found in the Pacific Northwest, have maximum life spans that are estimated at 3,000 years.

   Sequoias and redwoods, found in the Pacific Northwest, have maximum life spans that are estimated at 3,000 years.
2. There are bristlecone pines that are thought to be at least 4,500 years old.

   There are bristlecone pines thought to be at least 4,500 years old.
3. Perhaps even older than these pines are sea anemones, which are believed to have the potential for immortality.

   Perhaps even older than these pines are sea anemones, believed to have the potential for immortality.
4. This plantlike animal, which is intensively studied all over the world, stays "young" by constantly replacing parts of its simple anatomy.

   This plantlike animal, intensively studied all over the world, stays "young" by constantly replacing parts of its simple anatomy.
5. One group of sea anemones, which was transported to England in 1804 and placed in an aquarium, lived over 90 years without showing any sign of aging.

   One group of sea anemones, transported to England in 1804 and placed in an aquarium, lived over 90 years without showing any sign of aging.

D. Reduction of Adjective Clauses with Continuous-Tense Verbs in the Passive Voice

3 Page 353.

Answers:

1. Life extension experiments that are being performed on animals have shown promising results.

   Life extension experiments being performed on animals have shown promising results.
2. A number of tests that are being carried out concern the lowering of body temperature.

   A number of tests being carried out concern the lowering of body temperature.
3. The cold-blooded animals that are being subjected to lower temperatures live up to ten times longer.

   The cold-blooded animals being subjected to lower temperatures live up to ten times longer.
4. The mammals that are being given similar tests also show a significant increase in longevity.

   The mammals being given similar tests also show a significant increase in longevity.
5. Some monkeys and rats that are being fed temperature-lowering drugs have added years to their lives.

   Some monkeys and rats being fed temperature-lowering drugs have added years to their lives.

E. Reduction of Adjective Clauses with Verbs in Perfect Tenses

4 Page 354.

Answers:

1. He found that rats that had been fed only two-thirds of the normal number of calories lived twice as long as those that had followed a normal diet.

He found that rats having been fed only two-thirds of the normal number of calories lived twice as long as those that had followed a normal diet.

2. Other scientists who have studied McCay's findings are conducting similar experiments.

   Other scientists having studied McCay's findings are conducting similar experiments.

3. Roy Walford of the University of California at Los Angeles is running tests on rats that have fasted every other day for their entire lives.

   Roy Walford of the University of California at Los Angeles is running tests on rats having fasted every other day for their entire lives.

4. Walford, who has extended the lives of these rats, is convinced that his findings apply to humans.

   Walford, having extended the lives of these rats, is convinced that his findings apply to humans.

5. Walford and others who have seen the results of fasting in rats hope to find similar results in humans.

   Walford and others having seen the results of fasting in rats hope to find similar results in humans.

5 Page 354.

Answers:

1. Roy Walford is a pathologist who does research and teaches at U.C.L.A.

   Roy Walford is a pathologist who doing research and teaching at U.C.L.A.

2. Walford, who is considered an expert on aging, believes that the key to the fountain of youth is a lower body temperature.

   Walford, considered an expert on aging, believes that the key to the fountain of youth is a lower body temperature.

3. Walford bases his conclusions on his research that is being done with rats that have been systematically underfed.

   Walford bases his conclusions on his research being done with rats having been systematically underfed.

4. These rats, which are thought to be the oldest in history, weigh 25 percent less than "normal" rats but live twice as long.

   These rats, thought to be the oldest in history, weigh 25 percent less than "normal" rats but live twice as long.

5. Walford, who plans to live to be 130 to 140, has adopted a diet in some ways similar to the diet of his rats.

   Walford, planning to live to be 130 to 140, has adopted a diet in some ways similar to the diet of his rats.

6. Walford predicts that his diet, which consists mostly of vegetables, fruit, grains, and vitamin supplements, will help him lose an additional 30 pounds.

   Walford predicts that his diet, consisting mostly of vegetables, fruit, grains, and vitamin supplements, will help him lose an additional 30 pounds.

7. Scientists have known of evidence that supports the value of undernutrition for over 70 years.

   Scientists have known of evidence supporting the value of undernutrition for over 70 years.

8. However, Walford is the first scientist who has applied the principles to himself.

   However, Walford is the first scientist having applied the principles to himself.

G. Placement of Nonrestrictive Participial Phrases

6 Page 356.

Answers:

1. Walford, deciding not to wait for long-term studies is, in essence, acting as his own guinea pig.

Deciding not to wait for long-term studies, Walford is, in essence, acting as his own guinea pig.

Walford is, in essence, acting as his own guinea pig, deciding not to wait for long-term studies.

2. Most people, thinking that undereating would be too difficult, will probably never try undernutrition.

   Thinking that undereating would be too difficult, most people will probably never try undernutrition.

   Most people will probably never try undernutrition, thinking that undereating would be too difficult.

3. Walford, finding this type of diet enjoyable, plans to continue indefinitely.

   Finding this type of diet enjoyable, Walford plans to continue indefinitely.

   Walford plans to continue this diet indefinitely, finding it enjoyable.

4. Eating, often being done out of habit rather than need, may be our biggest health problem.

   Often being done out of habit rather than need, eating may be our biggest health problem.

   Eating may be our biggest health problem, often being done out of habit rather than need.

Using What You've Learned

7 Page 356.

Perceptions of the aging process are often culturally determined. Have students prepare for the group discussion by jotting down some notes about how they perceive aging. They might write down the characteristics of major age spans (infancy, childhood, adolescence, adulthood, and old age), for example. Ask students to think about these characteristics might be determined by the value systems of their cultures. Group members can then share their notes and ideas. Encourage students to continue to take notes during the discussions. Afterward, ask students to write a short composition on one aspect of the aging process. If you have a website or electronic bulletin board for the class, you can post students' papers there for publication.

Part 2 Verbs Followed by Participial Constructions; the Verbs *Lay/Lie, Raise/Rise*

Setting the Context

Invite students to respond to the Prereading Questions. Then tell students that they are going to read about a very old woman living in Abkhazia. Ask students to locate Abkhazia on the map, then read the "Khfaf" aloud for the class.

Discussing Ideas

Sample Answers:

Khfaf was 139 years old when the author met her. She seemed much more lively and alert than the author expected her to be, considering her age. Her face was also surprisingly smooth.

A. Verbs with Two-Part Objects

1 Page 357.

Answers: 1. The verification process kept researchers working for years. 2. In the end, the researchers caught some older people lying about their age. 3. Still, for every 100,000 people, they found 71 living past the age of 100. 4. The researchers left these elderly people working their fields and living their poor but healthy lives. 5. These findings about the elderly have sent many researchers looking into the keys to longevity.

B. Verbs of Perception

2 Page 359.
Answers: 1. The visitors have seen them swimming vigorously. 2. They have observed them working in the fields. 3. The visitors have noticed them participating in all family in community activities. 4. The have witnessed the elders being honored at feasts. 5. The have listened to these senior citizens talking to their great-great-great-grandchildren. 6. They have heard the old ones' advice being sought by young people. 7. They have witnessed true respect being given to them by younger people. 8. In Abkhazia, they've heard a few discussing their part in the Crimean War, fought in the 1850s.

3 Page 360.
Students' answers will vary. Invite volunteers to read some of their observations aloud for the class.

C. *By* with Phrases of Means or Manner

4 Page 360.
Answers: 1. leaving us alone 2. wearing two hats 3. explaining the reason 4. talking about his long life 5. bringing up his youngest child 6. farming his small piece of land 7. pointing to the green field 8. walking up this step path 9. taking my hand in his 10. working the ground with his primitive hoe 11. standing under his veranda 12. watching the glorious sunset

D. *Lay/Lie, Raise/Rise*

5 Page 362.
Answers: 1. lying 2. laid 3. raised 4. raise / lay 5. rise 6. rose

6 Page 362.
Answers: 1. lie 2. had already risen 3. finally raised 4. lied 5. lying 6. laid 7. lied 8. lying / to rise

Using What You've Learned

7 Page 363.
For a variation on this activity, you might ask partners to write a dialogue between an anthropologist and an elder of Vilcabamba or Abkhazia. Partners can then take turns reading their dialogues aloud in small groups.

Part 3 Adverb Clause to Phrase Reduction

Setting the Context

With students, brainstorm a list of factors contributing to good health and a long life. Tell students that the article "The Good Life" will speculate as to some of these contributing factors. Ask students to see if any items from their list are mentioned in the article as they read.

B. Elliptical Phrases

1 Page 366.
Answers: 1. The researchers assumed that diet was important even before arriving in the villages. 2. After examining hundreds of elderly people, doctors realized that the number-one killer in the West, heart disease, was virtually absent here. 3. Eating little meat and few dairy products, the villagers have no problem with cholesterol. 4. The villagers remain thin but amazingly healthy, consuming about 60 percent of the calories and 40 to 50 percent of the protein common in the Western diet. 5. Despite eating little protein, they have enormous amounts of energy. 6. If bored by their simple diet, they certainly disguise it well. 7. When offered Western food by visitors, the elderly were interested at first but preferred their own diet. 8. Illness is rare, but if sick, the villagers eat less, rest, and take herbal remedies.

2 Page 366.

Answers: 1. Since they don't have modern tools, they must devote much of their time to strenuous physical labor. 2. If they are tired of working to support themselves, few of the older people complain about this. 3. When they were questioned about their lifestyle, the older people saw nothing unusual about the way they lived. 4. After they move from their mountain villages to large cities, the children of the elderly rarely live past 80. 5. When they studied the people who had moved away from Abkhazia, scientists found a high incidence of heart disease. 6. Since they live the "good life," the people of Abkhazia almost never suffer from heart disease.

3 Page 366.

Answers: 1. After arriving, I found a small room to rent. 2. I talked to hundreds of people while wandering around. 3. Not knowing the local customs, I tried to be very polite.
4. Despite being a foreigner, I was accepted into the community almost immediately. 5. Getting ready to leave, I became sad. 6. Before departing, I packed my film and notes and said good-bye to them many friends I had made.

C. Dangling Phrases

4 Page 367.

Answers: 1. (no errors) 2. After shaking hands, we walked to a large tree and sat down. 3. While I was talking to José about his life and family, my horse stood nearby nibbling on the grass. 4. (no errors) 5. Since he lived a simple life and had few possessions, José was not concerned about money. 6. If ill, he takes a special type of herbal medicine prepared by his wife. 7. (no errors)
8. Although he was tired and hungry, José still had plenty of work to do. 9. While I was riding back to town, the view of the mountains was spectacular.

5 Page 367.

Sample Answers: 1. Having welcomed since early in the morning, I welcomed the chance for a rest. 2. After shaking my hand, I walked to a large tree and sat down.
3. While talking about his life and family, a cow stood nearby nibbling on the grass.
4. I had made my living as a farmer since coming to Vilcabamba some 90 years before.
5. Living a simple life and having few possessions, José didn't care about money.
6. If ill, José makes himself a special type of herbal medicine. 7. I had to get back to work after talking to José for over an hour.
8. Although tired and hungry, I still had plenty of work to do. 9. Riding back to town, the silence in the countryside was peaceful.

6 Page 368.

1. <u>Because most older people are less active and less productive</u>, society tends to regard them as useless.

   Being less active and less productive, society tends to regard most older people as useless.

2. Thus, as the aging process takes its toll, many senior citizens spend their last years away from their families in retirement communities or nursing homes <u>where they await the inevitable</u>.

   Thus, as the aging process takes its toll, many senior citizens spend their last years away from their families in retirement communities or nursing homes awaiting the inevitable.

3. <u>While the elderly are growing older</u> in these cultures, they gain social prestige and importance rather than lost it.

   While growing older in these cultures, the elderly gain social prestige and importance rather than lost it.

4. <u>Because they live in close-knit families</u>, the older citizens are never separated from their loved ones.

Living in close-knit families, the older citizens are never separated from their loved ones.

5. Even when they are very old, they continue to help with the household responsibilities.

   Even when very old, they continue to help with the household responsibilities.

6. And if they are sick, several generations of family are nearby to care for them.

   And if sick, several generations of family are nearby to care for them.

7. While they are surrounded by sons, daughters, grandchildren, and great-grandchildren, the old ones are constantly told, "You are the reason why we are here."

   While surrounded by sons, daughters, grandchildren, and great-grandchildren, the old ones are constantly told, "You are the reason why we are here."

8. Because many older people in the West believe they are useless, they age quickly and die young.

   Believing they are useless, many older people in the West age quickly and die young.

9. Because the old of Vilcabamba and Abkhazia know that they are not useless, they continue to lead productive lives well into their hundreds.

   Knowing that they are not useless, the old of Vilcabamba and Abkhazia continue to lead productive lives well into their hundreds.

Using What You've Learned

7 Page 368.
Form small groups of students and have groups debate chance versus destiny. Suggest that groups start by devoting five minutes to thoughts and observations in favor of chance. They can spend five minutes discussing destiny. Ask students to take notes during the discussion in preparation for a composition. After the discussion, students should be able to articulate where they stand on the issue and write a short composition arguing in favor of one or the other. Afterward, collect students' compositions, and organize them into two sections of a bound notebook: *Chance* and *Destiny*. Make the book available for students to read during breaks.

Part 4 Causative and Structurally Related Verbs

Setting the Context

Invite students to respond to the Prereading Questions. Encourage them to think not only of sound medical advice, but of superstitions, myths, and folk wisdom as well.

Discussing Ideas

Sample Answers: 1. In China, people believed that breath control led to immortality. 2. In Europe and the Middle East, the breath of virgins was believed to cure the problems of old age. 3. In ancient Rome, people drank human blood to stay young.

A. Causative and Structurally Related Verbs

1 Page 370.
Answers: 1. In Greek mythology, Zeus's wife Hera visited a spring that made the signs of age vanish. 2. Hera forced other beautiful women to stay away from this spring. 3. The Roman god Jupiter let certain people enter the special waters of Juventas. 4. Jupiter allowed these lucky bathers to regain their youth. 5. Of course, these waters helped the bathers feel young again. 6. The Bible mentions the "fountain of life" from which the Lord let Adam and Eve drink. 7. In search of the "fountain of youth," Ponce de León had native guides take him to present-day Florida in 1512. Unfortunately, he found an Indian arrow instead and died at age 61.

2 Page 370.
Answers: 1. The alchemists had gold and mercury brought to them because they believed these elements stopped aging. 2. Unfortunately, dissatisfied emperors had the alchemists executed. 3. Isabella and Ferdinand of Spain had stories about a fountain of youth investigated. 4. Several monarchs had potions created to make them young again. 5. Alfonso of Colombia had special jewelry designed to prolong his life.

3 Page 371.
Answers: 1. removed / packed 2. mince / put / inject 3. erected 4. run 5. injected 6. give 7. performed

4 Page 371.
Sample Answers: 1. I would not let my friends use too much of it. 2. I would not allow my family to pay for it. 3. I would make other people pay astronomical fees. 4. I would force my grammar teacher to ask my forgiveness before selling it to her. 5. I would have the police protect me. 6. I would have trespassers prosecuted. 7. I would not help scientists copy it.

5 Page 372.
Answers: 1. dying 2. gasping 3. finding 4. connect 5. and flood 6. injecting 7. freeze 8. packed 9. forming 10. disconnect 11. designed 12. being 13. being 14. become 15. to start

6 Page 373.
Answers:
1. While my wife and I were sitting in a roadside restaurant, I heard some people talking about a "rejuvenation machine" which was located in the middle of California desert.
2. After we had been in California for a few days, we drove out toward Twenty-Nine Palms, where we hoped to find this rejuvenation machine and its inventor, George Van Tassel.
3. I first saw George W. Van Tassel sitting by an impressive dome surrounded by desert.
4. As soon as I greeted him and explained my purpose, he let us examine his machine, the "Integratron," which Extraterrestrials had supposedly helped him design.
5. The Integratron was a dome 38 feet high and 53 feet in diameter resembling and old-fashioned observatory.
6. Van Tassel explained the machine inside the dome could produce up to 100,000,000 volts of electricity.
7. Van Tassel told us a person wanting to be young again needed only to walk under the arc of the electricity.
8. Van Tassel revealed to me the Integratron was financed by contributions from the Ministry of Universal Wisdom, Inc., a nonprofit organization owned by his family.
9. As Van Tassel wanted to get in touch with us in the future, we let him copy our address and phone number before returning to our car.
10. As we were leaving, I heard him talking to an older couple having just driven up.

7 Page 374.
For a variation on this activity, you can write a sentence continuing the story on a piece of paper. Give the paper to a student sitting in the front row and ask that student to write a sentence following up the action in your sentence. That student then passes the paper to the next student, only allowing him or her to see the previous sentence (i.e., the first student's sentence, not yours). The sentence you wrote can be hidden by folding the paper. Students continue in this way, adding sentences to the narrative based only on the preceding sentence. When all students have had a turn, read the completed

narrative to the class. The inevitable incongruity of it all should be good for a chuckle.

Using What You've Learned

8 **Page 374.**
Have small groups create and perform a skit based on one of the articles in the chapter. Before they begin writing, they should decide on a cast of characters equal to the number of group members. Groups should also choose a scribe to write down the script as dictated by other members, and a director.

Video Activities: Stealth Surgery

Before You Watch

Answers: 1. An X-ray machine takes pictures of one's skeletal structure. 2. MRIs and CAT scans are more sophisticated and much more costly imaging systems. Students will learn more about these procedures from the video.

Watch [on video]

Answers: 1. Novak's hobby is softball. It's unusual because he is 81 and has just had surgery. 2. c 3. the Stealth system 4. This is better than traditional surgery because it doesn't require so much cutting, is less painful, and requires less recovery time.

Watch Again [on video]

Answers: 1. MRI / CT scans / converted / images / placed / creates / anatomical
2. a 3. c 4. b 5. a 6. b

After You Watch

Answers: 1. having surgery 2. operating on Leonard 3. it is less invasive 4. an earlier operation 5. Leonard is unable to play softball

Focus on Testing

Answers:
Part 1: 1. d 2. b 3. a 4. a
Part 2: 1. c 2. c 3. b 4. c

Chapter 12

The Future

Goals

- Passive, continuous, and perfect infinitives
- Passive and perfect gerunds
- Review

Introduction

Read the article "A Glimpse of the Future" aloud for the class. Then write the following sentence on the board: *By the year 2050, we can expect many changes to have taken place. Underline the phrase to have taken place*. Explain that this phrase is in the passive perfect because the action is in a hypothetical point in the future in which it has been perfected, or completed. Ask students to brainstorm a list of predictions for the future and model how to cast these in the perfect passive. Some examples:

- Space stations will have been established on the moon.
- Nuclear weapons will have been eliminated.
- A vaccine for AIDS will have been developed.
- Public education will have been privatized.

Part 1 Passive, Continuous, and Perfect Infinitives

Setting the Context

Review the concept of *colony* with students, explaining that a colony is a territory that has been settled by people from a distant area. Then use the Prereading Questions to get students to speculate about the possibility of space colonies.

Discussing Ideas

Engage students in a discussion about the financial costs involved in the establishment of a space colony. In addition to the questions in the Student Book, you might ask the following: What priority should we currently give to space exploration? Should all nations be invited to participate in this process? Why or why not?

A. Review of Active and Passive Forms of Simple Infinitives

1 Page 380.
Answers: 1. to build 2. to be spread out 3. not to become 4. to be built 5. to enable 6. to take 7. to gather 8. to adjust 9. to be duplicated 10. to grow 11. to participate 12. not to be completed

B. Perfect and Continuous Forms of Active Infinitives

2 Page 381.
Answers: 1. to be (active simple) 2. to build (active simple) 3. to be spread out (passive simple) 4. not to become (active simple) 5. to be built (passive simple) 6. to enable (active simple) 7. to take (active simple) 8. to gather (active simple) 9. to adjust (active simple) 10. to be duplicated (passive simple) 11. to grow (active simple) 12. to participate (active simple) 13. to live (active simple) 14. not to be completed (passive simple)

3 Page 381.
Answers: 1. to be headed 2. to be gaining 3. to be 4. to keep up 5. to have stopped 6. to be malfunctioning 7. to come 8. to be aboard

4 Page 382.
Answers: 1. to be hurt 2. seem to be injured 3. to have been sent 4. to have

completed 5. seems to have developed 6. seems to be damaged

C. More Verbs Followed by Infinitive Objects

5 Page 383.
Answers: 1. to be taken 2. you not to resist 3. you to give 4. to be transferred 5. to kill 6. not to understand 7. to do 8. us to change

6 Page 384.
Sample Answers: 1. I will endeavor to have our fuel problems solved. 2. I must warn you to be careful. 3. I've directed our crew to build a transport system. 4. Crew members have volunteered to repair the gas leak. 5. You must consent to live by the rules of the colony. 6. I caution you not to stand near the engine. 7. I require you to follow my instructions. 8. Don't hesitate to ask questions.

7 Page 384.
Answers: 1. The universe is known to be expanding. 2. The earth is thought to be formed billions of years ago. 3. Aliens are assumed to be trying to communicate with us. 4. Sunspots are known to be thousands of miles in height. 5. Space travel is expected to be commonplace within 100 years. 6. The former Soviets are known to have sent the first woman into space. 7. The next satellite to Mars is supposed to be launched soon. 8. The Russians are believed to be training people to live in space permanently.

8 Page 384.
Answers: 1. will provide / will have provided 2. to expand / to be expanded 3. to telecommute 4. to have education be 5. to get married 6. to be made 7. to be eliminated 8. to be found 9. to develop / to have developed 10. not to have improved 11. will have gotten 12. governments to work

9 Page 385.
Answers: 1. to have completed 2. to work 3. to be sent 4. to go back / to work 5. that people will have found 6. to visit / to have 7. to be accepted / to become 8. to have not been drafted 9. to have reunited 10. to have earned / to have bought / to have started 11. to take over / not to work 12. to be finished / to spend

Using What You've Learned

10 Page 386.
Sample Answers: 1. So far, Earth is the only planet known to have intelligent forms of life. 2. The moon is expected to be the site of a space colony within the next century. 3. Mars was once thought to be inhabited by aliens known as Martians. 4. Jet streams on Saturn are calculated to reach as much as 1,000 miles per hour. 5. The Milky Way is believed to contain some 100 billion stars. 6. Space stations are expected to host permanent residents in the near future.

11 Page 386.
Students can use the dialogue in Activity 9 as a model for their discussions, as well as the list of verbs on page 383 of the Student Book. When groups are finished sharing, have each member tell the class about the hopes and plans of one member of his or her group.

Part 2 Passive and Perfect Gerunds

Setting the Context

The Prereading Questions ask students to think of robots they have seen in popular films. You can use the following film characters to prompt them:

- Hal in *2001: A Space Odyssey*
- R2D2 and C3P0 in *Star Wars*
- Klaatu in *The Day the Earth Stood Still*

- The title characters in *The Stepford Wives*
- The robots in *Westworld*
- The android in *Blade Runner*
- The title character in *Terminator*

Ask students to make generalizations about these characters and what they show about our hopes and fears in regards to technology.

Discussing Ideas

You can have students visit the websites listed in the Web Note on page 387 to facilitate this discussion. After asking the questions in the Student Book, ask students whether they can think of any ethical questions involved in assigning human tasks to computers.

B. Perfect Forms of Gerunds

1 Page 388.
Answers: 1. having been coined (verb; active perfect) 2. had begun producing (verb; active perfect) 3. boring (adjective) 4. welding (gerund) 5. spray painting (gerund) 6. handling (gerund) 7. combining (noun) 8. being replaced (verb; active simple) 9. not having taken (noun)

2 Page 388.
Answers: 1. The teacher was upset about the student's having lied to her. 2. I appreciate your having helped me with my math homework. 3. I regret not having gone to college when I had the chance. 4. Ana was pleased about having been chosen for the scholarship. 5. My husband was angry about not having given him an important message. 6. I don't remember having heard that man's name before. 7. I can't forgive your having taken my car without my permission. 8. John's having failed the entrance exam makes him ineligible to attend the college. 9. She felt hurt about not having been invited to the party. 10. Having not finished college did not stop Arthur from becoming a millionaire.

3 Page 388.
Answers: 1. having 2. having destroyed 3. functioning 4. dusting 5. watering 6. being used 7. disconnecting 8. being 9. seeing 10. getting 11. needing

4 Page 389.
Answers: 1. being surpassed 2. protecting 3. using (having used) 4. using / being / visiting (having visited) / producing / using / been made 5. developing / Accomplishing (Having accomplished) / being used

5 Page 390.
Students' answers will vary. Circulate as students interview each other and listen for their use of passive forms, modeling correct usage as necessary.

C. More Verbs Followed by Gerund Objects

6 Page 391.
Sample Answers: 1. profits going up 2. not being consulted (not having been consulted) 3. angering (having angered) 4. attempting (having attempted) 5. making 6. being replaced 7. explaining

7 Page 391.
Answers: 1. I won't tolerate your being tardy this time. 2. In fact, I can only recall having invited half that many. 3. We may have to postpone having dinner until nine. 4. You must try to prevent it from burning. We mustn't risk ruining dinner. 5. I hope my guests will forgive my sending them home without dinner. 6. Don't deny my having told you. I resent having to explain myself.

8 Page 392.
Answers: 1. to destroy (destroying) 2. to be taking away 3. to use 4. to appear (appearing) 5. to protect 6. to do 7. damaging 8. destroying 9. to slow down (slowing down) 10. to confuse 11. to cause (causing) 12. to break down 13. to destroy (destroying) 14. to be disappointed 15. to be

reduced 16. to face (to be faced) 17. to hold 18. to attend

Using What You've Learned

9 **Page 393.**
Form pairs of students or small groups to create skits using the prompts in the Student Book. Later, invite groups to perform their skits for the class.

10 **Page 393.**
Follow the directions in the book to play a game involving the on-the-spot creation of sentences with infinitives and gerunds. Give each team one point for each sentence that it forms correctly. If a team makes an ill-formed sentence, have the class help you identify and correct the error. Play continues until the first team achieves a score of 10.

Focus on Testing

Answers:
Part 1: 1. c 2. c 3. a 4. c
Part 2: 1. d 2. d 3. c 4. d

Part 3 Review

1 **Page 395.**
Answers: 1. living 2. marrying 3. to be 4. belonging 5. to be 6. to choose 7. to have 8. falling 9. get 10. to have 11. offering 12. to have 13. be 14. survive

2 **Page 396.**
Answers: 1. The 2. X 3. than 4. Although 5. a 6. may 7. surprising 8. where 9. and 10. if 11. or 12. the 13. that 14. when 15. work 16. One 17. X 18. may 19. of 20. cleaning 21. X 22. the 23. Over 24. a 25. from 26. to 27. However 28. inside 29. feel 30. may 31. by 32. a 33. to 34. For example 35. into 36. when 37. that 38. the 39. X

3 **Page 397.**
Sample Paragraph:
In the 21st century, an executive will be able to leave home in a single-seat car which gets 100 miles per gallon. As the executive steers the car into an automated traffic lane, she reads the news on a dashboard video monitor. Electronic sensors guide the vehicle to a "railport," where the executive boards a train. Once on board, the executive straps herself into a soft, pneumatic seat. The train levitates above the ground as it travels at 300 miles an hour. Within minutes, the train reaches the airport, and the executive boards a giant aircraft along with one thousand other passengers. The aircraft, which is made of plastic and is entirely controlled by computers, travels smoothly overseas at supersonic speed. The trip from the executive's front door in San Francisco, California, to Paris, France, has taken just three hours.

4 **Page 398.**
Sample Answers: 1. In the next 50 years, education will be revolutionized by the use of computers. 2. Computers will bring knowledge to people wherever they are-at home, on the job, by a hospital bed, in the car, or in a traditional classroom. 3. Education will be individualized on the basis of test that will reveal how each person can most easily learn. 4. Students who learn best by hearing information would receive much of their education orally. 5. If a learner has a visual orientation, he or she would spend more time reading on writing on computer screens. 6. By 2020, fewer people will study engineering and other applied skills since computers will do most of the work in these fields. 7. Although computers will be used to read and write, books will not completely disappear from many years. 8. Education expert David Brostrom

predicts that, by 2033, more than 60 percent of American adults will attend college, compared to today's 30 percent. 9. The revolution in genetics promises to transform the treatment of disease. 10. By the year 2010, researchers will not only have a complete map of all human genes, but they will also be able to make changes to some of those genes. 11. They will know how to regulate the normal growth of cells. 12. Medical advances will enable people to live longer, healthier lives. 13. Scientists will discover treatments for major diseases will allow people to live 100 years or more. 14. New techniques with lasers and advances in radiation will make many of today's medical operations obsolete. 15. Tremendous advances will be made in the treatment of disease; however, the cost of medical care will probably increase.

5 **Page 399.**

Answers: 1. began 2. lasted 3. were living (lived) 4. fed 5. was invented 6. had not yet ended 7. broke out 8. was 9. began 10. had been 11. rolled (were rolling) 12. remain 13. have been industrialized 14. is still spreading (is still being spread) 15. have been 16. have devoted 17. is still being felt 18. has been moving 19. is transforming 20. touches 21. is being called (has been called) 22. was initiated 23. has reached 24. are being shaken 25. are developing 26. has been successfully tested 27. is based (is being based) 28. will have already surpassed 29. will have been designed 30. was 31. will be 32. will live and work 33. will have come

Using What You've Learned

6 **Page 401.**

Tell students that they will conclude the chapter and the course with the writing of a poem. Have them read the text in the Student Book and decide on a subject for their poem. They can then follow the suggested format for their poem, or use a format of their own choosing. Encourage students to illustrate their poem on a separate page by creating a collage, drawing, or computer-generated graphic. Gather students' work and have an assistant help you bind the poems and illustrations together in a three-ring binder as a class publication. You can conclude the activity by having a "poetry slam," allowing each poet to read his or her work aloud to the class. Students may also wish to make copies of the bound work to take home.

Video Activities: Concept Cars

Before You Watch

Answers: 1. a 2. Students' answers will vary. Tell students that the video they are about to watch is about students who design their own fantasy cars.

Watch [on video]

Answers: 1. b 2. b 3. a. Lacrosse b. Prowler c. Avalanche

Watch Again [on video]

Answers: 1. a, c, d, f 2. a 3. b 4. c

After You Watch

Answers: 1. will have taken place 2. to increase 3. to own 4. cars to be

Focus on Testing

Answers:

Part 1: 1. b 2. d 3. b 4. a 5. d 6. c 7. c 8. b

Part 2: 1. b 2. a 3. a 4. c 5. a 6. c 7. d 8. a

Grammar Placement Test

Part 1 Complete the Sentence.

Circle the letter of the best word or words to complete each statement.

Example

I _____ from Boston.

(a.) am
b. were
c. are
d. is

1. Dick is the _______ determined person I have ever met.

a. much
b. most
c. more
d. many

2. His job was _______ than anyone could imagine.

a. hardly
b. harder
c. hard
d. not hard

3. She's a doctor and her life is never __________.

a. bored
b. boring
c. bore
d. board

4. They are ______ here.

a. new
b. new to
c. newly
d. news to

5. Yes, they ______.

a. haven't

b. hasn't

c. has

d. have

6. What does Natasha ________?

a. liked

b. likes

c. like to

d. like

7. Then, ________ June to September, it's very rainy.

a. in

b. on

c. at

d. from

8. Yes, she _______.

a. is

b. not

c. isn't

d. doesn't

9. The drugstore is to________ the movie theater.

a. next

b. the left of

c. left of

d. left and next

10. We are going _____________.

a. to a downtown

b. to the downtown

c. downtown

d. to downtown

11. Louisa loved the new book, and Jose ___________.

a. also does

b. does too

c. did too

d. didn't too

12. You went to the movies last night, ___________?

a. did you

b. didn't you

c. don't you

d. doesn't you

13. I found the movie last night to be very _______.

a. upset

b. upsets

c. unfulfilled

d. upsetting

14. Yes, he _______ at home last night.

a. were

b. was

c. weren't

d. wasn't

15. Excuse me, I need to buy ________ salt shakers.

a. some

b. an

c. a

d. this

16. Laura doesn't have _________ accounting experience.

a. any

b. some

c. the background in

d. knowledge of

17. Where are they ________?

a. gone to go

b. go

c. go to going

d. going to go

18. Yesterday, he said that his train will ________ at midnight.

a. arriving

b. arrived

c. arrive

d. arrives

19. They'll drop _____ their neighbor's house

a. in

b. on

c. at

d. by

20. Please ________________.

a. wake up her

b. wake him on

c. wake up your brother

d. wake up brother

21. I have a doctor's appointment _______ November 10.

a. at

b. on

c. in

d. from

22. I've ________ the Statue of Liberty.

a. visited often

b. visited recently

c. recently visited

d. ever visited

23. Mary doesn't like Indian food, __________.

a. and either does Bob

b. and Bob does too

c. and Bob doesn't neither

d. and Bob doesn't either

24. Well ________ for graduating with top grades.

a. yourself should be proud of you

b. you shouldn't be proud of yourself

c. yourself shouldn't be proud of you

d. you should be proud of yourself

25. You absolutely adore raspberries, ________?

a. do you

b. did you

c. don't you

d. didn't you

26. She didn't like the movie, ________?

a. did she

b. does she

c. didn't she

d. doesn't she

27. Her lemonade was ______ than his.

a. more sweet

b. sweeter

c. many sweeter

d. sweetest

28. We ______ them many times.

a. spoke

b. have spoken

c. spoken to

d. have spoken to

29. I'm nervous __________ taking the math test.

a. of

b. at

c. in

d. about

30. She's not intimidated __________ crowds of people.

a. speak

b. to speak to

c. to speak of

d. speak to

31. I'm __________ sitting at home with my dog, Winston.

a. content about

b. content from

c. content of

d. content with

32. I couldn't fathom how many ________ there were way up in the mountains.

a. oxes

b. ox

c. oxen

d. oxens

33. I couldn't believe it, but the high frequency noise caused my feline companion ______.

a. wince

b. to wince

c. wincing

d. winced

34. Tonight, Mrs. Adams is very sick because she is allergic to tomatoes and red chili peppers. At dinner, she ________ ordered the pasta with the white Alfredo sauce instead of with the red sauce.

a. should have

b. could have

c. might have

d. would have

35. Cynthia is _________ to make a major transition in her life.

a. readily

b. ready

c. prepared

d. readied

36. They haven't __________ anything being said.

a. understand

b. understood

c. understanding

d. understands

37. Will you look _________ my pet parrots while I am on vacation?

a. on

b. of

c. in

d. after

38. Do you have ______ milk at your house?

a. some

b. any

c. none

d. a

39. She is ecstatic whenever____________ going someplace new.

a. she thinks about

b. about she thinks

c. she about thinks

d. thinks about her

40. My Aunt Elizabeth ____________ the convent in 1985.

a. entered to

b. has entered

c. entered

d. entered in

41. She bathed ______ in a vat originally used to make wine.

a. himself
b. herself
c. hers
d. she

42. Many people believe that fine cheeses must be ______ in cellars.

a. ages
b. aged
c. aging
d. age

43. ______ the narrative, the men behaved very poorly.

a. By
b. According
c. According to
d. All accounts

44. She walked on ______ side of the street.

a. an right
b. a right
c. the right
d. right

45. ______ the high rate of inflation, it is very hard for individuals to save money.

a. Due
b. Due of
c. Due from
d. Due to

Part 2 Find the Errors.

Look at each item and select the letter below the word(s) containing the error.

Example

One of the reasons that I love him is that he go (a) to (b) visit his (c) mother every (d) Sunday.

(Answer: ⓐ)

1. Last night, the children were overly (a) concerned what (b) they weren't (c) going to get any (d) ice cream.

2. The latest (a) trends in (b) fashion designing (c) was (d) revealed in the magazine *Sharp Dresser*.

3. This (a) afternoon, I received an (b) extremely thoughtfully (c) e-mail message from a charming (d) young man.

4. Mary doesn't (a) like (b) watching football matches (c), and either (d) do I.

5. The jobless (a) rate for the (b) northern regions of the state, reported (c), will be published (d) in all of the local newspapers.

6. Contrary to (a) popular belief (b), some rabbits like to eat (c) fruits (d).

7. Statistics can be (a) very misleading (b), depending upon who (c) presents them and how their (d) presented.

8. She adored (a) hamsters and (b) guinea pigs but (c) detested mouses (d).

9. No one (a) was more surprising (b) than Henry to discover (c) that his riding buddy had become (d) engaged.

10. The (a) fever (b) had not yet broke (c) when the doctor came (d) to visit.

Placement Test

11. All of the students believe that they should get perfect score on their papers.
a b c d

12. When the telephone ring, I always race to answer it.
a b c d

13. I like them ever so much and do hope that they can go to vacation with us.
a b c d

14. It has been a very long time since she studied histories.
a b c d

15. My mother said that it was very long ago when Mr. Fujiyama decided to immigration to the United States.
a b c d

16. The working conditions at the factory were questionable by the human rights advocates.
a b c d

17. The textiles on display at the museum of applied arts were absolute stunning.
a b c d

18. I thoroughly enjoyed the visit to the aquarium; wherefore, the tour of the chocolate factory was a real disappointment
a b c d

19. Every individual diagnosed with sleep disorder should cut down on their caffeine intake and should see a medical doctor.
a b c d

20. Lisa is happiest than any of the other teen-age girls in the class.
a b c d

21. Tonight my mother will have a big (a) dinner and she will tell everyone to (b) eat as many (c) as they want or to have as many (d) servings as they like.

22. They would (a) have (b) gone to the concert, so (c) it started to rain (d) cats and dogs.

23. If I don't (a) have none (b) money, I won't be able to do any (c) shopping this (d) weekend.

24. Last (a) semester Dr. Miller taught a course (b) who (c) was nicknamed (d) Love and Glory.

25. I love sweets too (a) much (b) that (c) I'm ten pounds (d) overweight.

Chapter 1 Quiz

Name________________________________ Date__________

1. Identify the part of speech of each italicized word. (10 points)

1. *Although many* people around the world learn English in school at some point, not all of them may have had enough *opportunities* to practice speaking the language.
2. *Nearly* everyone *can* benefit personally *or professionally* from learning a foreign language at some point in *his* or her life.
3. Some people are *concerned* that *if* English becomes a global *language, other* languages will *eventually* be lost.
4. Already there are some countries that are *quite concerned with* the *increasing* amount of English words that are *replacing* words in *their* own languages.
5. *Nevertheless*, in *the* era of *globalization*, most people *feel* that having *a* common language will be extremely important.

2. Circle the correct words to complete each sentence. (10 points)

1. My English teacher gave (me / I) a pronunciation tape which so far seems (perfectly/perfect) for my needs.
2. When I was younger, I (used to / was used to) learn new languages very quickly, but as an adult I find it (is / be) much more difficult.
3. I (would begin / began) studying English when I was in primary school, and I (would / used to) love reading stories in English.
4. In order to learn a language, you (don't have to / must not) study in the country where people (speak / are speaking) it, since books and tapes are widely available.
5. Most people (would rather not / would prefer not) spend time doing homework for English class, but you (can / must) work hard if you want to improve.

3. Fill in the blanks with the correct form of the verb *travel.* (5 points)

1. These days, more and more college students in the United States ______________ to another country to study at some point during their education, usually in their third year.
2. Karen Lieberman and Anna Stern, who are now college seniors, ______________ to France during their third year of college.
3. "Before that trip, we ______________ out of the United States before," says Karen. "This was our first time."
4. While they ______________ throughout France, they had the opportunity to practice their French with many of the local people.

5. Karen and Anne enjoyed their experience so much that they are saving money for a trip to Europe after their graduation; by this time next year they hope that ________________ to many more places than France!

4. Fill in the blanks with an appropriate modal auxiliary or related structure to complete each sentence. In some cases, more than one modal may be possible. (5 points)

1. It seems impossible that Carlos has only been studying English for three years! His English sounds so fluent he __________ have been studying for such a short time!
2. We are not sure why Carlos is so fluent. He lives in Venezuela, but he __________ have spent some time in the past traveling or living in an English-speaking country.
3. __________ you mind lending me your grammar book? I forgot mine.
4. If you want my advice, I think you __________ try to study or travel in an English-speaking country if you want to learn English well.
5. Academic honesty is very important; you __________ cheat on an exam.

5. Fill in the blank with the appropriate form of the verbs in parentheses. In some cases, more than one verb form may be possible. (10 points)

The different ways in which people learn ______(1)______ (interest) researchers for many years. Some people learn best when they ______(2)______ (listen) to an instructorand write down notes. Others learn best visually; for them, they ______(3)______ (see) something—perhaps a picture or a written text—and from that point on they ______(4)______ (remember/always) it. Still others learn best when they ______(5)______ (do) hands-on activities: learning by doing. If you ______(6)______ (learn) a new language right now, knowing your own learning style can help you in this process. Think about your past learning strategies and experiences that ______(7)______ (work) well for you before you ______(8)______ (start) your current course of study. After you ______(9)______ (write down) some of the things you remember seeing, hearing, and doing in classroom situations, look at the learning style about which you wrote the most notes.This may be your dominant learning style. Knowing this means that as early as your next class, you ______(10)______ (begin) to pay more attention to how you learn, and you might even ask your teacher to help you do things that fit with your learning style.

6. Circle the errors and write your corrected sentences on the lines. Each sentence has two errors. (10 points)

1. Before we move to the United States in 1999, our family would live in Argentina.

   ____

2. Now that we live in the United States, we are knowing many other people who were used to live in South America like us.

   ____

3. When we were arriving in the U.S., the first thing my parents do is to sign up for English classes.

   ____

4. They felt that they should have not moved to an English-speaking country without learning the language better; they have not studied as much English as my brother and I back in Argentina.

   ____

5. Both my parents are improving their English for three years, and by this time next year I am sure that they will be going to speak English as well as my brother and I.

   ____

Name________________________ Date__________

1. Match the units of measurement in column 1 with the appropriate nouns in column 2. (10 points)

1. a tube of	a. water
2. a jar of	b. grapes
3. a gallon of	c. chips
4. a bar of	d. paper towels
5. a roll of	e. cheese
6. a bunch of	f. toothpaste
7. a dozen	g. eggs
8. two pounds of	h. jam
9. a bag of	i. soda pop
10. a six-pack of	j. soap

2. Circle the correct words to complete each sentence. (10 points)

1. One of (colleges / the colleges) I was interested in applying to offered excellent (classes / class) in international relations.
2. I visited the campus in the summer and although there were (a few / only a few) students there at that time, they gave me some good (informations / information) about the college.
3. They said that the professors are excellent, and even though they are very busy they can always find (little / a little) time to talk with you about your (work / works) and answer your questions.
4. They said that (moneys / money) is available to help students attend the college, though they did not know how (many / much) funding was available for international students.
5. Finally, to my surprise, they said I had a lot of (courages / courage) to travel so far to attend a college in another country; (much / many) of them said they would be too afraid to do that.

3. Fill in the blanks with an appropriate personal pronoun or possessive adjective. (5 points)

1. Columbus discovered America in 1492, and ________ discovery is celebrated in North America as "Columbus Day" every October.
2. However, many people object to this annual commemoration of the discovery; ________ claim that Columbus did not actually "discover" the continent.

3. ________ objections center around the fact that the region was already populated with native peoples, who had been living there for many years.

4. Because natives were already there, the land was ________ , but Columbus, motivated by greed, exploited the land for his own purposes.

5. However, other people object to this view, believing that Columbus's contribution was in bringing America to the attention of Western civilization; without ________, they argue, our culture would not be what it is today.

4. Complete the sentences by using the singular or plural forms of the nouns and verbs in parentheses. Use the past tense. (5 points)

1. Last year, my bicycling club ________ (be) interested in doing a long bicycle ride to raise money for charity.

2. Almost half of the ________ (member) ________ (be) interested in a fifty-mile ride to raise money for people suffering from cancer.

3. The majority ________ (be) interested in a two hundred mile ride to raise money for AIDS research, so we decided to do that one.

4. All of us ________ (be) a little worried, however, that we didn't have enough ________ (experience).

5. You see, none of our members ________ (be) used to riding more than forty miles at a time!

5. Complete the following passage by using *a, an, the,* or X (to indicate that no article is necessary). (10 points)

In ________ (1) spring of 1996, a writer named Jon Krakauer accepted ________ (2) assignment from *Outside* magazine. He agreed to try to climb to ________ (3) summit of ________ (4) Mount Everest, ________ (5) highest mountain peak in the world. He wanted to see if anyone could attempt ________ (6) climb or if only ________ (7) experts should do so. ________ (8) result, unfortunately, was disaster. His climbing team got caught in ________ (9) blinding snowstorm and nine climbers died. ________ (10) bestselling book called *Into Thin Air* describes his harrowing experience as a survivor.

6. Circle the errors and write your corrected sentences on the lines. Each sentence has two errors. In some cases there may be more than one way to correct the error. (10 points)

1. People who like to travel are people who like to enrich his life by learning about cultures that are different from his or her own.

   ____

2. A fearless traveler is one who will seek experiences that are quite different from their day-to-day life and who will get advices from local people about what to see and do.

   ____

3. Most of world's greatest explorers of fifteenth century were interested in expanding trade routes.

   ____

4. The most of early explorers had to overcome great public distrust in the expeditions, since in those days people believed the earth was flat and that the ships would fall off world.

   ____

5. Rarely the early explorers lost courage, even as they sailed to distant lands and preparing to meet unknown peoples.

   ____

Chapter 3 Quiz

Name________________________________ Date____________

1. Match the beginnings of sentences in Column 1 with the endings in Column 2. (10 points)

1. People either learn gender roles
2. Researchers find that both women
3. Some girls are neither encouraged
4. Not only are boys encouraged to be strong
5. My siblings and I were given toys for both girls
6. My friend Bill could neither play with dolls
7. Neither my son
8. Ed grew up with five sisters,
9. John grew up with no sisters,
10. Robert is not good at math,

a. nor helped to become assertive.
b. but he relates well to women.
c. and boys alike.
d. nor my daughter is good at math.
e. or are born knowing them.
f. so he relates well to women.
g. and men are equally good at math.
h. for he was never encouraged in it.
i. nor read books for girls.
j. but also they are told to be aggressive.

2. Circle the correct words to complete each sentence. (10 points)

1. (Because / Although) men and women seem to have so many problems communicating, some psychologists have theorized (what / that) men and women actually speak different languages.
2. Psychologists have come up with some communication tips (such that / so that) they may help couples (who / which) have difficult conversations.
3. First of all, it's important to understand (that / it) men like to solve problems; (otherwise / however), women may talk about a problem but not necessarily want advice.
4. Most women want a partner (which / who) will listen to them; (in addition / therefore), the best thing a man can do is to keep his comments to himself and only offer them if she says she would like advice.
5. (While / Since) most men are very tired or frustrated when they come home from work, they may need some quiet, solitary time (before / when) they answer their partner's questions about their day.

3. Fill in the blanks with affirmative or negative commands. (5 points)

1. __________ your hair; you look better with long hair than short hair.
2. __________ some exercise if you're feeling unhealthy.
3. __________ clothes that make you feel good about yourself when you date.
4. __________ seeing your friends even when you are in a new relationship.
5. __________ about not being married yet; many people wait until later in life.

4. Form exclamations from these statements. (5 points)

1. Sandra looks tired. ____
2. Sandra has an exhausted appearance. ______________________________

3. Pedro has an awful lot of free time these days. ______

4. Yee Yan is working very hard this week. ______

5. This chapter was incredibly difficult. ______

5. Link the following sentences with an appropriate transition to indicate addition, contrast, result, negative condition, or added comment/clarification. Add all necessary punctuation. (10 points)

1. Females in our society are socialized to be passive. They are encouraged to be beautiful rather than smart.
2. Feminism has a long and complicated history and has taken a variety of forms. Many people are unsure of the term and are hesitant to use the label, even if they do support equal rights for women.
3. Most people who call themselves feminists today simply want women to have the same opportunities and choices as men. There are still people who hear the word "feminist" and think of angry women or women who believe they are better than men.
4. Historically, the struggle for women's rights has been linked to the fight for civil rights in general. Many people in the women's movement used the same tactics that had proven successful in the struggle for civil rights for African Americans.
5. It is important for people to become educated about the history and meaning of feminism before they criticize it. They will remain confused about the concept.

6. Circle the errors and write your corrected sentences on the lines. Each sentence has two errors. In some cases there may be more than one way to correct the error. (10 points)

1. How happy are Marina and Vlad together! And what an adorable baby have they!

   ______

2. Jessica both was sad and lonely, so her relationship had ended.

   ______

3. Not only was Maria happy with her fiancé, but also was her family happy, but they decided to give her a large wedding to celebrate.

   ______

4. Ted didn't stop neither hoping nor believing that he would find the perfect woman for him, moreover, he made great efforts to try to meet people.

   ______

5. Marina and Vlad got married in 1999, they had a baby in 2001, as a matter of fact they hope to have another baby in the next two years.

   ______

Chapter 4 Quiz

Name________________________________ **Date**____________

1. Add the adjective clause to each sentence that follows, using appropriate punctuation. (10 points)

where most of the mysterious crop circles are found

1. The place __________________________ is the United Kingdom.
2. The United Kingdom __________________ has a lot of farmland.

who have tested plant and soil samples from within crop circles

3. Scientists ________________ have noticed physical changes to plant cell walls and to soil.
4. Crop circle researchers __________________ have noticed physical changes to plant cell walls and to soil.

who has done research on crop circles

5. My sister ______________ said that crop circles have become more complex in design and more frequent in occurrence since the 1990s. (I have only one sister)
6. My sister ______________ said that crop circles have become more complex in design and more frequent in occurrence since the 1990s. (I have three sisters)

when they were first discovered by farmers

7. Reports on crop circles in England date back to 1647____________________.
8. Reports on crop circles in England date back to the time ________________.

which include spacecrafts, hoaxes, and military experimentation

9. There are some scientific theories to explain crop circles, but the more popular theories are the ones ____________________.
10. To explain crop circles, people have developed theories _______________.

2. Match the independent clauses in section one with the dependent clauses in section two so that they form logical sentences. Write out the new sentences and add the correct punctuation. (10 points)

1. The Loch Ness Monster is a dinosaur-like animal
2. Sasquatch, or "Bigfoot," is a hairy, manlike creature
3. Many tourists come to Loch Ness
4. "Nessie" is a nickname for the legendary monster
5. It was believed to be Bigfoot

a. which is located in Scotland.
b. who startled some campers in the woods last week.
c. whose home is in Loch Ness in Scotland.
d. that is believed to live in a lake in Scotland.
e. who is thought to live in the mountains of the northwestern United States.

1. __________
2. __________
3. __________
4. __________
5. __________

3. Choose the best word to complete each sentence: (10 points)

1. Machu Picchu is one of the ancient (city / cities) of South America whose reasons for their demise (is / are) mysterious.
2. However, Machu Picchu is the only one of the ancient (city / cities) that (was / were) completely inaccessible to excavators until the 1940s.
3. Machu Picchu was one of the (temple / temples) that (was / were) inhabited mainly by priests, priestesses, and high functionaries.
4. The ruins, (which / that) are on a mountain, (is / are) accessible only by a long hike along the Inca Trail or a four-hour bus and train service.
5. The excavations at the site (has / have) revealed only 173 skeletons, (of which / which) 150 are female.

4. Combine each set of sentences. Change the second sentence into an adjective clause, adding all necessary punctuation. If there is a choice about degrees of formality with the structure or the choice of relative pronoun, use the most formal option. (10 points)

1. There are remains of over 30,000 ring forts in Ireland. Many of them date back to the Bronze Age.

   ____

2. The forts were built by ancient tribes. All of them wanted to protect their families from invaders.

   ____

3. The forts were located all over the countryside. Most of them were made of stone.

   ____

4. The Normans used forts for military purposes. Their newly conquered territory needed to be protected.

____

5. The ring forts were of varying sizes. One family or an entire tribe could live in them.

____

5. Circle the errors and write your corrected sentences on the lines. Each sentence has two errors. In some cases there may be more than one way to correct the error. (10 points)

1. It was the Incas which built its cities on narrow terraces on the steep mountainsides.

____

2. Many photos taken of UFOs (Unidentified Flying Objects), some of which is actually frisbees covered with tinfoil, has been proven to be hoaxes.

____

3. Today, all of the Egyptian pyramids is endangered by pollution, whose its harmful effects may destroy them eventually.

____

4. My friend Mohammed, whom works as a preservationist at the Egyptian pyramids, have worried about the harmful effects of tourism.

____

5. One of the most biggest concerns that it people have about our natural wonders is what they can be damaged by too many tourists.

____

Name_______________________________ **Date**___________

1. Complete the passage by using the present continuous, simple present, present perfect, future continuous, or simple future form of the verbs in parentheses. Add modal auxiliaries such as should, will, can, could may, might, where appropriate. In some cases, more than one verb form may be possible. (10 points)

Before you ______________ (go) to another country for an extended period of time, you
1

______________ (be) aware of a psychological condition called culture shock. When people
2

______________ (arrive / first) in another country, they ______________ (feel) excited at being in
3 4

a new place and on an "adventure." That excitement, however, ______________ (turn / soon) to
5

disorientation and "shock." As soon as people ______________ (realize) that basic, everyday activities
6

like buying groceries or going to the bank ______________ (be) totally different than in their home
7

country, they ______________ (begin) to feel frustrated and over-whelmed. Fortunately, by the time
8

most people ______________ (master) day-to-day activities in this new place, they
9

______________ (learn / probably) the language enough to feel more comfortable.
10

2. Choose the best words to complete each sentence. (10 points)

1. While our world (becomes / is becoming) more and more connected in the era of globalization, some people (worried / are worrying) about cultures losing their unique traits and languages.
2. (Since / Because) the development of the Internet, families and friends throughout the world (can / have been able to) communicate with each other more easily.
3. (As / Whenever) a society is in transition, there are always some people who (are resistant / are resisting) to change.
4. Once change (is beginning / has begun) to occur, however, people gradually (have incorporated / incorporate) change into their daily lives.
5. Years (before / after) people worried about possible negative effects of television and other technologies, they (worried / will worry) about the effects of radio.

Chapter 5 Quiz

3. Fill in the blanks with the best word from the list below to complete each sentence. Use words to introduce clauses or phrases, or use transitions, where appropriate. In all cases, more than one word will be possible. You do not need to use all of the words in your answers. Add appropriate punctuation to each sentence. (10 points)

as a result of	owing to	consequently	therefore	due to
due to the fact that	because of	because	hence	thus
as a result	since			

1. ____________ rapid changes that are occurring in their lives many teenagers suddenly become less communicative with their parents.

2. Teenagers are involved in the process of individuation from their parents ____________ they may wish to assert their differences from their parents and even prefer not to be seen with them in public.

3. ____________ teenagers can seem to withdraw more and more from the family parents often become quite alarmed and try harder to communicate with them.

4. Often their attempts at communication can sound more like interrogation ____________ teenagers may become even less communicative as they try harder to assert their independence.

5. However, a number of parents maintain good communication with their children throughout the teenage years ____________ good listening skills and expressions of emotional support.

4. Combine each set of sentences using the connecting words in parentheses. Change the verb tense to the past perfect in one of the clauses in each new sentence. Omit any repetitious information and add any necessary punctuation. (10 points)

1. Men's and women's roles were clearly defined as being centered around the workplace and the home, respectively. World War II began. (until)

2. The war began. Men were increasingly enlisted to help fight, leaving the women at home. (soon after)

3. So many men left to fight in the war. New employment and educational opportunities opened up for women. (after)

4. World War II broke out. There were very limited opportunities for women in factories or in professional occupations. (before)

5. The war ended. Many women found satisfaction in working outside the home, and were reluctant to give up their positions for the returning men. (by the time)

5. Circle the errors and write your corrected sentences on the lines. Each sentence has two errors. In some cases there may be more than one way to correct the error. (10 points)

1. Before you will make a major life decision make sure you are not under a lot of stress or feeling pressured by other people.

   ____

2. Soon after when cellular phones had been marketed at lower costs, more and more people, including teenagers, had begun buying them.

   ____

3. Due to she was such a devoted helper of the poor in India, many people to this day revere Mother Teresa as a result.

   ____

4. Because of Martin Luther King, Jr. was an incredible orator; therefore, huge crowds gathered to hear him speak about civil rights and nonviolent protest.

   ____

5. Within the first thirty years of the twentieth century occurred, Americans witnessed an explosion of technological innovations, including automobiles and radios.

   ____

Chapter 6 Quiz

Name________________________________ **Date**____________

1. Use *in spite of the fact that, in spite of, despite, even though,* or *nevertheless* to complete the following sentences. Add correct pronunciation where appropriate. (10 points)

1. ______________ attempts to reduce stress in their lives many people suffer from anxiety and panic.
2. They may suffer from insomnia at night ______________ they attempt to reduce caffeine in their diet.
3. Psychologists say that anxiety and panic disorders are on the rise ______________ there have been national campaigns to raise awareness about the effects of too much stress.
4. People are exercising more and trying to eat better ______________ they may need to modify their lifestyle even more if they want to see results.
5. ______________ some medications have proved helpful most people still prefer to try to improve their mental state through diet, exercise, and stress reduction.

2. Complete the passage by using *whereas, where, while, similar to, different from, like, unlike, instead of, in contrast, on the other hand,* or *on the contrary.* (10 points)

Maureen and Jessica are identical twins. ______________ (1) all identical twins, they have many similarities on the surface. Their faces and builds are the same, and they wear their short, dark hair in styles ______________ (2) each other. But physicality is where the similarities end. In terms of their academic interests and abilities, Maureen and Jessica are very ______________ (3) one another. ______________ (4) Maureen likes math and science classes, Jessica excels at literature and arts classes. ______________ (5) watching TV or wasting her spare time, Maureen likes to conduct scientific experiments or works on complicated math problems. ______________ (6) her sister, Jessica also prefers to keep busy during her spare time; ______________ (7), she would much rather read novels, write poetry, or paint. ______________ (8) presenting the twins with problems and conflicts, their differences seem to have brought them closer together. Many people wonder if the twins are always in conflict about their interests and ideas; ______________ (9), they enjoy learning about each others' interests. Maureen and Jessica's relationship suggests that people's differences can bringthem closer together ______________ (10) separating them.

3. Write the comparative and superlative forms of the following words. In some cases, more than one answer may be possible. (10 points)

1. clever ________________ ________________
2. difficult ________________ ________________
3. little ________________ ________________
4. far (distance) ________________ ________________
5. slowly ________________ ________________

4. Choose the best words to complete each sentence. (10 points)

1. Daniel speaks English as well (than / as) Roberta, but he doesn't study nearly as (hard / harder).
2. Rami gets higher grades (as / than) Takashi; in fact, she gets (highest / the highest) grades of anyone in the class.
3. Eduardo, (as well as / likewise) Sandra, forgot (their / his) grammar book today.
4. Milena has (the same / similar) trouble remembering dates and numbers as Joseph (do / does).
5. The grammar was (such / so) difficult that the students grew (most / more frustrated every day.

5. Circle the errors and write your corrected sentences on the lines. Each sentence has two errors. In some cases there may be more than one way to correct the error. (10 points)

1. Despite that we dream every night, many people could not remember their dreams.

   ____

2. Whereas my brother seems to be more left-brained because he is good at math, on the other hand I more right-brained because I am good at languages and art.

   ____

3. Where I am fascinated by theories of dream interpretation, my friends are enthusiastic.

   ____

4. Research on the mental abilities of elderly nuns is being conducted in order that learn most about how Alzheimer's Disease might be prevented.

   ____

5. The teacher had so extensive knowledge about grammar and gave so much good assignments that the students quickly mastered Chapter 6.

   ____

Chapter 7 Quiz

Name______________________________ **Date**__________

1. Write the correct form of the verb in parentheses. Include modals whenever necessary. (10 points)

1. His report concluded that technical jobs __________ (continue) to rise.
2. My boss told me that I _______ (be) extra careful.
3. I let my supervisor know that I ________ (stay) late if necessary.
4. Statistics show that white-collar jobs __________ (increase).
5. Union members complained that their working conditions ________ (be) unfair.

2. Change the quotations to reported speech. (10 points)

1. The secretary said, "Somebody just called."

   ____

2. Efraim told his wife "I'm going to get a promotion."

   ____

3. "You must wear your safety goggles," the supervisor told the workers.

   ____

4. "I will be on time tomorrow," Ruth promised herself.

   ____

5. I cried when Ginger said "I've decided to leave the company."

   ____

3. Circle the correct word to complete the sentence. (10 sentences, 10 points)

1. It is essential that you (take, took) notes during the meeting.
2. Mr. Alonso requested that his secretary (to make, make) the necessary arrangements.
3. I wonder (whether, if) I should stay or leave.
4. It (would be, is) vital for her to make a decision soon.
5. We suggest that all workers (attend, should attend) the meeting.
6. Do you know (if, when) Sachiko has arrived?
7. The union (demand, demands) that the company change its policies.
8. I insist that I (be paid, am paid) for extra work.
9. It is best if you (documented, document) your complaint.
10. It is unacceptable that sex or race (be used, is used) to discriminate in the workplace.

4. Circle the error in each sentence. Then, write the corrected sentence on the blank line. (10 points)

1. The technicians are trying to find out the reason for the computer virus got started.

   ____

2. Do you know whenever the meeting starts?

   ____

3. I wonder how many they pay secretaries.

   ____

4. I asked her what pages I should read.

   ____

5. Could you tell me whom is going to be my supervisor?

   ____

5. Circle the letter that best completes each sentence. (10 points)

1. That I am qualified for the job ______________.
   a. is not in question
   b. he asked
   c. on the application
2. How ________ the problem is the issue I want to address.
   a. difficult
   b. many times
   c. we solve
3. What he does with his time ______________
   a. do you know?
   b. is a mystery to me.
   c. while on break.
4. It's important ____ you to find the answer yourself.
   a. for
   b. that
   c. so
5. My lawyer urged me ______ all my records.
   a. that I keep
   b. to keep
   c. should I keep

Chapter 8 Quiz

Name________________________________ **Date**____________

1. Use the perfect form of each verb to complete the sentences. (10 points)

1. By the end of this century, we ________________ (colonize) the moon.
2. The world ___________ (go through) tremendous changes since WWII.
3. Until the 1950s, scientists ____________ (develop) few antibiotics.
4. Recent advances in medicine _____________ (give) cancer patients new hope.
5. It is hoped that within the next few years, world leaders ____________ (achieve) a major breakthrough in diplomacy.

2. Change these sentences to the passive voice. Omit the agent if appropriate. (10 points)

1. Alexander Graham Bell invented the telephone in 1876.

   ____

2. Technology has changed our lives forever.

   ____

3. Hopefully, we will find a cure for AIDs in the near future.

   ____

4. Electronic media will eventually replace books and newspapers.

   ____

5. Somebody reported the last case of smallpox in 1980.

   ____

3. Circle the correct word or phrase to complete the sentence. (10 points)

1. These days even farmers (have used, are using) computers.
2. I (have been living, am living) in the same house my whole life.
3. The most important invention of the last 100 years (have been, has been) the internal combustion engine.
4. In the future, houses (will have run, will be run) by computers.
5. You shouldn't get (worried, worry) about the situation.
6. Once upon a time, it was (believed, belief) that the earth was flat.

7. Before industrialization, people (had done, were doing) all their chores by hand.
8. More oil (could be, could have been) conserved in the past.
9. The first movie ever made (had been projected, was projected) in a theater in Paris.
10. We (would, should) be more conservative with fuel to avoid an energy crisis.

4. The following sentences are not well-formed. Write the corrected sentence on the blank line. (10 points)

1. By Samuel Morse the Morse Code was invented.

   ____

2. Many drugs recently derived from plants in the rain forest.

   ____

3. The modern family goes through many changes at present.

   ____

4. I have never heard of that procedure until I underwent surgery.

   ____

5. Native Americans had lived in longhouses when Europeans arrived in North America.

   ____

5. Circle the letter that best completes each sentence. (10 points)

1. Everybody ______________ more concerned about the environment.
   a. should have
   b. should be
   c. should show

2. We _________ still do something about global warming if we try.
   a. can
   b. ought
   c. must

3. Alternative energy sources ________________ a long time ago.
   a. will be developed
   b. have been developing
   c. should have been developed

4. Many species of animals ___________ if we don't protect them.
   a. might disappear
   b. could be saved
   c. will be born

5. The current government thinks we _______ drill oil fields in Alaska.
   a. ought
   b. ought to
   c. ought to have

Name______________________________ **Date**____________

1. Complete each sentence by writing the appropriate preposition. Choose from the following list. Some prepositions may be used more than once. (10 points)

about	after	at	by	of	on	to

1. She prepared for her performance ________ practicing everyday.
2. He is used ________ hearing loud music and staying up late.
3. I'm thinking ________ taking up the guitar.
4. Don't plan ________ getting a ticket this late.
5. Miguel and Jennifer were excited ________ the concert.
6. I look forward ________ hearing from you soon.
7. He was tired ________ practicing all day.
8. He seems to be good ________ improvising a tune.
9. The conductor insists ________ rehearsing right before the concert.
10. Minna was tired ________ playing so she took a break.

2. Complete each sentence by writing the gerund or infinitive form of the verb in parentheses. (10 points)

1. ________________ (Learn) how to play an instrument is a rewarding experience.
2. Gold is very easy ________________ (shape) because it's so soft.
3. It is useful ________________ (think) of Vincent Van Gogh as a colorist.
4. A good way to learn a foreign language is by ________________ (watch) films in that language.
5. A good novelist must learn how ________________ (listen) very closely to the way people speak.
6. Dancers use their bodies ________________ (communicate) feelings and to express their relationship to other dancers.
7. Painters spend a lot of time ________________ (observe) their surroundings.
8. Her way of ________________ (sing) sent shivers through my body.
9. The ________________ (make) of a film requires the collaboration of many different people.
10. Some people think that opera is ________________ (bore); others find it exciting beyond words.

3. Think of a particular activity that you enjoy and are good at. Write about it by completing each of the following sentences. Use infinitives or gerunds in your answers. (10 points)

1. I like ____
2. It involves ____
3. To be good at this, ____
4. My goal is ____
5. Other people might enjoy ____

4. The following sentences are not well-formed. Write the corrected sentence on the blank line. (10 points)

1. We agreed in order to practicing together.

   ____

2. Traditional art forms include sculpting, dancing, and stories.

   ____

3. It's important preserving and protecting native arts.

   ____

4. Public speech is a good way of the development of self-confidence.

   ____

5. High-quality writers, acting, and directors are all elements of a good film.

   ____

5. Circle the letter that best completes each sentence. (10 points)

1. I highly recommend ____________ this film.
   a. seeing
   b. to see
   c. for your seeing

2. Marcel is studying Arabic ________ an interpreter and translator.
   a. therefore being
   b. in order to become
   c. so to be

3. _______________ is better than knowing one language.
   a. Being bilingual
   b. To be bilingual
   c. He who knows two languages

4. The instructor expects her students ___________.
   a. of trying their best
   b. making their best effort
   c. to do their best

5. The author _____________ my ideas.
   a. persuaded me to reexamine
   b. convinced me rethinking
   c. made me changing

Chapter 10 Quiz

Name______________________________ **Date**__________

1. Complete each sentence with the correct form of *hope* or *wish*. (10 points)

1. I ______ that there is a peaceful resolution to the conflict.
2. The President shook my hand and _______ me good luck.
3. Van ________ he had spent more time preparing for the exam.
4. The rescue workers ________ they would be able to find survivors.
5. After trying their best, the team _______ for a victory, but they were defeated.
6. The family said a prayer, ______ for their son's safe return.
7. Don't you _______ you were able to go?
8. The tired traveler ________ somebody would be there to meet him at the station.
9. The defendant _________ that he will win the trial and gain his freedom.
10. I _______ that I could help you.

2. Choose the correct form of the verb in parentheses. (10 points)

1. I wish more people __________ (realized, will realize) how serious the situation is.
2. If we entered a war, the consequences _________ (would have been, would be) terrible.
3. I ____________ (had asked, would have asked) for your permission, but I couldn't contact you in time.
4. Everybody realized that they _____________ (should have prepared, would have prepared) for the hurricane before it arrived.
5. If we __________ (had not invented, would have invented) guns, we wouldn't have such a problem with violence today.
6. The strikers were hoping that the company _________ (could have taken, would take) their complaints seriously.
7. If I _______ (was, were) you, I would be more careful.
8. If everybody ___________ (would have listened, had listened) to each other, they might have been able to reach an agreement.
9. The young boy realized that he _________ (should pay attention, should have paid attention) to the old man's advice.
10. If Einstein ________ (had known, could know) that his theories would be used to develop an atomic bomb, he might have kept them a secret.

3. Change each of the following word pairs into a perfect modal auxiliary. (10 points)

Example: might listen: might have listened

1. can speak: ____________________
2. will sell: ____________________
3. should think: ____________________
4. must be concerned: ____________________
5. might not happen: ____________________
6. will not attempt: ____________________
7. can occur: ____________________
8. should not do: ____________________
9. ought to try: ____________________
10. might be alarmed: ____________________

4. The following sentences are not well formed. Write the corrected sentence on the blank line. (10 points)

1. Things were different today if we took a different course.

   ____

2. You shouldn't mix chemicals if you knew what you were doing.

   ____

3. The earth is able to purify itself when we stop polluting it.

   ____

4. I wish for my ability solving the world's problems.

   ____

5. Monique hopes she could go to protest rally yesterday.

   ____

Chapter 10 Quiz

5. Circle the letter that best completes each sentence. (10 points)

1. The city park is full of trash; ______________, it would be a perfect sanctuary.
   a. however
   b. unfortunately
   c. otherwise

2. If I had known it was illegal, I ____________.
   a. wouldn't have done it
   b. would otherwise do it
   c. won't keep doing it

3. Were you _________ early, I could drive you home.
   a. finishing
   b. to finish
   c. would have finished

4. Should the candidate _________, she would run again next term.
   a. have lost
   b. were to lose
   c. lose

5. He has often _______ he had gone to graduate school.
   a. hoped for
   b. wished that
   c. wished for

Name________________________________ Date____________

1. Complete each sentence with the correct form of *raise/rise* or *lay/lie*. (10 points)

1. In the equatorial zone, the sun ________________ at the same time every day.
2. The commander ordered his troops ________________ down their guns.
3. I was so tired I ________________ down for a little nap.
4. A member of the audience interrupted the speaker and ________________ an objection.
5. When I got home, I found a dog ________________ on my front step.
6. The girl's chores included ________________ silverware on the table before dinner.
7. People in the military are used ________________ very early in the morning.
8. When the teacher returned to her desk, she found that a student ________________ a note there for her to read.
9. He was so pale and ghostly it seemed as if he ________________ from the dead.
10. Flags around the country were ________________ half mast because of the national tragedy.

2. Expand each sentence by including the relative pronoun and the connecting verb. (15 points)

Example:

Harvard, one of the best schools in this country, has a well-earned reputation.

Harvard, which is one of the best schools in this country, has a well-earned reputation.

1. Ginseng, known for its healthful effects, is used by many people as a tonic.

   ____

2. People taking herbs should consult a doctor about possible side effects.

   ____

3. Researchers using live animals in their experiments should be supervised.

   ____

4. There are several good hospitals here specializing in child care.

   ____

5. A human being cannot be compared to a rat living in a maze.

   ____

6. This tree, over 4,000 years old, is being threatened by development.

____

7. The man running the experiment was startled by the results.

____

8. People eating less usually live longer.

____

9. Cancer, being studied around the world, may be cured one day.

____

10. The genome project may possibly identify the gene determining personality traits.

____

3. Circle the phrase that best completes each sentence. (15 points)

1. Rats _________ (that, which) have followed a special diet show a lower rate of heart disease.
2. Scientists, ___________ (have, having) studied the phenomenon for over a century, can draw no definitive conclusions about the purpose of dreaming.
3. Researchers watched the rats ________ (running, ran) in the maze.
4. We saw him ___________ (being rushed, having rushed) to the hospital.
5. Chantal hopes to make a living ______ (on, by) specializing in herbal treatments.
6. Before he left the lab, he ____________ (had collected, was collecting) his X-rays.
7. ________ (Despite, After) he had finished his research, he published his findings.
8. I _______ (had, should) the doctor give me a physical exam.
9. The patient ________ (let, led) the doctor look into her throat.
10. The nurses ___________ (could, helped) the patient get into the car.
11. After recovering from the operation, the ______________ (patient, doctor) was given a sedative.
12. _____________ (Exhausted, Having exhaust), the surgeon went into a private room to rest.
13. The patient sat in bed __________ (looked, looking) out the window.
14. The nurses caught him _________ (eating, having eaten) cake in bed.
15. The herbalist found an interesting fact ____________ (hidden, hid) in an old book.

4. The following sentences are not well-formed. Write the corrected sentence on the blank line. (10 points)

1. Since having lived for more than a century, the doctors astounded the old man.

   ____

2. The hospital has a specialist which is studying the age process.

   ____

3. Senior citizens, living a long time, can learn a lot from younger people.

   ____

4. Marie Curie, that is known for isolating radium, caught death from radiation.

   ____

5. Since losing a lot of blood, the patient just felt like laying in bed.

   ____

Chapter 12 Quiz

Name________________________________ Date___________

1. Complete the following table by filling in the correct form of the verb in each blank space. (15 points)

	Passive	Continuous Infinitive	Present Perfect	Perfect Passive
to delay		to be delaying		
to know	to be known			
to launch				to have been launched
to repair			to have repaired	
to think	to be thought			

2. Complete each sentence by circling the correct word or phrase in parentheses, then write it on the blank line. (15 points)

1. The spaceship is programmed __________ (to have traveled, to travel) all the way to Jupiter.
2. Many people appear __________ (to be contacting, to have been contacted) by aliens.
3. Some scientists expect the earth __________ (to hit, to be hit) by a meteor in the near future.
4. The space commander urged his crew __________ (to fasten, to be fastening) their seatbelts.
5. The alien pretended __________ (to be dying, death).
6. I make my robot do all the __________ (bored, boring) jobs.
7. Teachers shouldn't have to worry about __________ (replacing, being replaced) by robots.
8. She couldn't remember __________ (to get, getting) into a U.F.O. until she was hypnotized.
9. Many people can expect __________ (to be living, to have lived) in space within 100 years.
10. So far, nobody has programmed a computer __________ (thinking, to think) original thoughts.
11. After __________ (having examined, being examined) a meteor from Mars, scientists concluded that life may have existed on Mars billions of years ago.
12. Some people who have touched a meteor claim __________ (to have, having) special powers.
13. The "Big Bang" theory describes an __________ (expanded, expanding) universe that may one day come to a halt or reverse itself.
14. On spacecraft, cameras are used for __________ (filming, to film) take-offs and landings.
15. After __________ (being coined, to be coined) in 1921, the term robot was not widely used until the 1950s.

3. Read the following paragraph. Write the correct form of each verb in parentheses. (10 points)

We can expect many changes ____________ (1) (to take place) by the year 2050. Advances in gene therapy will allow defects ____________ (2) (to repair) before a baby is born. We probably will ____________ (3) (colonize) the moon by then. Many people will be ____________ (4) (live) and ____________ (5) (work) in space. In fact, there may be some people who will ____________ (6) (never visit) the earth. The moon may be an important source of new minerals that can be used ____________ (7) (develop) alternative sources of energy. With these advances, we may be able ____________ (8) (solve) a lot of our current problems. Hopefully, we will be able ____________ (9) (save) our precious planet before it is too late. Our technology won't be able to save us if we keep ____________ (10) (damage) the planet.

4. The following sentences are not well-formed. Write the corrected sentences on the blank lines. (10 points)

1. Everybody laughed at me having sighted a U.F.O.

   ____

2. Don't hesitate reporting any suspicious activity you have seeing.

   ____

3. The continued revolution in technology promises transforming our lives.

   ____

4. An alien spacecraft appearing to has landing in Central Park.

   ____

5. I won't tolerate you have ignored my orders.

   ____

Placement Test Answer Keys

Part 1

Example: a

1. b
2. b
3. b
4. a
5. d
6. d
7. d
8. a
9. b
10. c
11. c
12. b
13. d
14. b
15. a
16. a
17. d
18. c
19. d
20. c
21. b
22. c
23. d
24. d
25. c
26. a
27. b
28. d
29. d
30. b
31. d
32. c
33. b
34. a
35. b
36. b
37. d
38. b
39. a
40. c
41. b
42. b
43. c
44. c
45. d

Part 2

Example: a

1. b
2. d
3. c
4. d
5. c
6. d
7. d
8. d
9. b
10. c
11. d
12. b
13. c
14. d
15. c
16. c
17. c
18. b
19. b
20. a
21. c
22. c
23. b
24. c
25. a

Answer Keys for Chapter Quizzes

Chapter 1

1. Part of speech of each italicized word: (10 points)

1. although = conjunction; many = adjective, at = preposition; opportunities = noun
2. nearly = adjective; can = verb; or = conjunction; professionally = adverb, his = possessive adjective
3. concerned = adjective; if = conjunction; language = noun; other = adjective; eventually = adverb
4. quite = adverb; concerned = adjective; with = preposition; increasing = adjective; replacing = verb; their = possessive adjective
5. Nevertheless = conjunction; the = article; globalization = noun; feel = verb; a = article

2. Correct words: (10 points)

1. My English teacher gave me a pronunciation tape, which so far seems perfect for my needs.

2. When I was younger, I <u>used to</u> learn new languages very quickly, but as an adult I find it is much more difficult.
3. I <u>began</u> studying English when I was in primary school, and I <u>used to</u> love reading stories in English.
4. In order to learn a language, you <u>don't have to</u> study in the country where people <u>speak</u> it, since books and tapes are widely availabe.
5. Most people <u>would rather not</u> spend time doing homework for English class, but you <u>must</u> work hard if you want to improve.

3. Correct verb tenses: (10 points)

1. are traveling
2. traveled
3. had not traveled
4. were traveling
5. will have traveled

4. Correct modals: (5 points)

1. couldn't
2. might (or: may, could)
3. would
4. should (or: ought to, had better)
5. must not

5. Correct verb forms: (5 points)

1. has interested
2. listen
3. see
4. will always remember
5. do (or: are doing)
6. are learning
7. worked (or: had worked)
8. started
9. write down (or: have written down)
10. will begin

6. Errors are boldfaced; corrections appear below each sentence: (10 points)

1. Before we **move** to the United States in 1999, our family **would live** in Argentina.
   Correction: Before we moved to the United States in 1999, our family lived (or: used to live) in Argentina.
2. Now that we live in the United States, we **are knowing** many other people who **were used to live** in South America like us.
   Correction: Now that we live in the United States, we know (or: are getting to know) many other people who used to live in South America like us.
3. When we **were arriving** in the U.S., the first thing my parents **do was** to sign up for English classes.
   Correction: When we arrived in the U.S., the first thing my parents did was to sign up for English classes.
4. They felt that they **should have not moved** to an English-speaking country without learning the language better; they **have not studied** as much English as my brother and I back in Argentina.
   Correction: They felt that they should not have moved to an English-speaking country without learning the language better; they had not studied as much English as my brother and I back in Argentina.
5. Both my parents **are improving** their English for three years, and by this time next year I am sure that they **will be going to speak** English as well as my brother and I.
   Correction: Both my parents have been improving their English for three years, and by this time next year I am sure that they will be speaking English as well as my brother and I.

Chapter 2

1. Matching: units of measurement: (10 points)

1. f
2. h
3. a
4. j
5. d
6. b
7. g
8. e
9. c
10. i

2. Correct words: (10 points)

1. One of the colleges I was interested in applying to offered excellent classes in international relations.
2. I visited the campus in the summer and although there were only a few students there at that time, they gave me some good information about the college.
3. They said that the professors are excellent, and even though they are very busy they can always find a little time to talk with you about your work and answer your questions.
4. They said that money is available to help students attend the college, though they did not know how much funding was available for international students.
5. Finally, to my surprise, they said I had a lot of courage to travel so far to attend a college in another country; many of them said they would be too afraid to do that.

3. Correct pronouns and possessive adjectives: (5 points)

1. his
2. they
3. Their
4. theirs
5. it

4. Correct verb forms: (5 points)

1. was
2. members, were
3. was
4. were, experience
5. was

5. Correct articles: (10 points)

1. the
2. an
3. the
4. X
5. the
6. the
7. X
8. the
9. a
10. The

6. Errors are boldfaced; corrections appear below each sentence: (10 points)

1. People who like to travel are people who like to enrich **his** life by learning about cultures that are different from **his or her** own.
   Correction: People who like to travel are people who like to enrich their life by learning about cultures that are different from their own. (OR: A person who likes to travel is a person who likes to enrich his or her life by learning about cultures that are different from his or her own).
2. A fearless traveler is one who will seek experiences that are quite different from **their** day-to-day life and who will get **advices** from local people about what to see and do.
   Correction: A fearless traveler is one who will seek experiences that are quite different from his or her day-to-day life and who will get advice from local people about what to see and do. (OR: Fearless travelers are ones who will seek experiences that are quite different from their day-to-day life and who will get advices from local people about what to see and do).
3. **Most of world's** greatest explorers of **fifteenth century** were interested in expanding trade routes.
   Correction: Most of the world's greatest explorers of the fifteenth century were interested in expanding trade routes.
4. **The most of early explorers** had to overcome great public distrust in the expeditions, since in those days people believed the earth was flat and that the ships would fall off **world**.
   Correction: Most of the early explorers had to overcome great public distrust in the expeditions, since in those days people believed the earth was flat and that the ships would fall off the world.
5. **Rarely the early explorers lost** courage, even as they sailed to distant lands and **preparing** to meet unknown peoples.

Correction: Rarely did the early explorers lose courage, even as they sailed to distant lands and prepared to meet unknown peoples. (OR: The early explorers rarely lost courage, even as they were sailing to distant lands and preparing to meet unknown peoples).

Chapter 3

1. Matching (10 points)

1. e
2. g
3. a
4. j
5. c
6. i
7. d
8. f
9. b
10. h

2. Correct words: (10 points)

1. Because men and women seem to have so many problems communicating, some psychologists have theorized that men and women actually speak different languages.
2. Psychologists have come up with some communication tips so that they may help couples who have difficult conversations.
3. First of all, it's important to understand that men like to solve problems; however, women may talk about a problem but not necessarily want advice.
4. Most women want a partner who will listen to them; therefore, the best thing a man can do is to keep his comments to himself and only offer them if she says she would like advice.
5. Since most men are very tired or frustrated when they come home from work, they may need some quiet, solitary time before they answer their partner's questions about their day.

3. Correct commands: (5 points)

1. Don't cut
2. Get
3. Wear
4. Keep (or: Continue)
5. Don't worry

4. Correct exclamation: (5 points)

1. How tired Sandra looks!
2. What an exhausted appearance Sandra has!
3. What an awful lot of free time Pedro has these days!
4. How very hard Yee Yan is working this week!
5. How incredibly difficult this chapter was!

5. Correct transitions and punctuation: (10 points)

1. Females in our society are socialized to be passive; moreover, they are encouraged to be beautiful rather than smart. (Or any transition to show addition: furthermore, in addition, also).
2. Feminism has a long and complicated history and has taken a variety of forms; as a result, many people are unsure of the term and are hesitant to use the label, even if they do support equal rights for women. (Or any transition to show result: thus, therefore, hence, consequently).
3. Most people who call themselves feminists today simply want women to have the same opportunities and choices as men; however, there are still people who hear the word "feminist" and think of angry women or women who believe they are better than men. (Or any transition to show contrast: however, nevertheless)
4. Historically, the struggle for women's rights has been linked to the fight for civil rights in general; as a matter of fact, many people in the women's movement use the same grass-roots tactics that had proven successful in the struggle for civil rights for African Americans. (Or

any transition to show additional comment/clarification: in fact)

5. It is important for people to become educated about the history and meaning of feminism before they criticize it; otherwise, they will remain confused about the concept.

6. Errors are boldfaced; corrections appear below each sentence: (10 points)

1. How happy **are Marina and Vlad** together! And what an adorable baby **have they**!
   Correction: How happy Marina and Vlad are together! And what an adorable baby they have!
2. Jessica **both was** sad and lonely, **so** her relationship had ended.
   Correction: Jessica was both sad and lonely, for her relationship had ended.
3. Not only was Maria happy with her fiancé, **but also was her family happy, but** they decided to give her a large wedding to celebrate.
   Correction: Not only was Maria happy with her fiancé, but also her family was happy, so they decided to give her a large wedding to celebrate.
4. Ted **didn't stop neither** hoping nor believing that he would find the perfect woman for him, moreover, he made great efforts to try to meet people.
   Correction: Ted stopped neither hoping nor believing that he would find the perfect woman for him; moreover, he made great efforts to try to meet people. (OR: Ted didn't stop either hoping or believing that he would find the perfect woman for him. Moreover, he made great efforts to try to meet people).
5. Marina and Vlad got married in 1999**,** they had a baby in 2001**,** as a matter of fact they hope to have another baby in the next two years.
   Correction: Marina and Vlad got married in 1999, and they had a baby in 2001; as a matter of fact, they hope to have another baby in the next two years. (OR: Marina and Vlad got married in 1999; they had a baby in 2001. As a matter of fact, they hope to have another baby in the next two years).

Chapter 4

1. Correct punctuation of adjective clauses: (10 points)

1. The place where most of the mysterious crop circles are found is the United Kingdom.
2. The United Kingdom, where most of the mysterious crop circles are found, has a lot of farmland.
3. Scientists who have tested plant and soil samples from within crop circles have noticed physical changes to plant cell walls and to soil.
4. Crop circle researchers, who have tested plant and soil samples from within crop circles, have noticed physical changes to plant cell walls and to soil.
5. My sister, who has done research on crop circles, said that crop circles have become more complex in design and more frequent in occurrence since the 1990s.
6. My sister who has done research on crop circles said that crop circles have become more complex in design and more frequent in occurrence since the 1990s.
7. Reports on crop circles in England date back to 1647, when they were first discovered by farmers.
8. Reports on crop circles in England date back to the time when they were first discovered by farmers.
9. There are some scientific theories to explain crop circles, but the more popular theories are the ones which include spacecrafts, hoaxes, and military experimentation.
10. To explain crop circles, people have developed theories which include spacecrafts, hoaxes, and military

experimentation.

2. Matching. Correct sentences and punctuation: (10 points)

1. d
   The Loch Ness Monster is a dinosaur-like animal that is believed to live in a lake in Scotland.
2. e
   Sasquatch, or "Bigfoot," is a hairy, manlike creature who is thought to live in the mountains of the northwestern United States.
3. a
   Many tourists come to Loch Ness, which is located in Scotland.
4. c
   "Nessie" is a nickname for the legendary monster whose home is in Loch Ness in Scotland.
5. b
   It was believed to be Bigfoot who startled some campers in the woods last week.

3. Correct words: (10 points)

1. Machu Picchu is one of the ancient <u>cities</u> of South America whose reasons for their demise <u>are</u> mysterious.
2. However, Machu Picchu is the only one of the ancient <u>cities</u> that <u>was</u> completely inaccessible to excavators until the 1940s.
3. Machu Picchu was one of the <u>temples</u> that <u>were</u> inhabited mainly by priests, priestesses, and high functionaries.
4. The ruins, <u>which</u> are on a mountain, <u>are</u> accessible only by a long hike along the Inca Trail or a four-hour bus and train service.
5. The excavations at the site <u>have</u> revealed only 173 skeletons, <u>of which</u> 150 are female.

4. Sentence combinations with correct punctuation: (10 points)

1. There are remains of over 30,000 ring forts in Ireland, <u>many of which</u> date back to the Bronze Age.
2. The forts were built by ancient tribes, <u>all of whom</u> wanted to protect their families from invaders.
3. The forts, <u>most of which were made of stone</u>, were located all over the countryside.
4. The Normans, <u>whose newly conquered territory needed to be protected</u>, used forts for military purposes.
5. The ring forts, <u>in which one family or an entire tribe could live</u>, were of varying sizes.

5. Errors are boldfaced; corrections appear below each sentence: (10 points)

1. It was the Incas **which** built **its** cities on narrow terraces on the steep mountainsides.
   Correction: It was the Incas who built their cities on narrow terraces on the steep mountainsides.
2. Many photos taken of UFOs (Unidentified Flying Objects), some of which **is** actually frisbees covered with tinfoil, **has** been proven to be hoaxes.
   Correction: Many photos taken of UFOs (Unidentified Flying Objects), some of which are actually frisbees covered with tinfoil, have been proven to be hoaxes.
3. Today, all of the Egyptian pyramids **is** endangered by pollution, **whose its** harmful effects may destroy them eventually.
   Correction:Today, all of the Egyptian pyramids are endangered by pollution, whose harmful effects may destroy them eventually.
4. My friend Mohammed, **whom** works as a preservationist at the Egyptian pyramids, **have** worried about the harmful effects of tourism.
   Correction: My friend Mohammed, who works as a preservationist at the Egyptian pyramids, has worried about the harmful effects of tourism.
5. One of the most biggest concerns **that it** people have about our natural wonders is **what** they can be damaged

by too many tourists.
Correction: One of the most biggest concerns that people have about our natural wonders is that they can be damaged by too many tourists.

Chapter 5

1. Correct words: (10 points)

1. go
2. should be
3. first arrive
4. feel (or: may feel, might feel)
5. soon turns (or: can soon turn, may soon turn, might soon turn, will soon turn)
6. realize
7. are
8. begin (or: can begin, may begin, might begin, will begin)
9. master
10. will probably have learned

2. Correct words: (10 points)

1. While our world <u>is becoming</u> more and more connected in the era of globalization, some people <u>are worrying</u> about cultures losing their unique traits and languages.
2. <u>Since</u> the development of the Internet, families and friends throughout the world <u>have been able to</u> communicate with each other more easily.
3. <u>Whenever</u> a society is in transition, there are always some people who <u>are resistant</u> to change.
4. Once change <u>has begun</u> to occur, however, people gradually <u>incorporate</u> change into their daily lives.
5. Years <u>before</u> people worried about possible negative effects of television and other technologies, they <u>worried</u> about the effects of radio.

3. Correct words and punctuation: (10 points)

1. Due to (or: Owing to, As a result of, Because of) rapid changes that are occurring in their lives, many teenagers suddenly become less communicative with their parents. (note addition of comma after the dependent clause)
2. Teenagers are involved in the process of individuation from their parents; as a result, (or: consequently, hence, therefore, thus) they may wish to assert their differences from their parents and even prefer not to be seen with them in public.
3. Because (or: Due to the fact that, Since) teenagers can seem to withdraw more and more from the family, parents often become quite alarmed and try harder to communicate with them. (note addition of comma after the dependent clause)
4. Often their attempts at communication can sound more like interrogation; as a result, (or: consequently, hence, therefore, thus) teenagers may become even less communicative as they try harder to assert their independence.
5. However, a number of parents to maintain good communication with their children throughout the teenage years as a result of (or: because of, due to, owing to) good listening skills and expressions of emotional support. (no punctuation added)

4. Sentence combinations with correct punctuation: (10 points)

1. Men's and women's roles had been clearly defined as being centered around the workplace and the home, respectively, until World War II began.
2. Soon after the war had begun, men were increasingly enlisted to help fight, leaving the women at home.
3. After so many men had left to fight in the war, new employment and educational opportunities opened up for women.
4. Before World War II broke out, there had been very limited opportunities for women in factories or in professional occupations.
5. By the time the war ended, many women had found satisfaction in working outside the home and were

reluctant to give up their positions for the returning men.

5. Errors are boldfaced; corrections appear below each sentence: (10 points)

1. Before you **will make** a major life **decision make** sure you are not under a lot of stress or feeling pressured by other people. (2nd error: no comma after dependent clause)
   Correction: Before you make a major life decision, make sure you are not under a lot of stress or feeling pressured by other people.
2. Soon **after when** cellular phones had been marketed at lower costs, more and more people, including teenagers, **had begun buying** them.
   Correction: Soon after cellular phones had been marketed at lower costs, more and more people, including teenagers, began buying them.
3. **Due to she was** such a devoted helper of the poor in India, many people to this day revere Mother Teresa **as a result.**
   Correction: Due to the fact that she was such a devoted helper of the poor in India, many people to this day revere Mother Teresa. (OR: Mother Teresa was such a devoted helper of the poor in India; as a result, many people to this day revere her).
4. **Because of Martin Luther King, Jr. was** an incredible orator; **therefore**, huge crowds gathered to hear him speak about civil rights and nonviolent protest.
   Correction: Because Martin Luther King, Jr. was an incredible orator, huge crowds gathered to hear him speak about civil rights and nonviolent protest. (OR: Because of Martin Luther King Jr.'s incredible skill as an orator, huge crowds gathered to hear him speak about civil rights and nonviolent protest. OR: Martin Luther King, Jr. was an incredible orator; therefore, huge crowds gathered to hear him speak about civil rights and nonviolent protest).
5. **Within the first thirty years of the twentieth century occurred**, Americans **witnessed** an explosion of technological innovations, including automobiles and radios.
   Correction: Within the first thirty years of the twentieth century, Americans had witnessed an explosion of technological innovations, including automobiles and radios.

Chapter 6

1. Correct words and punctuation: (10 points)

1. <u>In spite of</u> (or: <u>despite</u>) attempts to reduce stress in their lives, many people suffer from anxiety and panic. (comma added after dependent clause)
2. They may suffer from insomnia at night <u>even though</u> (or: <u>in spite of the fact that</u>) they attempt to reduce caffeine in their diet. (no punctuation added)
3. Psychologists say that anxiety and panic disorders are on the rise <u>in spite of the fact that</u> there have been national campaigns to raise awareness about the effects of too much stress. (no punctuation added)
4. People are exercising more and trying to eat better<u>; nevertheless,</u> they may need to modify their lifestyle even more if they want to see results.
5. <u>In spite of the fact that</u> (or: <u>even though</u>) some medications have proved helpful, most people still prefer to try to improve their mental state through diet, exercise, and stress reduction. (comma added after dependent clause)

2. Correct words: (10 points)

1. Like (or: similar to)
2. similar to (or: like)
3. different from (or: unlike)
4. where (or: whereas, while)
5. instead of

6. Like (or: similar to)
7. on the other hand (or: in contrast)
8. Instead of
9. on the contrary
10. instead of

3. Correct comparative and superlative forms: (10 points)

1. cleverer, cleverest (or: more clever, the most clever)
2. more difficult, the most difficult
3. less, the least
4. farther, the farthest
5. more slowly, the most slowly

4. Correct words: (10 points)

1. Daniel speaks English as well as Roberta, but he doesn't study nearly as hard.
2. Rami gets higher grades than Takashi; in fact, she gets the highest grades of anyone in the class.
3. Eduardo, as well as Sandra, forgot his grammar book today.
4. Milena has the same trouble remembering dates and numbers as Joseph does.
5. The grammar was so difficult that the students grew more frustrated every day.

5. Errors are boldfaced; corrections appear below each sentence: (10 points)

1. **Despite that** we dream every night, many people **could** not remember their dreams. Correction: Despite the fact that we dream every night, many people cannot remember their dreams.
2. Whereas my brother seems to be more left-brained because he is good at math, **on the other hand I more** right-brained because I am good at languages and art. Correction: Whereas my brother seems to be more left-brained because he is good at math, I seem to be more right-brained because I am good at languages and art. (OR: My brother seems to be more left-brained because he is good at math; on the other hand, I seem to be (or: I am) more right-brained because I am good at languages and art.
3. Where I am fascinated by theories of dream interpretation, my friends are **enthusiastic**. Correction: Where I am fascinated by theories of dream interpretation, my friends are bored. (or: my friends are *not*).
4. Research on the mental abilities of elderly nuns is being conducted **in order that** learn **most** about how Alzheimer's Disease might be prevented. Correction: Research on the mental abilities of elderly nuns is being conducted in order to learn more about how Alzheimer's Disease might be prevented.
5. The teacher had **so extensive knowledge** about grammar and gave **so much good assignments** that the students quickly mastered Chapter 6. Correction: The teacher had such extensive knowledge about grammar and gave so many good assignments that the students quickly mastered Chapter 6.

Chapter 7

1. (10 points)

1. would continue
2. should be
3. could stay
4. are increasing
5. were

2. (10 points)

1. The secretary said that somebody had just called.
2. Efraim told his wife (that) he was going to get a promotion.
3. The supervisor told the workers (that) they had to wear their safety goggles.
4. Ruth promised herself that she would be on time the next day.
5. I cried when Ginger told me she had decided to leave the company. (OR: I cried when Ginger said (that) she had

decided to leave the company.)

3. (10 points)

1. take
2. make
3. whether
4. is
5. attend
6. if
7. demands
8. be paid
9. document
10. be used

4. (10 points)

1. The technicians are trying to find out **how** the computer virus got started.
2. Do you know **when (at what time)** the meeting starts?
3. I wonder how **much** they pay secretaries.
4. I asked her **which** pages I should read.
5. Could you tell me **who** is going to be my supervisor?

5. (10 points)

1. a
2. c
3. b
4. a
5. b

Chapter 8

1. (10 points)

I. Use the perfect form of each verb to complete the sentences. (10 points)

1. will have colonized
2. has gone through
3. had developed
4. have given
5. will have achieved

2. (10 points)

1. The telephone was invented by Alexander Graham Bell in 1876.
2. Our lives have been forever changed by technology.
3. Hopefully, a cure for AIDs will be found in the near future.
4. Books and newspapers will eventually be replaced by electronic media.
5. The last case of smallpox was reported in 1980.

3. (10 points)

1. are using
2. have been living
3. has been
4. will be run
5. worried
6. believed
7. were doing
8. could have been
9. was projected
10. should

4. (10 points)

1. The Morse Code was invented by Samuel Morse.
2. Many drugs have recently been derived from plants in the rain forest.
3. The modern family is going through many changes at present.
4. I had never heard of that procedure until I underwent surgery.
5. Native Americans were living in longhouses when Europeans arrived in North America.

5. (10 points)

1. b
2. a
3. c
4. a
5. b

Chapter 9

1. (10 points)

1. by
2. to
3. about
4. on
5. about
6. to
7. after
8. at
9. on
10. of

2. (10 points)

1. Learning
2. to shape
3. to think
4. watching
5. to listen
6. to communicate
7. observing
8. singing
9. making
10. boring

3. Answers will vary. The following are sample answers. (10 points)

1. I like playing basketball.
2. It involves a lot of dribbling, aiming, and shooting.
3. To be good at this, you have to practice as much as possib le.
4. My goal is to make the intramural varsity team.
5. Other people might enjoy watching a good game.

4. (10 points)

1. We agreed to practice together.
2. Traditional art forms include sculpting, dancing, and storytelling.
3. It's important to preserve and (to) protect native arts.
4. Public speaking is a good way of developing (to develop) self-confidence.
5. High-quality writing, acting, and directing are all elements of a good film.

5. (10 points)

1. a
2. b
3. a
4. c
5. a

Chapter 10

1. (10 points)

1. hope
2. wished
3. wished
4. hoped
5. had hoped
6. hoping
7. wish
8. hoped
9. hopes
10. wish

2. (10 points)

1. realized
2. would be
3. would have asked
4. should have prepared
5. had not invented
6. would take
7. were
8. had listened
9. should have paid attention
10. had known

3. (10 points)

1. could have spoken
2. would have sold
3. should have thought
4. must have been concerned
5. might not have happened
6. would not have attempted
7. could have occurred
8. should not have done
9. ought to have tried
10. might have been alarmed

4. (10 points)

1. Things might be different today if we had taken a different course.
2. You shouldn't mix chemicals unless you know what you are doing.
3. The earth would be able to purify itself if we stopped polluting it.
4. I wish I were able to solve the world's problems.
5. Monique wishes she could have gone to the protest rally yesterday.

5. (10 points)

1. c
2. a
3. b
4. c
5. b

Chapter 11

1. (10 points)

1. rises
2. to lay
3. lay
4. raised
5. lying
6. laying
7. to rising
8. had laid
9. had risen
10. raised

2. (15 points)

1. Ginseng, which is known for its healthful effects, is used by many people as a tonic.
2. People who take (that are taking) herbs should consult a doctor about possible side effects.
3. Researchers who use (that are using) live animals in their experiments should be supervised.
4. There are several good hospitals here that specialize in child care.
5. A human being cannot be compare to a rat that lives in a maze.
6. This tree, which is over 4,000 years old, is being threatened by development.
7. The man who ran (that was running) the experiment was startled by the results.
8. People who eat (that eat) less usually live longer.
9. Cancer, which is being studied around the world, may be cured one day.
10. The genome project may possibly identify the gene that determines personality traits.

3. (15 points)

1. that
2. having
3. running
4. being rushed
5. by
6. had collected
7. After
8. had
9. let
10. helped
11. patient
12. Exhausted
13. looking
14. eating
15. hidden

4. (10 points)

1. Since he had lived (Having lived) for more than a century, the old man astounded the doctors.
2. The hospital has a specialist that is (who is) studying the aging process.
3. Senior citizens, having lived a long time, can teach younger people a lot of things.
4. Marie Curie, who is known for isolating radium, died from radiation.
5. Since he had lost a lot of blood, the patient just felt like lying in bed.

Chapter 12

1. Complete the following table by filling in the correct form of the verb in each blank space. (15 points)

	Passive	Continuous Infinitive	Present Perfect	Perfect Passive
to delay	**to be delayed**	to be delaying	**to have delayed**	**to have been delayed**
to know	to be known	—	**to have known**	**to have been known**
to launch	**to be launched**	**to be launching**	**to have launched**	to have been launched
to repair	**to be repaired**	**to be repairing**	to have repaired	**to have been repaired**
to think	to be thought	**to be thinking**	**to have thought**	**to have been thought**

2. Correct words: (15 points)

1. The spaceship is programmed to travel all the way to Jupiter.
2. Many people appear to have been contacted by aliens.
3. Some scientists expect the earth to be hit by a meteor in the near future.
4. The space commander urged his crew to fasten their seatbelts.
5. The alien pretended to be dying.
6. I make my robot do all the boring jobs.
7. Teachers shouldn't have to worry about being replaced by robots.
8. She couldn't remember getting into a U.F.O. until she was hypnotized.
9. Many people can expect to be living in space within 100 years.
10. So far, nobody has programmed a computer to think original thoughts.
11. After having examined a meteor from Mars, scientists concluded that life may have existed on Mars billions of years ago.
12. Some people who have touched a meteor claim to have special powers.
13. The "Big Bang" theory describes an expanding universe that may one day come to a halt or reverse itself.
14. On spacecraft, cameras are used for filming take-offs and landings.
15. After being coined in 1921, the term robot was not widely used until the 1950s.

3. (10 points)

We can expect many changes to take place (1) by the year 2050. Advances in gene therapy will allow defects to be repaired (2) before a baby is born. We probably will colonize (3) the moon by then. Many people will be living (4) and working (5) in space. In fact, there may be some people who will never visit (6) the earth. The moon may be an important source of new minerals that can be used to develop (7) alternative sources of energy. With these advances, we may be able to solve (8) a lot of our current problems. Hopefully, we will be able to save (9) our precious planet before it is too late. Our technology won't be able to save us if we keep damaging (10) the planet.

4. (10 points)

1. Everybody laughed at my having seen (sighted) a U.F.O.
2. Don't hesitate to report any suspicious activity (that) you have seen.
3. The continuing revolution in technology promises to transform our lives.
4. An alien spacecraft appears to have landed in Central Park.
5. I won't tolerate your ignoring my orders.